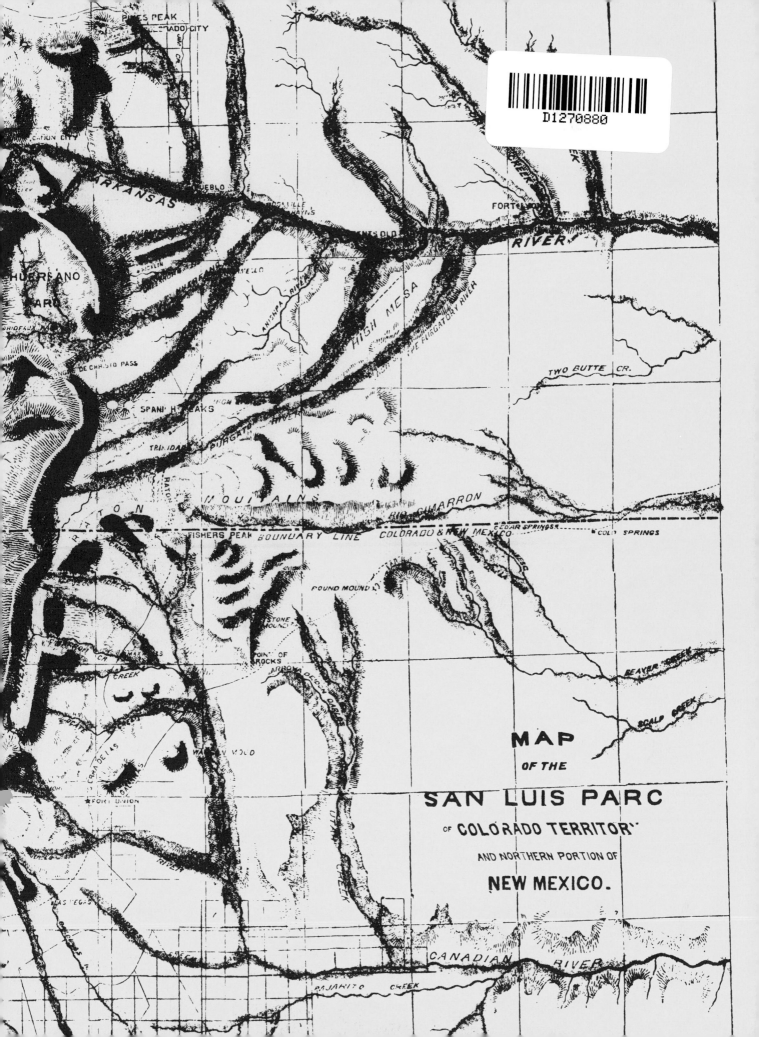

MAP

OF THE

SAN LUIS PARC

OF COLORADO TERRITORY

AND NORTHERN PORTION OF

NEW MEXICO.

D1270880

THE SAN LUIS VALLEY

For George

THE SAN LUIS VALLEY
Land of the Six-Armed Cross

By

Virginia McConnell Simmons

PRUETT **P** *PUBLISHING COMPANY*

Boulder, Colorado

Library of Congress Cataloging in Publication Data

Simmons, Virginia McConnell, 1928-
    San Luis Valley.

    Bibliography: p.
    1. San Luis Valley—History. I. Title.
F782.S2S56   987.8'33   79-24315
ISBN 0-87108-548-8

First Edition

1 2 3 4 5 6 7 8 9

Printed in the United States of America

Photo Credits

Archival photographs are from the collections of the State Historical Society of Colorado unless otherwise credited. Prints of sketches are from Heap's *Central Route to the Pacific,* *Harper's New Monthly Magazine,* Darley's *Passionists of the Southwest,* and the Denver *Journal of Commerce.*

Four recent photographs were made by Thomas J. Noel and George C. Simmons, these being credited in the captions. All others are by the author.

Acknowledgments

This book offers not a first look but a fresh look, it is hoped, at the history of the San Luis Valley of Colorado. It is a synthesis of a mass of material about the region. The bibliography and footnotes in this volume indicate many of the books, articles, and other records which the author consulted. In addition, the names of several individuals and repositories deserve special mention because of their assistance.

During the past decade members of the San Luis Valley Historical Society have given generously of their time and energy to the collecting of documents and interviews. Much of this work appears in *The San Luis Valley Historian,* their quarterly which has been used extensively in the writing of this book. One individual whose name, by chance, does not appear in my bibliography, but who should be recognized for her devoted work in the society, is Ruth Marie Colville.

At Adams State College the library contains files on regional history which were made available through the helpfulness of Christine Moeny, special collections librarian. The faculty and graduate students of the history department at Adams State College, also, are commended for the many excellent theses, which are available to subsequent researchers.

The State Historical Society of Colorado possesses extensive files and documents, and Enid Thompson, librarian there at the time of my research, was most helpful in locating papers which were related to this study. Of special value at the same society was *The Colorado Magazine,* the quarterly in which have appeared many useful manuscripts about the San Luis Valley. Also, Dr. LeRoy R. Hafen, who for many years was historian of the society, is saluted for the remarkable service he performed in collecting, compiling, editing, and publishing an enormous amount of material on state and local history and for his encouragement of contributions by those who were part of that history.

The Denver Public Library's Western History Department offered much assistance through its efficient and friendly staff. Alys Freeze, formerly head of the department, and her successor, Eleanor Gehres, especially are thanked. Robert Svenningsen, chief of the archives branch of the Federal Archives and Records Center in Denver, was very helpful in guiding me to material at the center. Other repositories in Colorado which were useful for research in regional history were located at the U.S. Geological Survey, at Colorado College's Tutt Library in Colorado Springs, and in the Colorado history collections at the University of Colorado Libraries in Boulder.

Both the New Mexico State Records Center and Archives and the New Mexico State Library contain much material related to Colorado's San Luis Valley. Dr. Myra Ellen Jenkins, chief of the historical services division, provided excellent guidance to the documents in the Records Center and Archives, while Virginia Jennings helped me with materials at the State Library.

For their reading the manuscript and offering many suggestions, my deep appreciation is extended to Dorothy D. Wilson, former curator of the museum of Adams State College and a director of the San Luis Valley Historical Society; to Dr. Duane A. Smith, Department of History, Fort Lewis College; and to Thomas C. McConnell, my son.

Fred A. Pruett and Gerald Keenan of the Pruett Publishing Company are thanked for their publication of my manuscript, as well as for their patience in awaiting its arrival.

Finally, I wish to express my gratitude to my husband, George C. Simmons, whose encouragement helped bring this undertaking to fruition. His skillful drafting of the San Luis Valley maps in their final form was a major contribution to the book.

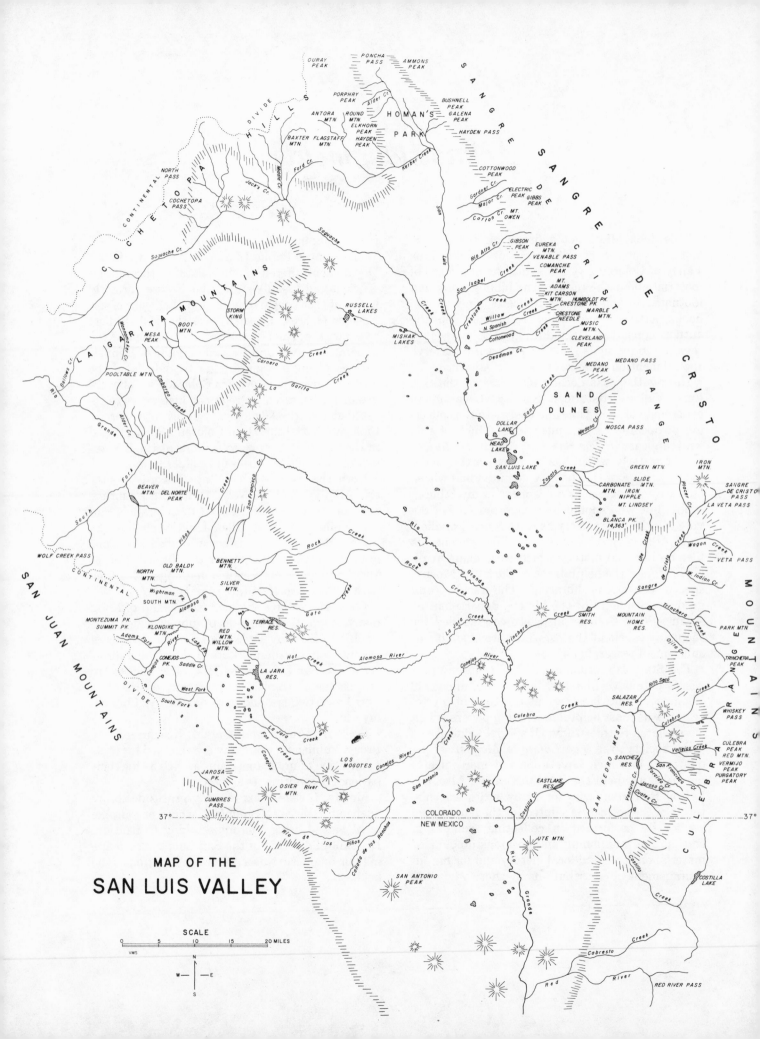

MAP OF THE
SAN LUIS VALLEY

SCALE

0   5   10   15   20 MILES

VMS

N
W — E
S

Contents

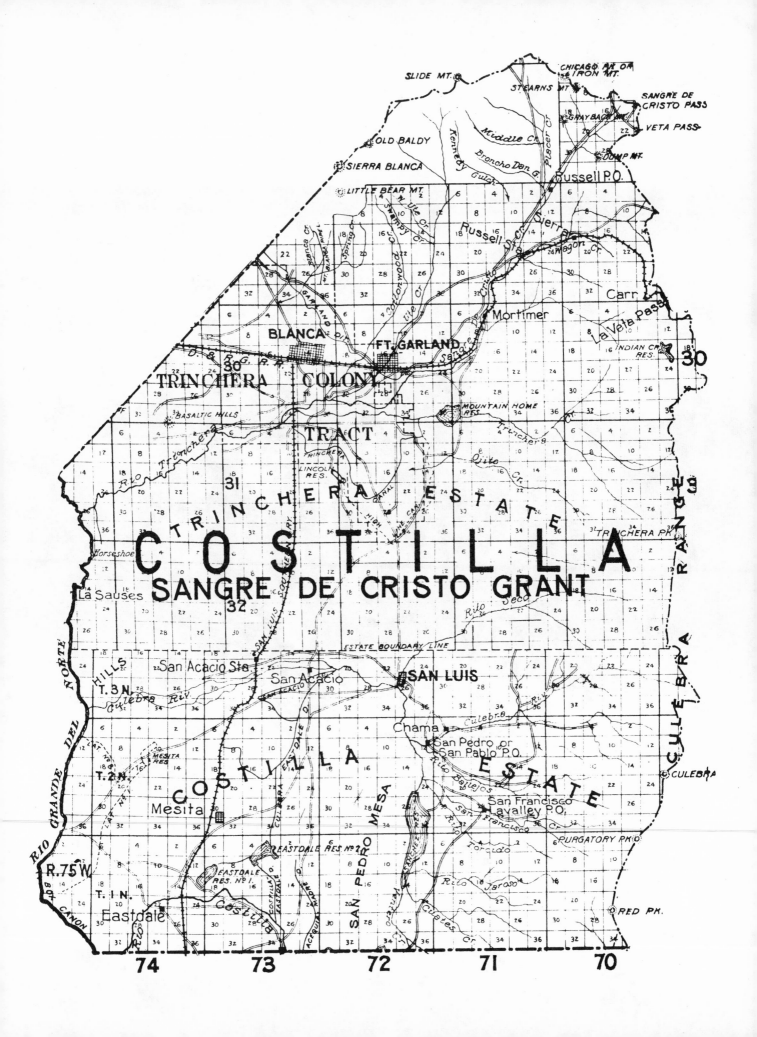

The Rio Grande, photographed at Stewart's Crossing, flows down the San Luis Valley on its long journey from the Continental Divide to the Gulf of Mexico.

Prologue

The Land—Indian, Chicano, or Anglo?

A place has as many histories as it has had people. Each individual and each culture understand that place and its story differently. And each believes it to have been his.

Each occupant of the San Luis Valley has identified with it according to his own needs for survival and according to his own hates, fears, hopes, and knowledge. But did living in the valley make it, in fact, his own irrevocably? Or did the man belong to the place?

One man scratched petroglyphs on a cliff and hunted buffalo for his food and shelter. Another built a hut of mud and logs and channeled a stream to irrigate his crop. Another laid iron rails across the fields and dug the gold from the mountains.

The valley gave each one his sustenance, and he left the scars of his passing on the land. For that matter, the land left its share of scars on the man. Scars or not, a place never becomes the exclusive possession of any culture or individual. Places, though, have a fair chance of getting hold of people and of bending their wills and energies to fit the land. The San Luis Valley is one of those places. In it a lot of people have learned many things about courage and honor, hope and endurance. A history of the valley must be, thus, a composite of many stories, bound together by a unity of place.

1

Following the course of the Rio Grande, thousands of birds, including these sandhill cranes, migrate through the San Luis Valley each spring and autumn.

I

"A Most Beautiful Inland Prospect"

After a bad day's march, through snow some places three feet deep, we struck on a brook which led west, which I followed down and shortly came to a small run, running west. . . .

Followed down the ravine and discovered after some time that there had been a road cut out, and on many trees were various hieroglyphics painted. After marching some miles we discovered through the lengthy vista at a distance another chain of mountains and nearer by at the foot of the White Mountains, which we were descending, sandy hills. We marched on [to] the outlet of the mountains and left the sandy desert to our right. . . . When we encamped I ascended one of the highest hills of sand and with my glass could discover a large river flowing nearly north by west and south by east through the plain which came out of the third chain of mountains. . . . The prairie between . . . bore nearly north and south. The sand hills extended up and down at the foot of the White Mountains . . . and appeared to be about five miles in width. Their appearance was exactly that of the sea in a storm, except as to color, not the least sign of vegetation existing thereon. . . .

We marched obliquely to a copse of woods which made down a considerable distance from the mountains. . . . We marched hard and arrived in the evening on the banks of the Rio del Norte. . . .

As there was no timber here we determined on descending until we found timber. We descended thirteen miles when we met a large west branch into the main stream, up which about five miles we took up our station. . . .

We ascended a high hill which lay south of our camp, from whence we had a view of all the prairie and rivers to the north of us. It was at the same time one of the most beautiful and sublime inland prospects ever presented to the eyes of man. . . .

The main river, bursting out of the western mountains and meeting from the northeast a large branch which divides the chain of mountains, proceeds down the prairie, making many large and beautiful islands, one of which I judged contains 100,000 acres of land, all meadow ground, covered with innumerable herds of deer. . . .

The great and lofty mountains, covered with eternal snows, seemed to surround the luxuriant vale, crowned with perennial flowers, like a terrestrial paradise, shut out from the view of man.[1]

Lieutenant Zebulon Montgomery Pike wrote this first English description of the San Luis Valley in south-central Colorado in 1807. Despite the intrusions of man's handiworks since then, this intermontane basin remains a "terrestrial paradise." The great sweep of the valley shimmers beneath its soaring rim of peaks, the over-all magnitude of the scene bestowing a sense of solidity to its mystic beauty.

Pike's first view was from Medano Pass in the Sangre de Cristo Range. His midwinter crossing followed a well-worn trail used by Indians and Spaniards of Nuevo Mexico to enter and to leave the valley.

The San Luis Valley is larger than Colorado's three other great intermontane basins—North Park, Middle Park, and South Park, all lying west of the Front Range. The elliptically shaped San Luis Valley, at an elevation of 7,000 to 8,000 feet above sea level, stretches its ample girth approximately one hundred miles from north to south and sixty-five miles from east to west.[2] The three other valleys are surrounded entirely by mountains, but this southernmost one is not. Its distinct northern limit is the meeting of the Sangre de Cristo and San Juan mountain ranges; the Sangre de Cristos form the eastern border, and the San Juans form the western; but the San Luis Valley has no definite southern limit. The most convenient demarcations on the south are Ute Peak and San Antonio Mountain, both rising just below the Colorado-New Mexico state line and serving as large, round gateposts for the valley. Beyond them lie New Mexico's Sunshine Valley and the Taos Plateau.

The outline of the San Luis Valley resembles an irregular, inverted horseshoe or Indian *najahe* design. The rim of the mountains is studded with several 13,000- and 14,000-foot summits, of which Blanca Peak is the highest at 14,343 feet. These mountains forming the rim are divided by passes that provide routes in and out of the valley. The main Sangre de Cristo Range is separated from a southern branch, the Culebra Mountains, by Sangre de Cristo Creek and La Veta Pass. Through this route the prairies of eastern Colorado can be reached. In the Culebra Mountains is San Francisco Pass, a high route to New Mexico's Cimarron country. In the northern Sangre de Cristos are Mosca Pass, leading to the Huerfano River; Medano and Music passes to the Wet Mountain Valley; and Hayden Pass to the Arkansas River. This northern group of the Sangre de Cristos, only ten to twenty miles wide in places but rising a mile or more above the valley floor, was Pike's "White Mountains."

The Sangre de Cristos and the San Juans meet at Poncha Pass, the main gateway to the upper Arkansas Valley. Although the latter mountains form the divide between the Pacific and Atlantic watersheds, the portions of the range that abut the valley are only 8,000 to 10,000 feet above sea level and are much less rugged in appearance than the peaks on the east side of the valley. Subgroups of the San Juan Range, which extends west and southwest tier on tier, are divided along the valley by three principal passages. Between the Cochetopa Hills to the north and La Garita Mountains lie Saguache Creek and Cochetopa Pass to the Gunnison country.[3] Midway down the west side is the Rio Grande, the major river of the San Luis Valley, with three forks forming its headwaters high in the Continental Divide; via these headwaters is reached southwestern Colorado. Farther south along the mountains is Cumbres Pass, which leads to the regions of the Chama and San Juan rivers. And through the great gateway on the south, the Rio Grande leaves the valley, tracing an ancient route to New Mexico and Old Mexico, and ending its career finally in the Gulf of Mexico.

The valley that lies within this mountainous frame is not a featureless monotone. In fact, the valley consists of four geologic and geographic divisions—the Alamosa Basin, the San Luis Hills, the Costilla Plains, and the Culebra Re-entrant.[4] The Alamosa Basin, occupying the northern and west-central parts of the valley, is the "prairie" that Pike described. It slopes gently inward toward the east side from the Rio Grande's alluvial fan, a build-up of deposits left by the stream. Sands, gravels, and volcanic debris from stream and mountain erosion have filled some parts of the Alamosa Basin to depths of 4,000 to 7,000 feet through millions of years to create the nearly level surface seen in this portion of the valley today.

The "sandy desert" that Pike's party passed is at a point in the Alamosa Basin where Medano Creek flows from the Sangre de Cristos just north of Blanca Peak. This giant sandpile runs about ten miles along the mountains and rises to nearly 700 feet above the valley's floor. These are the highest inland dunes in the United States.[5]

About such a setting legends cluster. Entire flocks of sheep, together with their shepherds, are said to have been swallowed up in the dunes. Wagons with their mule teams have suffered the same mysterious fate. And horses with webbed feet have been seen racing over the sculptured slopes when the moon is full.

But dunes are made of more earthly stuff, too—grains of sand eroded from igneous and metamorphic rock of the Sangre de Cristos and from volcanic rock of the San Juans. When strong, southwesterly winds blow across the dry valley—and they frequently do—dust storms gather in the basin and hurl their burden against the Sangre de Cristos, piling up loose sand in the trap created by Medano Pass.[6]

Near the town of Blanca, only a short distance south of the sand dunes, barren hills and mesas, capped with lava, appear and extend southwest nearly to Antonito. These are the San Luis Hills. Volcanic in origin, they are 500 to 1,000 feet higher than the valley floor.[7] The largest of the mesas is called Flat Top while the highest of the hills are called the Pinyon Hills, though most of the trees were cut long ago. Between the hills and the San Juan Mountains on the west, the Alamosa Basin reaches south to the Taos Plateau.

East of the San Luis Hills are the Costilla Plains. Bound on the east by the foothills of the Culebra Mountains, the Costilla Plains consist of a deposit-filled strip running south from Blanca Peak into New Mexico.

The fourth division of the valley, the Culebra Re-entrant, lies between the Costilla Plains and the Culebra Mountains in a curve where the

Above, the San Luis Valley's dunes are the highest inland sand accumulations in the United States; *below,* blown by southwesterly winds, the dunes shift in constantly changing patterns.

mountains swing back to the east. Because this area was formed earlier, it has eroded into a more diversified topography than the Alamosa Basin or the Costilla Plains. In the Culebra Re-entrant are foothills forested with pinyon and juniper. In the southern part San Pedro Mesa rises 5,000 feet, and two smaller but prominent mesas occur southeast of Fort Garland. All three are capped with basalt from a lava flow.[8]

The valley itself was created by faulting, or fracturing, of the earth's crust, which took place in a zone running from southern New Mexico into central Colorado. Although sediment has buried the evidence deeply, the valley was caused by a down-dropped block between uplifted mountain ranges. The slight slope of the valley floor to the east results from an eastward tilt of the faulted block. More recent than the faulting was volcanic action in and adjacent to the valley.[9] La Garita Mountains, San Antonio Mountain, Ute Peak,

and the San Luis Hills are conspicuous examples of volcanic formation.[10]

Water in the form of streams, wells, and springs is of great importance to the San Luis Valley. In its southern half a few year-round streams join the Rio Grande. Among these are Rock Creek, Alamosa River, La Jara Creek, the Conejos River, and San Antonio River from the west; and Trinchera, Culebra, and Costilla on the east. The Rio Grande and all of these tributaries have been used extensively for irrigation.

From the north no tributary reaches the Rio Grande, because the entire upper portion of the valley is a closed basin from which no water drains except by seepage. The streams which do flow down from the surrounding mountains disappear into the gravels and sands of the valley floor. Even Saguache Creek, draining an extensive area of La Garita Mountains, becomes lost in the sands of the north end of the valley. San Luis

A national monument was established in 1932 to protect the dunes. *Colorado Department of Highways photo.*

Creek, with numerous intermittent tributaries from the Sangre de Cristos and Poncha Pass, occupies a seemingly predictable course as it flows south toward the San Luis Lakes, but the water frequently disappears before reaching this goal.

Surprisingly, the San Luis Lakes, just west of the dunes, remain full, even when often feeder streams and other nearby ponds dry up after their occasional appearances. This puzzling phenomenon is due to the location of the San Luis Lakes at the lowest point in the closed basin, in what is called a sump, fed by seepage and underground reservoirs of water.

Other areas of the north end of the valley appear to be equally out of place, being wet and marshy. This condition is caused by the water table's closeness to the surface of the land. When the valley's streams sink into the porous floor, seepage does not continue downward unobstructed but is impounded by relatively impermeable layers of sediment. This water table seeps up in many areas and causes serious problems for agriculture, since large portions of land are damaged by alkali and hardpan as a result.

In addition to these naturally wet spots, hundreds of ponds mark the locations of artesian wells, primarily in the north end of the valley but in the south end also. Beneath the upper water table and sedimentary beds is a much deeper and larger reservoir, contained by harder, less porous rock than in the case of the upper water table. During the late 1800s and early 1900s scores of artesian wells were drilled into this deep aquifer for irrigation and domestic purposes. Unfortunately, this added surface water compounded soil problems in a number of localities where the water table normally was too high.[11]

A third source of surface water other than from streams is from natural springs, which abound in the valley, most seeming to occur where the water table abuts hard, volcanic formations. Among these are Los Ojos, or McIntire's Springs, near which Pike built his stockade because the warm spring kept the Conejos River thawed even in February; Russell Springs near La Garita Mountains and south of the town of Saguache; Hunt Springs northeast of the same town; and Medano Springs near the sand dunes. Some were the favored campsites of Indians and, later, of pioneers; some have provided year-round lakes for cattle ranches; and some were developed into health and recreational resorts, a few of which still operate from time to time. One of these, Valley View Hot Springs east of Villa Grove, was a popular attraction a century ago.

In a region with low quantities of precipitation—less than ten inches annually—these underground waters and the mountain streams are essential to give life to the valley. Pike's description of a "luxuriant vale" borders on literary hyperbole, for the "perennial flowers" which "crowned the valley," according to his pen, were merely the dried flower heads of rabbitbrush. The potential was there, though, to bring forth abundant crops when the land was irrigated. And the mountainsides were cloaked with evergreens then as now, while water-bearing clouds veiled snow-packed summits.

Earth, sky, water, and life—ever becoming, ever changing in time and in space, without beginning and without end.

Cliffs along Rock Creek exhibit the graffiti left by prehistoric people and by Ute Indians.

II

"When The Sun Stands Still"

During the winter solstice, at "the time when the sun stands still," Indian priests chant songs which tell of the origin of the earth, the ordaining of the seasons, the coming of animals, and the birth of human beings—the genesis when all was set in order.[1] From tribe to tribe many of these myths describe the emergence of the first creatures from the underworld through a small hole, known as the *Sipapu.*

A Tewa Pueblo legend says that the first humans, after their birth in the underworld, climbed a tree to a lake called *Sip'ophe,* the *Sipapu,* and from the lake into this world. The spirits of the dead also re-enter the underworld through this lake, which thus contains many spirits. According to the Tewa legend, *Sip'ophe* is a definite place—a small, brackish lake near the Sand Dunes in the San Luis Valley.[2]

When anthropologist Edgar L. Hewett visited the valley in 1892, he found a black lake, one hundred yards in diameter, its shores ringed with dead cattle. He was told by an old resident of the area that every year cattle who drank this water, which never dried up, died in great numbers. Hewett was satisfied that he had found the Tewas' *Sip'ophe.*

The San Luis Lakes near the dunes are logical candidates to be this sacred spot. San Luis Lake and Head Lake, which together are called the San Luis Lakes, are larger than the lake which Hewett found, however. Dollar Lake, just north of these two, is nearly the size described by Hewett. Like the others, it does not dry up, and its perfect symmetry seems to recommend it for supernatural events. In the pursuit of anthropological lore, Blanca Peak itself should not be overlooked as another possible location of *Sip'ophe,* though. The mountain is near the sand dunes, and on its summit are a number of small lakes which might have been suited to mythology.

Blanca Peak figures in other Indian legends. The Navajos of the Southwest describe their traditional home as being confined within boundaries defined by four mountains at the points of the magnetic compass. On the north is Big Sheep Mountain in Colorado's La Plata Mountains, and on the south is Mount Taylor near Grants, New Mexico. On the west are the San Francisco Peaks of Arizona. The mountain on the east is said to be banded with black rock and crowned with white shell, but the location is not precise enough, in fact, to be pinpointed. Blanca Peak often has been suggested as the eastern landmark.[3] Pioneer settlers near Blanca Peak understood that this mountain had religious significance for Indians who still visited it in the late 1800s. A ring of stones on its summit, 7,000 feet above the valley floor, is thought to have been used in their ceremonials.

These tales, handed down through the generations of prehistoric and recent peoples, are young in the total spectrum of occupation of the valley. Toward the end of the last Ice Age, while large portions of the continent still were covered by ice, a corridor of land along the eastern slopes of the Rocky Mountains enabled nomadic hunters from the north to enter the plains of what is now Colorado, northeastern New Mexico, and western Texas. Known as Folsom Man, this ancient race survived by hunting bison, camels, and mammoths, as well as a few smaller animals which still exist today. Bones of five extinct animals, believed to have been *Bison taylori,* and stone tools belonging to Folsom Man have been found in the San Luis Valley, where game was pursued from the plains about 8000 B.C.[4]

The first discovery of Folsom artifacts in the valley occurred in the vicinity of the sand dunes and was made by Clarence T. Hurst. A second location, on the west side of Blanca Peak, was

9

called the Zapata Site. In pockets between low dunes, around the San Luis Lakes, the Dry Lakes and elsewhere, archaeologists have found large bones and beautiful, fluted points typical of those used by Folsom Man. Most of these discoveries were made in the 1930s and 1940s. Other projectile points belonging to the Yuma Culture also have been found in the valley, but occupation seems to have died out after 5000 B.C., probably because of unfavorable weather conditions, such as prolonged drought or excessive heat.[5] Varieties of game, which had attracted hunters for hundreds of years, then may have moved to moister and cooler land, and the valley was left with only a handful of artifacts and a few bones to mark the passing of 3,000 years of sporadic occupation.

It once was believed that the next visitors to the valley were Pueblo Indians from New Mexico, after a gap of 6,000 years while the valley remained unoccupied; but beneath an excavation of Pueblo artifacts another type of projectile point was unearthed, definitely establishing a previous occupation.[6] This group was given the name "Upper Rio Grande Culture." In addition to the artifacts found at the original site in the southeastern part of the valley, other locations were found on the east side of the valley in the large area extending between the sand dunes and Arroyo Hondo in New Mexico. Other sites were located on the west side of the valley from south of Monte Vista to Tres Piedras in New Mexico. Since the northern end of the valley yielded no evidence of artifacts from this culture, it is assumed that these people came from the south.[7]

The people of the Upper Rio Grande Culture were migratory hunters, who brought no pottery and raised no crops during their trips into the valley. They hunted rabbit, deer, antelope, and buffalo with points that were rather crudely fashioned from black and grey volcanic stone. Dwellings were merely temporary camps and shelters made of rock, the locations of which have been found on knolls and canyon rims affording good views of game, aggressors, or both.[8] Although no definite date has been given for the valley's occupation by these people, they are supposed to have predated the birth of Christ.[9]

Evidence of yet another long-vanished culture has since come to light. These people were called the "Hogan Builders" because of the numerous circular- and horseshoe-shaped shelters which they built by laying up slabs of lava. Pottery has been found at these sites. Although it is a type found in northern New Mexico, it is thought not to be of Pueblo origin. It has been dated about A.D. 1100 and may be an early type of Navajo and Paiute ware.[10]

The activity of this culture centered on the west side of the valley, where at least fifty enclosures have been found on high ground south of Saguache, and a few were south of Monte Vista. The area of occupation also includes several sites north and east of Alamosa.[11] Near some of the "hogan" sites in Rock Creek Canyon, petroglyphs were pecked out of the volcanic cliffs along the stream. Because some of the chipped designs were embellished with pigment, the area became known as Piedra Pintada. The Utes claimed that the petroglyphs were old when their fathers came into the region.[12] However, more recent art is intermingled with the ancient. For example, pictures of horses, firearms, headdresses, and a large spear belong to the work of historic Indians, such as the Utes themselves; but some of the petroglyphs are thought to belong to the Hogan Builders. Other petroglyphs can be seen along Carnero Creek.

The Tewa Indians, who now live in pueblos north of Santa Fe, New Mexico, tell legends about *Sip'ophe* and even about living in the San Luis Valley, but no firm evidence exists of Pueblo Indians having had permanent dwellings there. However, Taos Pueblo Indians describe bird-hunting expeditions into the valley. So many Pueblo-type bird points have been found near the sand dunes, San Luis Lakes, and the area around Alamosa that Pueblos probably procured feathers for garments there. These hunting expeditions by the Pueblo people began, most likely, about A.D. 1300, after the migration of the cliff dwellers from Mesa Verde, Chaco Canyon, and Canyon de Chelly, when some of these people moved into north-central New Mexico and built the pueblo-type villages of the Rio Grande valley and neighboring areas.[13]

These Pueblo Indians were attracted to visit the San Luis Valley not only by game and fowl but also by turquoise, a material which they especially prized. Spaniards arriving in New Mexico in the late 1500s found Indians adorned with blue and green turquoise in their nostrils as well as on their ears. The Pueblo people also used the stone as a trade item and offered gifts of it to their gods.[14] This turquoise came from mines scattered throughout the Southwest and the San Luis Valley.

The San Luis Valley has at least two turquoise mines, one of which may be the oldest worked by prehistoric people of North America. Now called the King Mine, this deposit is nine miles east of Manassa. In a refuse heap at the mine prehistoric tools of bone and stone have been found.[15] Further indication of this mine's use by ancient people has been the discovery of turquoise of the same type in archaeological digs west of the San Juan Mountains. The people there either obtained it by trade or traveled to the mine.[16] Apparently the Zunis also knew this turquoise very early, for one of their legends tells of Turquoise Man and Salt-Old-Woman bringing stones from the north to start the Cerillos Mines northwest of Santa Fe, New Mexico. Ethnologists believe that this legend refers to the King Mine.[17] Although the mine became at one time the largest turquoise producer in the world, it is worked only sporadically now, and the material mined is not of the remarkable quality of former times.[18]

The Hall Mine and other nearby deposits of turquoise are about five miles northwest of Villa Grove. This area also appears to have been worked by Indians. The bright, robin's-egg blue stone of Villa Grove was once very popular, but it no longer is being mined.[19]

By A.D. 1300 Indian tribes in southern Colorado and northern New Mexico were becoming distributed and aligned much as the Spaniards found them in the late 1500s. Drought and encroachment by Apache and Ute Indians had forced the Pueblos from their cliff dwellings; and these aggressors, too, had moved as the result of territorial pressure. As early as A.D. 800 the Utes had entered western Colorado in search of better hunting and more easily defended territory than they had experienced previously in the Great Basin of Utah.[20] When they moved eastward into Colorado, they took over most of the mountain areas and remained there.

Although the Utes traveled in small family groups and bands to hunt or to fight, they belonged to two distinct tribal units—the Southern Utes and the Northern Utes—who remained separate geographically. Although any of the Southern Ute bands might visit the San Luis Valley to hunt from time to time, the Tabeguache band—also known as the Uncompahgres—claimed the valley as their particular domain. The Southern Ute claim to the valley was not unchallenged, however, as Navajo Apaches pressed from the west while Jicarilla Apaches pressed from the east. Later the Comanches, the Arapahos, the Cheyennes, and the Kiowas came from time to time from the plains to contest the Southern Ute claim.

The Utes differed from their neighbors in language, physical appearance, and way of life. In language they were related to Shoshoni-tongued people to the northwest. In appearance they were short, stocky, and dark-skinned. In customs they differed more from the Pueblos than from the Plains Indians or even the Navajos, who also depended on nomadic hunting for their sustenance.

The Pueblos, on the other hand, had permanent homes with utilitarian crafts and agriculture. As a result, the Utes and the Pueblos found mutual benefit in getting along with each other and trading occasionally. From time to time the Utes brought meat and hides to the Pueblos in exchange for corn, beans, and squash.[21]

Usually, though, when the Utes wanted to supplement their standard diet of meat from big and small game, they ate berries, yucca, cactus, and insects. Because of their dependence on foot travel when they first entered the area, the Utes were limited in their ability to gather food. When winter approached and game became scarce, the Utes were forced to move *en masse* to warmer areas such as Pagosa Springs or along the Gunnison and Uncompahgre rivers between Montrose and Grand Junction. In the spring the buffalo, elk, deer, and antelope returned to the San Luis Valley. Ducks, geese, cranes, herons, and dozens of other birds flew up the Rio Grande to nest among the ponds and marshes of the valley.[22] Then the Utes returned, but so too did their enemies. It was a life of seemingly immense freedom on the one hand but of continual menace, natural or human, on the other.

Several routes were used regularly by these migrants. The Arkansas Valley and South Park, another hunting ground enjoyed by the Utes, were reached by Poncha Pass and trails to the northeast. Journeys to and from Gunnison and Uncompahgre River country were made by way of Cochetopa Pass, or Buffalo Pass as the Utes called it. Wolf Creek and Cumbres Pass led in and out of the Southwest country. Pagosa Springs, one of the tribe's favorite "resorts," was often reached by these routes; but another trail, little known today, led almost directly from the San Luis Valley to Pagosa Springs by way of Rock Creek. Encampments along this route account for the numerous pieces of art work added by the Utes to the ancient cliff drawings at Piedra Pintada. Their trail descended the west side of the mountains along the Navajo River.[23] Similarly, evidence of much-used campsites and rock art at the mouth of Carnero Canyon reveal that the Utes frequently used Carnero Creek as a route into the mountains.

Behind them these people left their dead, but only a few have been found. Skeletons of ancient miners were found at the King Mine. Another burial was unearthed by a plow at the foot of Blanca Peak, where the corpse had been placed in a seated position facing the west. Over his face was an abalone shell, secured with leather thongs.[24] Who buried him in this manner? Was he perhaps fearful that the dead man's spirit would

Sand and wood in the dry bed of Medano Creek.

return from the underworld to gather companions
to relieve his loneliness?

The people who once lived in the valley did not
believe that they came from dust and returned to
dust but that their spirits re-entered the *Sipapu*
from which they had come originally. The dead
were like rain returning water to a river. The
circle continued without end. So said the legends,
when the sun stood still.

III

"Those Who Are Considered Subjects of the King"

On April 30, 1598, Don Juan de Oñate took possession of New Mexico in *Tierra Nueva*, the Spanish New World, claiming the land "from the leaves of the trees in the forest to the stones and sands of the river," the Rio del Norte.[1] Thereby, all territory drained by the Rio Grande, including the San Luis Valley, became the possession of King Phillip II of Spain, and the people in it were considered his subjects.

That spring day in 1598 was only a century after Columbus's discovery of America. It was about eighty years since Cortez had entered Mexico City. Only about sixty years had passed since Coronado's penetration of the American Southwest and since Hernando de Soto, discoverer of both the Rio Grande and the Mississippi, had died on the shores of the latter.

Before he died de Soto appointed Luis Moscoso de Alvarado as the leader of their expedition. Moscoso and his men attempted to find an overland route from the Mississippi to Mexico City through what is now Texas. Failing this, they arrived at their destination by way of the Gulf of Mexico and a route across Mexico's mountains and central plateau.[2] They never were in or near Colorado, as is sometimes said. They did not cross the Sangre de Cristo Mountains. They did not discover the San Luis Valley. They did not mine gold from a cave on Marble Mountain. And the name for Mosca Pass did not derive from Moscoso but from the Spanish word for flies or mosquitoes.

In fact, almost nothing was known about the vast territory called *tierra incognita* by the Spaniards when they set out to claim it. Although Cabeza de Vaca, Fray Marcos de Niza, and Coronado had given a few names to rivers, mountains, and Indian villages, none of these men had entered Colorado unless Coronado possibly crossed the extreme southeastern corner of the state. Instead of useful geographical information, fables about rich mines and potential converts to the Church were the lore which drew the Spaniards north in the 1580s to occupy New Mexico and to find the Seven Cities of Cibola and the land of Grand Quivira.

Early in that decade two missionary parties set forth, one reaching as far as Taos. Hostility among the natives and the murder of two of the holy men halted these enterprises for a few years. Meanwhile, two unauthorized expeditions left Mexico in search of Cibola and Quivira, but these also failed. Oñate, the son of a wealthy citizen of Mexico, next was awarded an official contract to conquer and occupy the lands to the north. As part of this contract he agreed to outfit about four hundred soldiers, settlers, and priests and to provide about one thousand head each of cattle, sheep for wool and for mutton, and goats. In exchange the crown would give him artillery, a six-year loan of funds, titles of civil and military command, and the right to assign Indians to serve him, his heirs for two generations, and companions who merited reward. Within a few years the *conquistadores*, who had set forth for New Mexico with high expectations, learned that their rewards, compared to the hardships, would be disappointing.

When he arrived at the junction of the Rio Grande and the Rio Chama in northern New Mexico, Oñate established two villages, San Juan de los Caballeros and San Gabriel del Yungue, the first European settlements in North America after St. Augustine. Nearby San Juan Pueblo extended a hospitable reception to their new neighbors, thinking that the Spaniards might herald the return of one of the Pueblo savior gods.[3] While the padres dealt with this spiritual misconception, an exploring party left almost immediately in search of gold on the eastern plains. Another group, learning of buffalo to the north, set out to capture some for domestication. Although both of these improbable pursuits failed, the buffalo hunt offered the first recorded description of the San Luis Valley and the Indians who were found there.[4]

The buffalo hunters discovered about fifty lodges, apparently Ute, toward the east side of the valley. Each tepee was made of buffalo hide, weighing about fifty pounds. Bundled up, these could be pulled on the lodge poles by large dogs. On these *travois* the Spaniards also saw meat and corn, the latter probably having come from the Pueblos. The Indians' hunting weapons were described as being exceptionally large bows with arrows tipped by comparably large, thick points—a type that we know was used by Colorado's Utes for hunting buffalo. The Spaniards enjoyed a demonstration of buffalo hunting by the Indians. However, the newcomers found it easier to make friends with the Indians than to corral buffalo. With a herd of about five hundred in sight, the would-be *vaqueros* stampeded the buffalo. Some Spanish horses were killed in the melee, and the expedition returned to Onate in failure.

The original friendliness between the Pueblos and the Spaniards deteriorated almost at once. The conquerors needed food and shelter, so, with winter descending, the Spaniards commandeered the corn supply of the natives and impressed them into service. Such policies could be rationalized in New Mexico, as in Old Mexico, by the rights of possession by a superior civilization. After New Mexico became a colony and headquarters were moved to Santa Fe in 1609, the original Spanish policies remained the rule in dealing with the Pueblos.

Contact with Utes to the north remained friendly until the late 1630s when Spanish soldiers attacked a band and led off about eighty members to augment the conquerors' slave force. Thereafter the Utes began to raid Spanish livestock and goods, adding to the herds of horses that had first been acquired through trade. Ute trade commodities consisted not only of game but also of Ute children who were impressed into the service of the Spaniards.

Until 1680 this harsh but relatively undramatic balance continued. The Spaniards themselves regimented their lives under the absolute rule of their government and religion and were not the stuff of colorful frontiersmen.[5] Nor did it appear that the Pueblos were any more imaginative and cunning than the Spaniards until 1680, when nearly every Indian pueblo rose up simultaneously and drove their conquerors from New Mexico in one desperate blow. Following this unusual venture in cooperation, the Pueblo villages settled into their own separate lives, with little further interest in united action. Consequently, with the Spaniards out of the way, the Utes and other nomadic tribes were able to plunder the helpless Pueblos almost at will. When the Spaniards returned in 1692, they found the Pueblos submissive for the most part, but the nomadic Indians to the north had become more powerful through the horses and other loot that they had seized.[6]

In 1694 General Don Diego de Vargas, having restored Spanish possession of Santa Fe, set forth to the few northern pueblos that had not yet capitulated to the reconquest. At Taos the pueblo was found deserted with the Indians in hiding. The general took as much grain as could be loaded on his animals and burned the rest. He then decided to return to Santa Fe by way of a long detour to the north to avoid meeting Pueblos who might seek reprisal for his looting. The chosen route lay through the San Luis Valley, the land of the Utes who were believed to be friendly to the Spaniards.

The army moved north to Culebra Creek, then turned west to cross the Rio Grande, and camped on the San Antonio River, where de Vargas was able to catch up with making entries in his diary. This diary not only described events and routes of the expedition but also indicated Spanish place names which already were in use in the San Luis Valley. While encamped on the San Antonio River, the Spaniards hunted elk and buffalo. De Vargas reported one herd of about five hundred of the latter seen near San Antonio Mountain. A surprise attack by about three hundred Utes shattered the peace of the Spanish camp, and six Spaniards were wounded before the tide was turned. Immediately after eight Utes were killed, the Indians waved a buckskin flag of truce and reentered the camp to trade. The Spaniards gave them some of the maize from Taos, a horse, some dried meat, and a few odds and ends, which seemed to satisfy everyone.[7]

On the whole, perpetuation of friendship with both the Utes and the Jicarilla Apaches was useful to the Spaniards in their dealings with the Pueblos and also with the Comanches. To assure a balance of power against the latter especially, the Spaniards helped other tribes. In 1720, for example, the governor ordered his soldiers to destroy the Picuris Pueblo, "which lies between the settlements of Xicarilla and Sierra blanca, where they received me with the Image of Our Blessed Lady."[8] Four years later another governor was contemplating war against the Comanches because they have "wasted and pillaged those of the Xicarilla nation who are considered Subjects of the King."[9]

No small part of such considerations was related to the search for mineral wealth. Spanish policy was to convert the Indians and to develop mines wherever possible.[10] Personnel to carry out both purposes were sent hand in hand, as is seen in a legend about the naming of the San Luis Valley and the Sangre de Cristo Mountains. Francisco Torres, a missionary to the Pueblo Indians, accompanied a party searching for gold in and around the valley. He is said to have climbed a hill near the place where the Rio Grande leaves the mountains, and, moved by the view of the valley at his feet, he named it in honor of the patron saint of his native city, San Luis in Seville. Moving across the valley, the party entered the mountains to reach a mine located in one of the passes. Indians, who had been brought with the party for this purpose, were compelled to perform the labor of working it. These slaves, reinforced by other Indians, rebelled and drove the Spaniards down to the sand dunes and then to San Luis Lake. There a makeshift raft was built for escape onto the lake. Torres, who had been wounded in one of the skirmishes, was among those on the raft, but he was dying. Looking up at the snow-capped mountains, aglow in the flush of sunset, he exclaimed, "Sangre de Cristo, Sangre de Cristo," meaning "blood of Christ."[11]

Perhaps this legend refers to a Spanish mine that is involved in countless tales about Marble Mountain's caves. This mine is purported to have been found in a big cave, the entrance marked with a Maltese cross. Stories of the Spanish Cave of Marble Mountain tell of the discovery of an ancient ladder, a windlass, a skeleton in chains, and bottomless pits that conceal what may be a mine.[12] Since the Spanish Cave is reached from the Wet Mountain Valley, not the San Luis, it seems more likely that the mining which took place during Torres' last journey was at some other location. Early American traders and trappers referred to the "Sangry de Christy" gold mine; a mine worked in the nineteenth century in Sangre de Cristo Pass is said to have been opened by Spaniards; another mine in the Culebra Moun-

tains showed evidence of earlier Spanish working; Spanish arrastras for milling ore were found by early settlers directly south of the sand dunes at North Arrastra Creek and high in the San Juan Mountains near Summitville. It seems apparent that the Spaniards did find minerals around the San Luis Valley, but precisely when they were mined is unknown.

The interest in finding gold may have blinded the Spaniards to another resource which was drawing French explorers deeper and deeper into the North American wilderness—fur. After the French began to settle in the Mississippi Valley in the early 1700s, they made efforts to investigate the rivers which flowed from the west. The French, in fact, had claimed all of the Mississippi drainage basin, which included everything east of the Continental Divide and north of the Rio Grande's drainage. Although the Plains Indians blocked French incursions for a while, Uribarri reported as early as 1706 that French trade goods had made their way into eastern Colorado.

By 1720 the Comanches had obtained firearms through this French trade, and, in possession of the Europeans' weapons as well as their horses, the Comanches went on a raiding binge that grew into the scourge of the entire southern plains, Texas, and Mexico as far south as Durango. Moreover, negotiations between the French and the Comanches in 1746 opened new trade routes closer to New Mexico than those previously developed. Because of this economic and political threat, the Spaniards now for the first time attempted to establish some evidence of occupation north of New Mexico on the plains. They set up a handful of small posts on the Arkansas and Huerfano rivers for this purpose. Because of these outposts, routes that crossed the mountains on the east side of the San Luis Valley saw increased use for a few years.

The French challenge did not last long, though. When France seemed about to lose its North American claims to England in 1762, France preferred to make an outright gift to Spain of all its territory west of the Mississippi. This event spurred the Spaniards of New Mexico at last to take an interest in exploring the lands to the north. One of these expeditions, led by Don Juan Maria de Rivera, set out in 1765 to search the mountains of southwest Colorado for minerals. The party entered the area by way of the Rio Chama, the route that became known as the Spanish Trail. They returned along the Gunnison, across Cochetopa Pass, and down through the San Luis Valley.

Increasingly, however, Indian hostilities commanded Spanish attention. In 1768, to protect Pueblo and Spanish settlements at Ojo Caliente from raids, Governor Mendinueta ordered a fort built on top of San Antonio Mountain, where a wide expanse to the north and east could be watched.[13] For the next few years depredations still continued. More than one hundred New Mexicans were killed in 1771, and thousands of horses, mules, cattle, and sheep were stolen or destroyed.[14]

Such was the state of affairs in 1778 when Don Juan Bautista de Anza was sent to Santa Fe as the new governor, charged particularly with a campaign to quell the Comanche trouble. A native of Sonora, Anza had apprenticed as a volunteer Indian fighter in campaigns against the Apaches, and he had achieved special recognition as a leader in opening an overland route from Sonora to California.[15] Arriving in New Mexico as governor, Anza wasted no time in setting up a multifaceted program of defense against the Indians. Whenever possible he attempted to establish friendship with them through trade negotiations, but at the same time he was quick to send military units to punish any bands who proved troublesome. The Comanches under Chief Cuerno Verde were the most unruly of all.

On August 15, 1779, the governor himself, being the captain general of New Mexico, headed north with an army of about six hundred recruits in pursuit of Cuerno Verde. Being poorly equipped, Anza's army moved up the west side of the Rio Grande, instead of taking the usual route through Taos, in hopes of surprising the Comanches. Anza's journal, which uses many Spanish place names, describes this expedition, which passed through the San Luis Valley. After an encampment on the "Rio de San Antonio" they came to the "Rio de los Conejos" (Rabbit River, if translated into English). Here the Spaniards found two hundred Utes and Jicarillas who were eager to ride with them. Traveling at night to conceal their movements, the entire force moved north, crossing the "Rio del Pino," "Las Jaras" (named for either the wild roses or the reeds that grew along that river), "Timbres" (later called the Alamosa River, referring to its cottonwoods), and "San Lorenzo" (later called Rock Creek and Piedra Pintada). They crossed the Rio Grande at "El Paso de San Bartolomé." This crossing most likely was the ford east of Del Norte used by early settlers as part of a toll road.[16] At this point Anza entered in his journal that his Indians told him the river originated in a large marsh fed by springs, which in turn were filled by "the melting of snow from some volcanos which are very close."

Instead of investigating this phenomenon, the army with its Indian recruits proceeded toward the east to a "pleasant pond" called "la Cienga de San Luis." The Utes, who now were accompanying Anza, had been camped at San Luis Lake prior to their meeting on the Conejos River. The Comanches had raided the Ute camp at the lake and had made off with the Utes' horses. The Utes had recovered their stock and had killed about a dozen Comanches, whose remains Anza saw when he arrived at the lake. But the Utes were eager to exact further toll, and, thus, they had joined with Anza's force.

Moving north from the lake, the army next camped at a spring called "Aguage de los Yutas," or "watering place of the Utes," near the top of Poncha Pass. The crossing to the Arkansas River Valley was made on August 28. After pursuing the enemy across South Park, Anza marched around the south slopes of Pikes Peak and finally caught up with his quarry near the later site of Pueblo, Colorado. Although most of the Utes deserted Anza when the showdown was at hand, the Spaniards engaged the Comanches and killed eight of them.

The next encounter with the Comanches, who fled southward, was east of the peak now called "Greenhorn," the English translation of Cuerno Verde. Although the Comanches had been reinforced, they were defeated again, this time decisively. Chief Cuerno Verde, his son, and four renowned captains were among those killed. When Anza returned to Santa Fe after this victory, the Comanche threat to New Mexico had been broken.

His return route crossed La Veta Pass and the "Rio de la Culebra," where some of the Ute deserters were found. But these seemingly timorous campaigners, Anza learned, had encountered another party of Comanches, had killed sixteen of them, and had captured forty horses for their trouble.[17]

Henceforth the Comanches gave the Spaniards so little trouble that they were accorded a treaty of peace in 1786, a treaty in which the Utes shared lest the Santa Fe government be accused of favoritism. Unfortunately, peace with the Spaniards did not mean peace among Indians, and as late as 1809 these tribes again met in a major battle. Some Jicarillas and Utes, including those of the San Luis Valley, had decided to hunt buffalo together in the "Sierra de Almagre," which is the Front Range around Pikes Peak. During this hunt a large party of Comanches, Kiowas, and other Plains Indians attacked the hunters. Mano Mocha, chief of the Utes, was one of those killed. Upon hearing this news in Santa

Mule deer still abound in the foothills surrounding the valley.

Fe, the governor commented that "great loss and disadvantage regarding peace" would result from the death of "General Mano Mocha."[18] The old quarrels between the tribes did, in fact, revive.

Though more than two hundred years had passed since Spanish acquisition of New Mexico, little had changed in the San Luis Valley. Indians still occupied it, hunting, fighting, and raiding. Only the presence of horses and firearms was different, but this was an important difference to future settlers.

The Spanish descendants had left only a few mines and some of their dead—the bones of a soldier found near Deadman Creek and, on Ute Creek, the headstone of a padre who died in 1660.[19] Despite the fact that Spaniards had lived on the threshold of the valley for two centuries, they never assumed the strength or initiative to occupy this northern stronghold of the *indios barbaros.*

When Pike entered the San Luis Valley in 1807, he found an uninhabited place as large as the state of Connecticut. "Those who were considered subjects of the King" were, as usual, wintering elsewhere in their traditional haunts.

17

Poorly equipped for a long journey through deserts and mountains, Pike's men suffered severely from cold, hunger, and nuisances such as strange vegetation bearing spines but no food.

IV

"Refreshing My French Grammar and Overseeing the Works"

After 1800 the San Luis Valley was to emerge from its long seclusion, and the early years of the nineteenth century would witness the first official expedition of Americans into the valley.

After Spain had acquired French claims to Louisiana in 1762, the Spanish government had awakened to the possibilities of territorial exploitation. A Spanish fur trade developed with its center in St. Louis and with field personnel consisting largely of French and American trappers. Hoping to locate a route by which they could compete with other fur enterprises, the Spaniards even offered rewards for locating a northwest passage to the Pacific. But this interest in a northern empire had come too late. English fur companies, French traders, and even American frontiersmen were pressing their interests in Louisiana. Although they repeatedly penetrated Spanish territory illegally, cultivating the friendship and aid of Indians, the Sangre de Cristo Mountains remained the limit beyond which these intruders had been able to travel without the certainty of arrest.[1]

In 1800 France traded the state of Tuscany to Spain in exchange for the return of Louisiana, but French enterprises had little opportunity to develop before Napoleon sold the entire territory to the United States in 1803. The young republic, scarcely a quarter of a century old, eagerly set about exploring this bonanza, which took in all the land west of the Mississippi as far south as the Arkansas River's drainage and north to British territory.

During the first year or two after the Louisiana Purchase, a few French traders and trappers continued to roam the plains and found their way into New Mexico, which still belonged to Spain.

New Mexican authorities detained such interlopers and sometimes pressed them into the service of the government as scouts, interpreters, or spies.

One such example of Spanish vigilance during this period stemmed from an incident in the San Luis Valley in 1805. In October a Spanish soldier and a Frenchman named Tarvet were sent on a scouting party to the valley. At the Rio de Una del Gato (the Rio Gato, or "Cat's Claw River") they found four Frenchmen, who were escorted to Santa Fe for questioning. They testified that during their travels they had been fired upon by Pawnee Indians dressed in leather jackets. These garments, it was supposed, had been supplied by either American or French traders. Further evidence of illegal activity by traders had been reported from the Arkansas River, where the tracks of horses and mules crossed and recrossed the stream.[2]

When he first arrived in New Mexico a year earlier, Tarvet had revealed that Americans were encouraging the loyalty of Indians, and traders to the tribes on the plains, he said, were being licensed to treat with any Indians whose friendship might be important to the Spanish. Tarvet's reports were reinforced by two other Frenchmen, Baptiste La Lande and one Durocher, who wandered into New Mexico at about the same time.[3] A month or two later Governor Real Alencaster attempted to counteract such threats by urging that a fort and settlement be established on the Arkansas for trade with the Indians not only in that area but also as far away as the Missouri River.[4]

During this period Americans entering the Louisiana Territory did so without benefit of adequate maps. Whatever Spanish maps existed were carefully kept out of the hands of rivals, while the first American maps printed after the Louisiana Purchase provided almost no geographical details of practical use. The names of the Platte River, the Arkansas River, and the Red River were known to cartographers, but the origins of these streams were obscure. The Red River presented special problems in terms of boundary claims, because it does not empty into either the Mississippi system or the Rio Grande but flows into the Gulf of Mexico itself.

Although the Red River actually heads in the Texas Panhandle, the Spanish thought that its source was near the Rio Grande.[5] President Thomas Jefferson probably shared this notion, but he discreetly avoided discussions of the Red River in relation to boundary questions.[6] Instead, American expeditions were sent to investigate the river sources. Following an exploration of the headwaters of the Mississippi River, young Lieutenant Zebulon Montgomery Pike of the United States Army was assigned to investigate the western portions of Louisiana and the sources of the Red River.

Pike's orders also incorporated some business with Indian tribes through whose land he would be passing. He was to return a group of Indian captives to their Osage village in Missouri, to arrange peace between certain tribes, and to treat with the Comanches. As he traveled across the plains and toward the headwaters of the Arkansas and the Red rivers, he was to describe the geography, the navigability of the rivers, the natural history, and the people occupying the regions visited. (Obviously, the government in Washington wanted the most for its meager money.) Finally, Pike was cautioned by his commander, General James Wilkinson, to move carefully so as to avoid detection and cause for offense while near New Mexican territory.[7]

On October 9, 1806, Pike left Belle Fontaine, near St. Louis. In his party were eighteen men from the Mississippi expedition plus the son of General Wilkinson, a volunteer surgeon, an interpreter, two soldiers, and the fifty-one Osage In-

This log stockade near Sanford commemorates the location of Pike's winter camp in the San Luis Valley.

dians who were being returned to their home. Provisions were sufficient for a four-month tour of duty. Instead, Pike was gone nearly eleven months, some of his men even longer, and the absence of any cold-weather equipment was to be a severe handicap.

The expedition went according to plan for several weeks. Even when Pike learned from the Pawnees that six hundred dragoons from Santa Fe had been looking for him, he was not surprised, for he had been warned by Wilkinson that the Spanish probably would try to stop him. He was disturbed, though, to observe that the Pawnees were much more favorably impressed by the Spaniards' display than by his little party.[8]

The most puzzling aspect of Pike's journey up the Arkansas River is that he seems to have been bent on reaching Spanish territory above all else. Although he dutifully kept careful notes on every riffle in the river, as well as other features of geography, he was peculiarly intent on following the trail of the Spaniards. Near present-day Pueblo, Colorado, he digressed long enough for a vain attempt to climb Pikes Peak and then returned to his pursuit of the Spanish trace.

November had arrived and the strength of the men had diminished. Caught in an early snowstorm, some of the horses nearly died from starvation. While a few men were sent back to the Mississippi to report the progress of the expedition, the remainder entered the mountains. Still following the Arkansas and the trail of the Spaniards, they reached what was to become the site of Canon City. There they left the river and moved north into South Park, where the Spanish tracks led. Pike, oddly, was sure enough of his geography to identify correctly the sources of the South Platte River; but, descending from South Park into the Upper Arkansas River Valley near Buena Vista, he believed that he had found the headwaters of the Red River. He explored this stream northward to its source and then turned downstream. On December 26, when Pike was in the vicinity of Salida, he was only a day's march from Poncha Pass and the San Luis Valley.

Still under the impression that he was following the Red River, Pike continued downstream. Reaching the Royal Gorge, he crossed the hills through which the Arkansas knifes, and then found himself, much to his mortification, back at his former campsite near Canon City. At least, he consoled himself, he had found the source of the Arkansas River.

Despite this reversal Pike clung to the goal of finding the headwaters of the Red River, although he had lost the Spanish trail that he apparently thought would lead to this objective. His men had been marching with reduced gear since leaving the area of Pueblo, their clothing was inadequate for winter travel, and their food was gone. At the Canon City campsite two men and more of the equipment had to be left. The rest of the horses also remained there.

On January 14, 1807, Pike, Dr. Robinson, and twelve men headed south on foot, following Grape Creek. Struggling through deeper and deeper snow, the men labored with forty-five-pound packs containing presents for Indians and ammunition. Reaching the Wet Mountain Valley, they went without food for three days when they were unable to bring down any game, until they succeeded in killing both buffalo and deer. In this valley nine of the men suffered frozen feet, and two individuals were unable to travel farther. Reluctantly leaving these two behind, Pike and the others moved into the Sangre de Cristos, or the "White Mountains" as he called them. During the approach to the mountains, another man had to be left behind, but the main party crossed Medano Pass and entered the San Luis Valley on January 28.

When Pike saw the valley and the Rio Grande in the distance, he was sure that he had found the Red River at last. In fact, he used that name instead of the Rio Grande on his maps. Reaching the banks of this stream near Alamosa and finding no timber, Pike proposed that the group move downstream until wood was found for building rafts. Perhaps he was planning to float down the Red River to the Gulf of Mexico, or perhaps his real goal was Santa Fe, as some claim.

Downstream Pike found cottonwood groves crowding the banks of the Conejos River. Moving up this stream about five miles, he also found that mineral springs kept the Conejos River thawed and assured a water supply.[9] Here Pike decided to build a stockade "that four or five might defend, against the insolence, cupidity, and barbarity of the savages whilst others returned to assist on the poor fellows who were left behind at different points."[10]

Although Pike had seen signs of horses near the sand dunes, there is no evidence that he found any "savages" in the valley. Nevertheless, he had the stockade built as strongly as possible under the existing circumstances. Logs twelve feet long were set up on end to form the outer walls, and an inner tier of stakes slanted outward toward the exterior walls. The entire construction was only about thirty-six feet square.[11] This was the first building, however rude, set up by Americans in Spanish territory, as well as in the San Luis

Valley, and over it the American flag was flown for the first time in what became Colorado.[12]

While his men built the stockade, Pike hunted and kept up his journal. Among his notations were descriptions of a large, Spanish road along Culebra Creek. He also mentioned using this road when he went out hunting, but he never expressed concern about the possibility that he was in Spanish territory.

On February 7 Dr. Robinson set forth alone for Santa Fe. Pike confided to his journal that he wondered whether he ever would see again this able companion who would be marching directly into the hands of the Spanish. The professed reason for Robinson's taking this risk was to collect a debt from Baptiste La Lande for William Morrison of Illinois, who had outfitted La Lande's trading expedition. If Morrison knew that La Lande was in New Mexico and if La Lande was, in fact, detained there by the provincial authorities, it seems unlikely that Robinson went to Santa Fe expecting to collect any cash from the profits of the trading venture.

Much discussion has been devoted to Robinson's melodramatic journey from the San Luis Valley to Santa Fe and to the real purpose of the entire Pike expedition for that matter. To understand these arguments, one must know something about General Wilkinson, who had ordered the expedition.

Wilkinson was originally a commissioner of Louisiana Territory and later governor and commander of the army, during which time he sold information to the Spanish government concerning the plans of the United States in the Southwest. He also was an acquaintance of Aaron Burr, Jefferson's vice-president. After Burr's political career had been ruined by his killing Alexander Hamilton in a duel, Burr turned his ambitions toward separating the western states and Louisiana from the United States. When Burr appeared in Louisiana in 1805, an alliance between Burr and Wilkinson was suspected. Perhaps to clear his own name, Wilkinson revealed Burr's plot to Jefferson in 1806. Pike had left for the Southwest before Burr was brought to trial. Upon Pike's return, he found himself under suspicion for his affiliation with anything connected with Wilkinson. Robinson, who had been a close friend of Wilkinson, was even more suspect.[13]

One theory about the Pike expedition is that it was merely a ploy for Wilkinson to get word to the Spanish government about Burr's plot so that it would fail. On the other hand, if Wilkinson himself, indeed, entertained treasonous schemes, he might have sent Robinson to gather information about New Mexico. In either case it seems apparent that Robinson planned from the outset to reach the San Luis Valley and, from there, Santa Fe. Pike may have been in league with Robinson, or he may have been a dupe in the scheme. His knowledge of Robinson's plans has never been determined.

Following Robinson's departure for Santa Fe, the young commander settled down to the quiet routine of playing the waiting game. According to his journal, he spent the hours "refreshing my memory as to the French grammar, and overseeing the works." The former activity ironically was well chosen, for on February 26 two Frenchmen appeared.

These were foreign scouts who had been sent to the San Luis Valley, they said, to inform Pike that Governor Alencaster in Santa Fe was sending fifty dragoons to protect the Pike party from Ute Indians, for the Utes were threatening a raid. Pike had seen no Utes, but within a few minutes he did observe the approach of fifty-nine Spanish dragoons and fifty mounted militia. The "protective" force was armed with lances, carbines, and pistols. Unruffled, Pike requested through the French interpreters that the troops remain outside and that the officers be invited into the stockade for breakfast. The two Spanish lieutenants, Don Ignacio Saltelo and Don Bartholemew Fernandez, were astonished to discover that to enter they were obliged "to crawl on their bellies over a small drawbridge."

After a breakfast of venison, goose, and biscuits, the following conversation took place, Pike recorded:

> The commanding officer [Saltelo] addressed me as follows: "Sir, the governor of New Mexico, being informed you had missed your route, ordered me to offer you in his name mules, horses, money, or whatever you may stand in need of to conduct you to the head of the Red River, as from Santa Fe to where it is sometimes navigable is eight days' journey and we have guides and the routes of the traders to conduct us."
>
> "What," said I, interrupting him, "is not this the Red River?"
>
> "No Sir! the Rio del Norte."
>
> I immediately ordered my flag to be taken down and rolled up, feeling how sensibly I had committed myself in entering their territory, and was conscious that they must have positive orders to take me in.[14]

As Pike suspected, Lieutenant Saltelo did have

orders to take Pike to Santa Fe. In fact, Governor Alencaster had sent two scouting parties looking for Pike long before he entered the San Luis Valley. Scouts had watched Almagre and Sangre de Cristo creeks, each party being composed of a captain, eight soldiers, and about two dozen civilian volunteers with their Indian friends. Every third day the scouts had sent a courier to Santa Fe to report whether or not Pike had appeared. The commanders of each party had been instructed to invite Pike, if he were found, to come to Santa Fe, and they were to insinuate that his compliance would be in the best interests of harmony. If he should decline to come, he was to be told that other less cordial soldiers might not let him pass.[15]

Pike circumspectly accepted the invitation extended by Saltelo. While some of the Spanish soldiers remained in the valley with Pike's men, the American explorer was escorted down the west side of the Rio Grande and out of the valley. At San Juan he met Baptiste La Lande, who made no mention of having seen Robinson, nor did Pike's journal give any hint that he thought this to be the man for whom Robinson was looking. They talked of La Lande's detention in New Mexico, but Pike felt that the Frenchman's remarks were designed to disarm Pike and that La Lande actually was a spy for the Spanish government. La Lande accompanied Pike and his escort the rest of the way to Santa Fe. At the New Mexican capital, where Pike stayed for one day and night, the Spaniards' guest was politely questioned and entertained. Pike seems to have been as discomfitted by his shabby appearance at dinner in the governor's palace as he was by the official interrogation regarding his expedition.

The next day he again set off to the south under escort and was reunited with Robinson at Albuquerque. After being taken to Mexico, they were released to return to Louisiana by way of Texas. Pike's men, too, eventually were escorted through New Mexico and sent homeward.

Nothing in Pike's papers, found a century later in Spanish archives, and nothing in his future military career indicate that he was less than loyal to the United States. His expedition contributed to the nation's understanding of its new frontier, and, when his journal was published, it was illustrated with a map that for the first time described correctly the locations of the Platte and Arkansas rivers and the Rio Grande, although he perpetuated the errors about the Red River by placing its source in the neighborhood of the New Mexican Sangre de Cristos. His notes conscientiously reported in detail all that he had observed on his long journey to the Southwest and Mexico.[16]

A few of the descendants of the Spanish party that had arrested Pike later lived in the San Luis Valley. The child of one soldier, Julian Sanchez, had a home on Culebra Creek; and the children of Antonio Domingo Lucero, a drummer boy, also lived in the valley.[17] But for several years after Pike's visit the valley remained unsettled. It continued under the dominion of Spain until 1821, and occupation by New Mexicans was not encouraged.

Even after Mexico, including New Mexico, became independent of Spain, the Arkansas River remained the boundary beyond which Americans rarely traveled. When Spain found its North American claims about to slip from its grasp, a last-ditch effort to establish its northern boundary had been made. In 1820 the Adams-Onis Treaty was ratified, recognizing the Arkansas River as that border.[18] This formal agreement acted as an effective buffer for the next several years, long after Americans finally were permitted to enter New Mexico.

San Luis Valley Counties and Communities
x—Former   O—Existing   ★—County Seat

o Alder

o Rawley
Exchequerville x
o Bonanza
Bonita x   x Kerber City   o VILLA GROVE
Spook City x   x Sedgwick
                         Parkville x   x Claytonia   x Orient City
                                                           o Valley View Hot Springs (Haumann)
                                                      x Bismark (?)
                                                      o Mineral Hot Springs
x Rockcliff
                                             x Cotton Creek
              ★ SAGUACHE   x Mirage
              x Milton   x Rio Alto
S A G U A C H E   x San Isabel
                                                      x Teton
              o Swede Corners   o MOFFAT   o CRESTONE
                                           Julia City x   x Spanish
                                             Lucky x   x Sangre de Cristo
              Veteran x   Cottonwood x
                                                      x Duncan
              La Garita Station x   X Liberty
x Sky City   x Biedell   Dune x   x Music City
              x Los Mogotes   Gibson x
              x Carnero
              o LA GARITA

                                   o CENTER ——— o HOOPER ——————————— ★
                                                (Garrison)
o Masonic Park
   o Agua Ramon   x Loma   o Ansel   x Medano Springs
Granger o   o Hanna   x La Loma   o Sargent   x Goudy (Garnett)   x Old Mosca (Montville)
   o SOUTH FORK   DEL NORTE ★   x Del Norte   o Dunul Coryell (Stanley)
              San Jose x   x Seven-Mile Plaza   x   o MOSCA (Streator)
              San Francisco x   x Haywood   x Zapata
                                o Torres   X Uracca   x Placer
                             o HOMELAKE   x Russell
R I O   G R A N D E   o MONTE VISTA   A L A M O S A   o Sierra
                                                         Fort   x Trinchera
                             o Parma   x McGinty   Massachusetts
                                           x Wayside (Riverside)   x   x Garland City
o Summitville   o Bowen   ★ ALAMOSA x Washington Springs
   x Jasper (Cornwall)   o Baldy   o BLANCA
                             o Waverly   o FORT GARLAND
x Stunner   o Henry   x Rio Grande
   o Platoro   o Estrella
                                                                C O S T I L L A
                             o Morgan
Centro x   o CAPULIN   x Richfield   x Pike's Stockade
                         o LA JARA   o La Sauses (Stewart's Crossing)
                         o SANFORD
                         o BOUNTIFUL   San Acacio o   x Old San Acacio
C O N E J O S   ★ SAN LUIS
              ROMEO o   o MANASSA   SAN PEDRO o   o CHAMA
                         o Los Cerritos   o SAN PABLO
              Servietta x   x Rincones   o LOS FUERTES (Vallejos)
              Guadalupe o   x Raza de Brazos   o SAN FRANCISCO (La Valley)
         SAN RAFAEL o   ★ CONEJOS   o Mesita
         LAS MESITAS o o ANTONITO   (Hamburg)
              o MOGOTE   o Lobatos   x Myers Ferry
              o Canon   (Cenicero) (Paso del Puerto)
   o Los Pinos   x Eastdale
Cumbres o   o Osier   o SAN ANTONIO
                ORTIZ o   JAROSA o   o GARCIA (Manzanares)

V

"In the Nibor Hood of Touse"

For two centuries French *voyageurs* and Indians with whom they traded harvested millions of beaver pelts from the upper regions of North America to feed the international fur market. Yet, for only a quarter of a century did "mountain men" trap in the San Luis Valley before the beaver industry died out. During its brief heyday in the Southern Rockies trapping was neither the large-scale economic venture nor the same kind of experience which it had been on the rivers of the North. But what the southern beaver industry lacked in durability, profit, and birch bark canoes, it made up for in the liveliness of Taos.

Shortly after Pike's expedition to the Southwest, fur hunters had begun to appear more frequently along the Arkansas and Platte rivers. Spanish officials, nervous about this activity and by alliances made between the fur traders and the Plains Indians, had pressed their boundary claims and arrested any trappers found near the Arkansas as trespassers.

Later, in the second decade of the 1800s, a trapping party led by Joseph Philibert crossed the mountains in the San Luis Valley. These eighteen French trappers had been assembled by Philibert in St. Louis to trap and trade with the Arapahos. In the autumn of 1814 forty Spaniards in search of horses in the San Luis Valley came upon two men of this party. They were taken to Santa Fe for questioning, and 250 soldiers were sent out to arrest the others and to confiscate their goods. All were held in Santa Fe for a month and a half and then were allowed to remain in Taos for the rest of the winter prior to their retreat across the mountains to the plains.[1]

Philibert's trapping was successful enough that he encouraged others to try to enter the valley. Although the New Mexican government was persuaded occasionally to permit trapping east of the mountains, licenses still were not issued for the valleys along the Rio Grande. To prevent unauthorized activity there, the Spaniards established a post on the Rio Colorado, or the "Little Red River," north of Taos where Questa now is located. The Rio Colorado outpost was noted by Jules De Mun in 1816, when he traveled to the "Rio de la Culevra" (Culebra Creek) with a party of Spanish traders and two trappers from St. Louis.[2]

Traders and trappers may have observed the formalities of seeking permission to work east of the mountains, but from time to time rumors of an American takeover of the plains reached Santa Fe.[3] In 1818 while the Arkansas River boundary was being negotiated by the United States and Spain, relations between the two countries deteriorated abruptly when American notes, describing routes into New Mexico and the resources of the province, were apprehended by the Spanish. The viceroy in Mexico City sent orders that the mountain passes on these routes be fortified to prevent an invasion. Foremost of these passes was Sangre de Cristo, which the notes reported to be practicable for artillery and easy defense. Another pass into the San Luis Valley also was considered for a fortification. This may have been Mosca Pass, which the notes called a very bad route, seldom used even by Indians.[4] Apparently a fort was built only on Sangre de Cristo Pass. It was a triangular stone enclosure on a hill about five miles east of the pass's summit.[5] The fort was built by 1819, for in that year one hundred Indians attacked a small detachment of Spaniards there.[6] Although a large troop was sent to reinforce the site after this incident, the fort appeared to have been abandoned for about a year when Jacob Fowler, an American trapper, passed it in 1822.

Although Spain did acquire the region east of the mountains north to the Arkansas River under the terms of the boundary agreement of 1820, Spanish possession was short-lived. Discontent with Spain's rule was strong in Mexico. Following the examples of the French and American revolutions, Mexico rebelled in 1821 and became independent of the crown.

As soon as Spain's rule in New Mexico was terminated, American traders turned their efforts toward the new market, Santa Fe. The third party to reach New Mexico, following those of Baird and McKnight, was led by Hugh Glenn, a trader among the Osage Indians. When he learned from Spanish soldiers that Mexico had declared her independence, Glenn was camped with about twenty men near Pueblo. He immediately decided to seek permission to trap in the Rio Grande area, and he and four of his men joined the soldiers who were bound for Santa Fe. They followed the well-worn Sangre de Cristo trail, which lay along the Huerfano, past Badito Cone, and up Pass Creek to Pass Creek Pass. From there they continued to Sangre de Cristo Pass, then down Sangre de Cristo Creek, and along the east side of the San Luis Valley to Taos. This route became so frequently used by trappers in subsequent years that it was known as the "Trappers' Trail," as well as the "Taos Trail."

While Glenn was getting the license, his men remained on the east side of the mountains under the leadership of Jacob Fowler, second in command of the Glenn expedition. Fowler is of particular interest because he kept a journal of the venture in 1821-22, including a description of trapping in the San Luis Valley. His faithfulness to the principles of phonetic spelling was equalled by an accurate eye for detail. His record provides both the first American description of the San Luis Valley after Pike and also information about the fur-trade years.[7]

Predictably, soldiers arrived to escort the Fowler contingent from Pueblo to Taos. They set forth on January 29, 1822. Crossing Sangre de Cristo Pass, on February 5 they entered the San Luis Valley, "an oppen plain of great Extent." En route Fowler observed not only the abandoned fort on the pass but also the settlement at Rio Colorado, which had been deserted by "the Inhabetance for feer of the Indeans now at War With them." At Taos the trapping party learned that 700 soldiers were then battling Navajos east of the mountains. These Indian troubles, together with a three-year drought and scarcity of flour, probably were responsible, in part at least, for the encouragement of American trade in Santa Fe.

Arriving "in the nibor Hood of touse," Fowler's brigade was introduced quickly to the local customs—from infamous grain alcohol to local hospitality, which began with a fandango and ended with a "Close Huge" from which they escaped only after considerable embarrassment.

Four days "in the nibor Hood of touse" were enough. On February 12, splitting into three parties, the men left town to trap. Two of the groups, led by Isaac Slover and Jesse van Bibber, went directly to the San Luis Valley, while the third, led by Fowler, investigated the streams to the south. Finding the beaver already taken there, he and his men also went north to the valley.

Here they trapped along the Conejos, called by Fowler "Pikes forke of the Delnort." Their camp was "about three miles below His Block House Whear He was taken by the Spanierds." The trappers worked the San Juan Mountains to the west, La Garita Mountains, Wagon Wheel Gap, across the passes and down the Lake Fork of the Gunnison River. On the east side of the San Luis Valley they trapped along Trinchera and Culebra creeks. They met with fair success despite ice on some streams. In addition to beaver they took a few "aughter," probably marten. Game brought in for the camp pot included mountain sheep, deer, elk, "cabery" (antelope), geese, and one sandhill crane. When hunting was bad once, they killed a horse for supper, but the poor beast was not yet skinned out before a hunter brought in some venison. On Culebra Creek they bagged a wolf—perhaps a coyote.

The first of their encounters with Indians occurred near South Fork. While the trappers were out of camp, Utes stole two "Buffelow Roabes Some lead and two knives." This tribe, Fowler observed, "live alltogether on the Chase Raising no grain." Another camp near the Conejos found itself hemmed in between two large Indian encampments. The traps of one man were stolen, but he rode after the culprits and recovered all but two. On Culebra Creek Jicarilla Apaches came into Fowler's camp to warn him that Utes had stolen three of the Americans' horses and intended to take more. To avoid this raid, the men moved their camp a few miles and spent a cheerless night without a campfire but without an Indian incident either.

In the early summer of 1822 the Glenn expedition packed 1,100 pounds of furs back to St. Louis and sold them to the American Fur Company.[8] Trapping had been sufficiently good that other independent parties were encouraged to head for the Southern Rockies. Here they could operate without competition from the great trading companies of the North. Furthermore, furs traded in New Mexico were not taxed.[9] Many of these trappers who came in the 1820s and 1830s worked the San Luis Valley. Others used the valley as a route to the Gunnison and Uncompahgre river regions.

In addition to trails left by the trappers, a rudimentary wagon road appeared in the valley. By the mid-twenties, when trade between the Missouri River and New Mexico was becoming active, some shippers used the Sangre de Cristo Pass route to Taos. However, the main branch of the Santa Fe Trail lay far to the east on the plains. Most traffic to Santa Fe stayed on the main branch or else used the Mountain Branch that crossed Raton Pass, south of present-day Trinidad, Colorado, bypassing both the San Luis Valley and Taos.

For trappers, however, Taos was the principal trade and supply center in the Southern Rockies. Many of the mountain men headquartered in or near Taos, married Mexican or Indian women or both, and chose to remain in the area after the fur industry declined.

Originally, about half of the trappers were of French extraction.[10] Most of the American trappers were frontiersmen, who, like the French, came out through Missouri.[11] Among the early mountain men was Antoine Robidoux, whose father, a French-Canadian, founded St. Joseph, Missouri. Antoine Robidoux arrived in New Mexico in 1824 and was responsible for bringing several colorful men into the area. He operated posts on the Uintah River in Utah and on the Gunnison River, the latter being reached by a short cut across the Sangre de Cristos through Mosca Pass and then across the San Luis Valley to Cochetopa Pass. The use of Mosca Pass by Robidoux's supply trains resulted in its being called Robidoux Pass for a while. The name was still in use when Americans surveyed the area in the 1850s.

One of the men attracted to the Southern Rockies by Robidoux was Antoine Leroux, who arrived in Taos in 1824.[12] Leroux was back and forth through the San Luis Valley continually in the following years. Kit Carson came to Taos in 1826.[13] He worked on wagon trains for two years and then became cook for Ewing Young, a Taos storekeeper, who organized a trapping party in 1829.[14] It was a large party of about forty men. Intending to go to western New Mexico, they set out through the San Luis Valley to conceal their real destination.[15] Later Carson achieved success as an independent operator and had his own

coterie of trappers and scouts. Already a central character in Taos, Kit married the Spanish sister-in-law of Charles Bent, a prominent American entrepreneur, in the 1840s, thereby assuring Carson's social acceptance.

Tom Tobin, who came west in the 1830s, worked with Carson from time to time. He is known to have trapped in the San Luis Valley in 1838, on one of many probable trips to the area. After marrying a señorita at Arroyo Hondo north of Taos, Tom settled down to farming a plot given to the couple by his mother-in-law. Tobin was the half-brother of another famous mountain man, Charles Autobees.[16] Tom and Charlie both worked at times for Simeon Turley at Arroyo Hondo, where a potent beverage called Taos Lightning was distilled at Turley's place of business. Charlie's assignment was to haul shipments of this frontier necessity to trading posts which had been built east of the mountains.[17] Without question, Charlie's trips through the San Luis Valley were the most eagerly anticipated missions of the entire fur-trade era.

As inflammatory as Taos Lightning was the personality known as "Peg-leg" Smith. "Peg-leg," whose given name was Thomas, and Aaron B. Lewis crossed the San Luis Valley from Taos in the early 1830s with the intention of trapping between the Gunnison and Colorado rivers. When Ute Indians attempted to appropriate their catch, "Peg-leg" discouraged the thieves with a barrage of colorful language, but the trapping expedition was abandoned. The men returned to Taos by way of Poncha Pass and the valley.[18]

Among the legendary trappers are found only a few Mexican names. Domingo Lamelas was one of these exceptions. In 1827 Lamelas was granted a license to trap on the Rio Colorado (the "Little Red") and on the Moro, provided that he took no foreigners with him. Instead he trapped in the San Luis Valley with Simon Carat and Antoine Leroux. The furs were impounded and the men were questioned by government officials. In their testimony Leroux revealed that the operation had been under contract to Sylvestre Pratte.[19] Despite such efforts by the New Mexican government to maintain some control of the industry, it obviously was in the hands of "foreigners," who were only slightly inconvenienced by officialdom on the one hand and hostile Indians on the other.[20]

By the 1840s the decline in beaver prices affected the amount of trapping being done, although the industry did not die out abruptly. In 1842, for example, John Hawkins and Dick Wootton hauled a valuable mixed cargo of beaver pelts and Spanish silver across Sangre de Cristo Pass to Bent's Fort on the Arkansas River. Hawkins may have been the son of Jacob Hawken, renowned gunsmith of Missouri. Wootton became well known as a resident of territorial Colorado. Both Hawkins and Wootton were employed by Bent, St. Vrain and Company in the 1840s.[21] From this company's adobe fort on the Arkansas River, trade with Indians of the plains and mountains took place.

As the profit in beaver declined and trapping dropped off in the 1840s, the buffalo trade gave many mountain men jobs.[22] The mood of various Indians often determined their success. When Charles Town of Taos went to the San Luis Valley in 1846 to trade on Culebra Creek, the Utes stole his horses.[23]

Nevertheless, traders and Indians are known to have camped together harmoniously several times on Saguache Creek, about twenty miles above the present town of Saguache. This location was one of the most popular and beautiful of the Ute camps. Its Indian name, *Saguguachipa*, meant "blue water," referring to a spring that rose from a basin of blue-stained earth. Because the traders who visited this camp could not pronounce the name, they abridged it to "Saguache," the name applied later to the creek and the pioneer town.[24] In October 1846 Alexander Barclay came to the valley from the post on Hardscrabble Creek to trade with the Utes for buffalo hides at two encampments, one on the west side of the valley between the Rio Grande and Saguache Creek, the other between Saguache Creek and Poncha Pass.[25]

Almost no information about New Mexico appeared in print in the States through these years. Jacob Fowler's journal was not published until many years later, in 1898. Pike's record remained the most available source, with the exception of a few newspaper stories repeating the tales of mountain men. A map prepared by the United States government in 1839 named only a few mountains and streams, one being the Rio Bravo del Norte, or the Rio Grande. Where the San Luis Valley might have been shown, but was not, were these words: "Of this Country the little that is known is learned from the Trappers of Santa Fe. They represent the Country from the Colorado to the sources of the Arkansas & Platte as very Mountainous and the Vallies narrow."[26]

Ignorance about the area soon came to an end, though. In 1836, when Texas gained its independence from Mexico, Texas claimed that its western boundary was the Rio Grande, which incidentally would have included the east side of the San Luis Valley. When Texas became one of the United States, the boundary claim along the Rio Grande was adopted by the American government. Not surprisingly, Mexico contested the matter, and this dispute, coupled with a problem of debts owed the United States by Mexico, precipitated the outbreak of war in 1846. On August 19 of that year General Stephen Watts Kearny took possession of New Mexico for the United States by marching into Santa Fe. By virtue of this military occupation the San Luis Valley became part of the United States.

Among the first American citizens to visit the valley thereafter were Mormons of Nauvoo, Illinois, who had left that place because of harassment there. The mustering of volunteers for the Mexican War provided some of these Mormons with an opportunity to enlist as volunteer infantrymen with the promise of going to California. Taking along a few families, they marched to Santa Fe, arriving after Kearny had taken the capital. Although the Mormons had not come through the journey in very good shape, some were determined to continue to California, while eighty or ninety others were sent back to Pueblo for the winter. These men and their families were joined in December by several members of the Mormon Battalion, which had been beset by illness after it started for California. This addition, which nearly doubled the contingent at Pueblo, arrived after a difficult trip through the San Luis Valley and across Sangre de Cristo Pass in deep snow. A few of them who were too ill to complete the journey with the others laid over with Simeon Turley at Arroyo Hondo for several days, but all were in Pueblo by the middle of January 1847.[27] They were fortunate to have left Turley's when they did.

As might be expected, the sudden take-over of New Mexico by Americans was not well accepted by most local citizens. The Mormon Battalion reported a lack of cooperation in obtaining food and equipment in villages which they passed. In the area around Taos, where isolation had bred independence for scores of years, the New Mexicans rebelled against the American settlers in January 1847. New Mexico's new governor, Charles Bent, was one of the "foreigners" killed in the Taos uprising. At Arroyo Hondo, where the last Mormons had just left, Simeon Turley and others escaped by digging a hole from the distillery into the granary. Turley was captured and killed, but Tom Tobin made it to Santa Fe, where he joined the volunteers who were organizing to put down the rebellion.[28] Another survivor from Arroyo Hondo was John D. Albert, who, like Tobin, had married a Mexican and was working for Turley. Albert escaped to the north, passing "the settlements on the little Red River." Discovering them to be in league with the uprising, he continued through the San Luis Valley, across Sangre de Cristo Pass, and so to Pueblo.[29]

Since Fowler had passed through this area in 1822 and reported Rio Colorado deserted, it had been resettled. A description of the "Plaza of the Colorado" was written by George Frederick Ruxton, Esq., an Englishman who traveled through Mexico and the· Rocky Mountains in 1846 and 1847. In New Mexico only a few days before the rebellion, Ruxton visited Taos, Arroyo Hondo, and Rio Colorado. He found the inhabitants of Rio Colorado living in the most deplorable conditions he had seen anywhere. "Growing a bare sufficiency for their own support, they hold the little land they cultivate, and their wretched hovels, on sufferance from the barbarous Yutas, who actually tolerate their presence in their country for the sole purpose of having at their command a stock of grain and a herd of mules and horses."[30]

Between this settlement and Pueblo he found no other dwellings. With a half-breed guide, Ruxton spent his first night out from Rio Colorado in a "state of congelation" from the cold. This camp on "Rib Creek" (Costilla) was not improved by the "wolves" that prowled around all night. When Ruxton crossed "La Culebra, or Snake Creek" the next day, he noticed that the Mormons had camped there only a few days earlier. Ruxton and his guide continued to "La Trinchera, or Bowl Creek" and then entered an exceptionally windy valley, called El Vallecito. It was known also as the "Wind Trap" by mountain men, Ruxton noted. From this uncomfortable place they climbed Sangre de Cristo Pass and left the valley.[31]

During the quarter century since New Mexico had first welcomed traders and trappers, the San Luis Valley had become a familiar place to mountain men, to a large number of Mormons, and to one world traveler. The self-reliant, buckskin-clad trappers were not about to leave the West just because the beaver trade had given out. They remained as hunters, scouts, and Indian fighters, their names reappearing subsequently in records of American exploration and military campaigns. The Mormons would return, though several years later, to this valley that they first saw under such inauspicious circumstances. And the journalist-on-horseback, the gentleman adventurer who appeared at a climactic moment in history, would be followed by a host of other reporters, and rich men, poor men, doctors, lawyers, and even a few lingering Indian chiefs.

Explorers in the West often published extravagant descriptions of its geography, as seen in this view of Blanca Peak at the entrance to the San Luis Valley, from Heap's *Central Route to the Pacific.*

VI

"Mule Tail Soup, Baked White Mule, and Boiled Gray Mule"

A preacher is expected to guide his followers to the portals of heaven, but Parson Bill Williams led thirty-two men straight into the gates of hell in the winter of 1848-49. William Sherley Williams had given up a pulpit in the States many years prior to this disaster and had trapped all over the West with Jedediah Smith. Assuming the ways of the land like many other mountain men, Williams had taken a squaw for his wife and had stayed in the West when the fur trade waned. When John Charles Frémont met him at the trading post at Pueblo in November 1848, "Old Bill" was sixty-one years old.[1]

Despite his age Williams was hired at Pueblo to guide Frémont's reconnaissance of a route for a transcontinental railroad, because it was generally believed that he knew the country involved better than anyone else.[2] Had this notion been true, he would have been a most appropriate successor to Kit Carson and Thomas Fitzpatrick, mountain men who had guided Frémont's expeditions to Oregon and California earlier in the 1840s. With their help Frémont had completed the most extensive investigations till then of the western territories, and his staff had prepared the first map of the West that could be considered reliable, so to work for the famed Frémont was a prestige which any aging trapper would consider an honor.

After the Treaty of Guadalupe Hidalgo formally ceded New Mexico to the United States in 1848, Americans needed to know more about their new territory. Although Frémont had traveled through Colorado earlier in the 1840s, he had not been south of the Arkansas River. Frémont's influential father-in-law, Senator Thomas H. Benton of Missouri, who had financed the two earlier trips, now sent him to investigate New

Mexico in hopes of finding a route near the thirty-eighth parallel for a railroad, the "central route to the Pacific," which Missourians believed to be the key to America's westward expansion.[3] In addition to Benton's investment, other St. Louis businessmen put up cash and equipment for the reconnaissance of 1848-49.[4]

The thirty-eighth parallel lies a little north of Medano Pass in the Sangre de Cristo Mountains. It crosses the San Luis Valley near Crestone on the east and lies south of Saguache on the west. Cochetopa Pass is north of this parallel, and the Rio Grande heads just south of it. Lake City, north of the Continental Divide, is quite near the thirty-eighth parallel. Apparently, Frémont intended to reach the Lake Fork of the Gunnison River, on which Lake City is located, by crossing the San Luis Valley and traveling up the Rio Grande. In November 1848, while Frémont was at Bent's Fort, he wrote to Senator Benton that his route would take him to the head of the "Del Norte."[5] This would not have been an unusual choice, although Cochetopa Pass was used more frequently for winter travel into the Gunnison country.

With the exception of a guide, Frémont's expedition was fully manned when it left Bent's Fort. In this force were a physician, a millwright, a gunsmith, a cartographer, and an artist who would perform the functions now filled by photographers. Frémont had expected to hire Kit Carson at Bent's Fort for another tour in the vital role of guide, but Kit was confined in Taos by illness. There were assurances that a substitute could be found farther up the Arkansas at Pueblo, for several mountain men were known to be wintering there. Thus, Williams came to be chosen.

When the party left Pueblo, they headed west

Kit Carson, left, posed with the Pathfinder, John Charles Frémont, who met disaster in the San Juan Mountains.

through the outpost at Hardscrabble and then crossed the Wet Mountains into the Wet Mountain Valley. In the Wet Mountains the men encountered deep snow, although it was still only late November. Because of this early onset of winter the expedition found itself moving more slowly and consuming more of its food supply than had been planned for this stage.[6] In hindsight it seems that Frémont should have abandoned at this point the impractical goal of a winter crossing through the mountains.

Instead, Williams led the men into the Sangre de Cristos from the Wet Mountain Valley, evidently planning to use Medano Pass as Pike had done in 1807. But, as the expedition's cartographer, Charles Preuss, observed in his journal, "Bill's vacillations showed that he was not very much at home, at least in these parts," and in crossing the range he "definitely missed the promised *good* pass."[7] When they finally reached the top, where they could see the San Luis Valley, they had to make a "wide detour through fresh-fallen snow to the real pass."[8] It has been suggested that the pass which they descended was Mosca, or Robidoux Pass; but since their trail led along the north side of the sand dunes, it seems clear that they used Medano.[9] In fact, Medano has been called Williams Pass, along with another name, Sand Hill Pass.

On December 4 when they circumvented the dunes, snow lay three feet deep. More snow fell and was drifted by strong wind while the men and their 120 mules struggled across the San Luis Valley in a much more difficult traverse than usually encountered. They arrived at the river "where the valley narrows down to a canyon," the water glistening "rather deep below." According to Frémont's account, this stream was La Garita Creek. Preuss remarked, "It was obvious that Bill had never been here."[10]

Despite such doubts about Williams' ability to guide, the expedition entered the mountains here. As the snow became deeper and deeper, the mules were unable to find anything to eat, and most of the grain carried for them was gone. Nevertheless, the party pressed farther into the mountains, while the old trapper assured them that a snowless mesa lay beyond the divide. Seven mules had died by December 16 when the expedition reached a summit that they hoped would be the Continental Divide. It was not, and more mountains lay ahead. The next day the strongest men pushed on, attempting to break a trail for the others, but wind and snow drove them back to camp.

The party occupied this place, called "Camp Desolation," for several days. Here the hands and feet of a number of men froze. Even the eyelids of Dr. Benjamin Kern were frosted shut one day. Many of the animals died in this camp, and "Old Bill" lay down and wanted to die himself.[11] In a vain effort to save the remaining mules, they were driven onto a promontory from which the snow had been blown, exposing a little grass. But nearly all of them froze to death on this unsheltered knoll. The men began to survive by eating frozen mule meat, while the mules that were still alive ate blankets, ropes, pack saddles, and each others' tails and manes.

Finally, on December 22 Frémont admitted defeat and turned the expedition back. Using a different route than the one by which they had entered the mountains, they struggled through the snow, hauling baggage and equipment in relays and on wooden sleds that they had made. On December 24 they had to dig through six feet of snow with pots and dinner plates. At "Camp Hope" on December 25, according to Fremont, they feasted on elk stew, doughnuts, biscuits, coffee, and mule-meat pie. But one of his men reminisced in later years that the Christmas menu had consisted of "mule tail soup, baked white mule, and boiled gray mule." Relishes were tallow candles.[12] Aside from concern for historical accuracy, one might accept the second as symptomatic of the men's morale.

By December 27 conditions had become so desperate that a party of four set out for help. In this group were Williams, Henry King, Thomas Breckenridge, and botanist Frederick Creutzfeldt. Their destination was Abiquiu, which they thought was the "next Spanish town," where they hoped to obtain animals and food. Estimating the distance to be about one hundred miles, they expected to reach it in about four days by traveling at night. Agreeing to this plan, Frémont sent them off with $1,800 for their purchases. The fact that Williams thought that Abiquiu was the most accessible Spanish town is further evidence of his unfamiliarity with New Mexico.

After the rescue party set off on December 28, the others continued their slow progress with the baggage and equipment. "A sled came to grief, we could not find material for snowshoes, ... we had to leave the animals behind."[13] At this time the men broke up into three groups, called "messes," each of which was to carry or scavenge its own food supplies.

By New Year's Eve one of the messes already

had dropped about three miles behind the others. In it were the Kern brothers, Captain Andrew Cathcart, who had been with Ruxton during some of his travels, and a few Indians who were returning to California with Frémont. To celebrate New Year's Eve, this motley little band "sang several songs in our crude way," read aloud to each other, and minced some mule meat for the next day's "treat."[14]

As the three messes worked their way down through the mountains, they passed several campfire sites left by their would-be rescuers. It soon became apparent that the rescue party had become lost before reaching the Rio Grande and had spent more than four or five days getting out of the mountains. Later it was learned that all four men had been frostbitten and that their food had given out. For several days they subsisted on a hawk, an otter, and a boot, until, when King died from exhaustion, the survivors ate some of his flesh. Finally, on their twenty-first day out, Breckenridge killed a deer, and on the following day the "rescue party" was rescued by Frémont, whose mess reached the San Luis Valley on January 11.[15]

Finding Indian tracks on January 12, the Frémont mess followed them and arrived at an Indian camp on the fifth day. Here they were able to obtain horses and an Indian guide who would take them down through the valley to the settlement on the Rio Colorado. One day out from the Indian encampment, they found Williams, Creutzfeldt, and Breckenridge, looking like apparitions.

When the party reached Rio Colorado, preparations were begun immediately to assist the men who had been left behind in the mountains. Local women set about baking large quantities of bread to be carried by the rescue party. Since the village had no mules—only a few goats—Alexander Godey rode down to Arroyo Hondo, thirteen miles to the south, to get some. He brought back thirty, plus one well-received hog.

Godey seems to have been one of the hardiest and ablest members of the expedition. He had been with Frémont previously. Godey was twenty-five years old when he met Frémont in the summer of 1843 at Fort St. Vrain, a fur-trade post on the South Platte River. The young man then had been in the Rockies for six or seven years, working as a hunter for the trading posts near the mountains and occasionally undertaking trading expeditions into Indian territory. Godey hired on with Frémont to accompany the survey in 1843. Despite his many other qualifications the young mountain man apparently did not have sufficient experience in the Southern Rockies to qualify as a guide in 1848-49.

However, the self-reliant Godey was chosen now to lead the rescue attempt, which began on January 23 from Rio Colorado. Accompanied by four Mexicans, he headed back toward the mountains, while Frémont recuperated in Taos at the home of Kit Carson and the other two men waited in Rio Colorado.[16]

Eighteen miles above the mouth of the Conejos the rescue team found the first of the survivors. To this group Frémont had given the unrealistic task of bringing out the baggage, an assignment that was impossible for them to fulfill, of course. Not only the baggage but also the weaker members of the mess had been abandoned. Quarrels about the division of food had arisen, and finally the mess's leader, Lorenzo Vincenthaler, had declared each man for himself. Seven of this group died.

As the rescuers pressed north, they found a few of the deserted men still alive. The Kern team also was found in severe condition but still resolved to stay together. Although two of their men had died, they resisted the decision to eat human flesh, choosing instead a diet of bugs, moccasin soles, rosehips, and the carcass of a dead wolf. A final survivor, one of the California Indians, was found in the shelter of a cave. By February the heroic rescue party had brought out the men, Frémont's trunk, and some of the other baggage, but ten men and all of the expedition's mules were dead.

Still the disaster was not complete. Frémont, who had shown such an exaggerated concern for the expedition's equipment, remained unwilling to give it up as a loss. In the spring Dr. Kern and "Old Bill" were sent to recover it. They both were killed by Indians during their return to the tragedy-filled mountains. Although Ute Indians were seen wearing the Americans' clothing in the summer of 1849, Frémont's equipment never was found.[17]

The area where the ill-fated Frémont expedition foundered has been pinpointed by the discovery of two campsites. One of these was high on Wannamaker Creek, the other at the head of Embargo Creek. At both sites were found a number of tree stumps, cut about six feet above the ground, presumably at snow level. At the camp on Embargo Creek two sleds that had been made to haul Frémont's gear were found. Albert Pfeiffer, the son of a mountain man of the same name, first saw the sleds while he was trailing a deer about 1880. One sled was about four feet long, and the other was about six and one-half feet long. Both had been made of spruce wood without metal fastenings. In 1930 a U.S. Forest Service ranger, E. S. Erickson, was guided to the location of the sleds by a sheepherder, Epimenio Romero.[18] At the Wannamaker Creek camp, called Camp Desolation by the expedition, forty-three tree stumps were found.[19] After camping here for several days, the men had started with their improvised sleds toward the Rio Grande via Embargo Creek, where the sleds were abandoned.[20]

The route by which the expedition reached the Wannamaker Creek encampment never has been established, although Frémont's contemporaries accepted the fact that the men were headed for the headwaters of the Rio Grande when they became lost. The pass that they would have been seeking has been called variously Leroux, Summer, or Williams Pass, as well as the Pass of the Del Norte. When they reached the headwaters of Wannamaker Creek, they still were about twenty-five miles east of this pass. Despite Williams's faults as a guide, the severe weather alone could have been responsible for his confusion, as he easily might have mistaken one landmark for another in the blinding snow.

In the winter of 1806-07 Zebulon Pike undertook a crossing of the Sangre de Cristos without a retinue of experts, without special equipment, without pack animals, and without a guide, and he appears to have reached his intended destination. Still, he has been referred to as the "lost pathfinder." Compared to Frémont's disaster of 1848-49, Pike's accomplishments probably have deserved more credit. For his part, Frémont did succeed eventually in reaching California, though not by a central route. Instead, he followed Kit Carson's advice and used a southern route. Although the renowned "Pathfinder," as Frémont came to be called, returned to the San Luis Valley once more during his fifth and final venture in exploration, his energies thereafter were directed toward politics, mining, and railroad building, all of which won him additional fame as well as controversy.

History will not permit Parson Bill Williams to vindicate himself, for he had no second chance. For him there was no escape from the devilish fate that the San Juan Mountains had stored up.

The site on Ute Creek where Fort Massachusetts was built in 1852 is overgrown with sagebrush and chamiso.

VII

More Mule Meat

The fulfillment of America's "manifest destiny," westward expansion, owes an enormous debt to that inglorious beast the mule. Exploration of western territories frequently depended on the availability and the stamina of this long-eared symbol of stubbornness. When a mule was ready to give up, his human counterpart also was apt to be in desperate straits. Thus, the mule often was called upon to make one more sacrifice—to be eaten—as Frémont's expedition proved. Others would do the same.

In the year when the "Pathfinder" from Missouri had left the bones of 120 mules in the San Juans, all of present Colorado officially became United States territory. In 1851 the Territory of New Mexico was organized, incorporating what is now Arizona, New Mexico, and part of Colorado. In practice most of the San Luis Valley was considered to be within the Territory of New Mexico, but the law creating this territory was imprecise in the boundary description. In it the northern limit was drawn along the thirty-eighth parallel, but when the boundary reached the Continental Divide, it went south to the thirty-seventh parallel and then continued west. North of this boundary the land was part of the Territory of Utah, also organized in 1851. Confusion stemmed from the fact that the mountains where the boundary was supposed to drop south from the thirty-eighth to the thirty-seventh parallel was called the Sierre Madre. Unfortunately, some maps of the day showed the Sierra Madre at the location of the Continental Divide, while others placed it at the Sangre de Cristos.

This point about the boundary is pedantic, however. In effect the intention of Congress is clear, for new settlements south of the thirty-eighth parallel in the San Luis Valley were placed under the jurisdiction of Taos County, New Mexico Territory.[1] Further evidence to support New

Mexico's jurisdiction is found in military organization for the area. In 1851 the United States Army set up a system of defense for the Southwest. Headquarters were at Fort Union, about one hundred miles east of Santa Fe. Under its charge were several smaller posts, the northernmost of these being Fort Massachusetts, built in 1852 in the San Luis Valley. Its purpose was to offer protection to routes through the valley and to settlers who had begun to move into New Mexico's northern frontier.

It was the responsibility of the commander of the Ninth Military Department at Fort Union to select locations for such forts.[2] However, Major George A. H. Blake was assigned to take Company F, First Dragoons, and Company H, Third Infantry, to the San Luis Valley in "Ute Country," where Blake chose the location of Fort Massachusetts on Ute Creek beneath Blanca Peak. The site implies that Blake had little concern for defending either trails or settlements, for it was well removed from both, but it was the first adequate location north of privately owned land, the Sangre de Cristo Grant. The fort enjoyed sufficient timber, clear running water, and scenery, but the surrounding hills made it a more likely spot for surprise attack than a convenient place from which to protect citizens. Consequently, the garrison was relocated later at Fort Garland, when that site was leased from the owners of the land grant.

With rudimentary government and defense organized in the West, Americans were eager to begin its exploitation. Despite Frémont's experience in 1848-49 Senator Benton remained steadfast in his hope that the thirty-eighth parallel would yield a transcontinental rail route through St. Louis to the Pacific. Contending that this would be the shortest possible line between Washington and California, he led a campaign to secure congressional appropriations for surveying this route, while his competitors were doing the same for northern and southern routes.

To reinforce his arguments favoring the central route, Senator Benton obtained a statement from Antoine Leroux of Taos. Benton sent Leroux's letter to the New York *Daily Tribune,* where it appeared on March 16, 1853. Leroux's information was, of course, everything that the senator's sympathizers could have wanted. Leroux stated unequivocally that the central route was the best to California, as he and other traders and trappers could prove from personal experience. Also, since the army had provided protection against Indian depredations, the San Luis Valley quickly would become the most prosperous section of New Mexico, he said, and would provide traffic for the proposed railroad. West of the valley Cochetopa Pass afforded a year-round passage, which was suitable even for wagon traffic, it was so gentle. This pass had been used by wagons since 1837, he claimed, when two families "named Sloover [perhaps Isaac Slover] and Pope" had used it en route to California.[3]

An opportunity to investigate this route came as an adjunct to the journey of E. F. Beale, newly appointed superintendent of Indian affairs in California, who would be traveling to his new post. Benton sent—and paid the expenses of—Beale's cousin, Gwinn Harris Heap, whose duty it was to prepare written reports and artist's sketches of his observations about possible locations for a railroad. Since Beale's expedition was small and not equipped with appropriate instruments for such work, Heap was merely expected to make a preliminary reconnaissance. Nevertheless, his report yielded an excellent description not only of the Beale route but also of the surrounding area and its people. Illustrated with lithographs from Heap's sketches, the published report became a major tool in Benton's continued campaign for a central route.[4]

Beale and Heap left Washington in April 1853. By May 15 they had assembled a force of ten men, enough light equipment for the rapid trip that they planned, and a string of pack animals. From Westport, Missouri, the supply point, they headed west on a route along the "Kanzas" and Arkansas rivers to the Huerfano, which they followed into the mountains. Entering the San Luis Valley by way of Sangre de Cristo Pass, Heap wrote:

> We were now travelling on an Indian trail; for the wagon trail, which I believe was made by Roubideau's wagons, deviated to the right, and went through the pass

named after him. This pass is so low that we perceived through it a range of sand hills of moderate height in San Luis Valley; to have gone through it, however, would have occasioned us the loss of a day in reaching Fort Massachusetts, though it is the shortest and the most direct route to the Coochatope; and Mr. Beale's views constrained him to take the most direct route to Fort Massachusetts, where he expected to obtain a guide through the unexplored country between New Mexico and Utah, and also to procure some mules. We were therefore very reluctantly compelled to forego the examination of Roubideau's Pass. . . . An excellent wagon road might be made over these mountains, by the Sangre de Cristo Pass, and a still better one through Roubideau's. . . .

> Continued our course to the southwestward through thick pine woods, and in one mile we reached the head waters of Sangre de Cristo Creek, flowing into the Del Norte after its junction with the Trinchera. The Sangre de Cristo mountains, and the Sierras Blanca and Mojada [referring to the northern Sangre de Cristos] were covered with snow. . . .

> On our maps, the Sangre de Cristo is improperly named Indian Creek, which is a fork of the Sangre de Cristo, and is not named at all on them. Up Indian Creek, I am informed, there exists an excellent pass from the San Luis valley to the plains on the eastern side of the mountains [Veta Pass]. . . .

> We arrived [at Fort Massachusetts] late in the afternoon, and received a warm and hospitable welcome from Major Blake, the officer in command, Lieutenants Jackson and Johnson, and Dr. Magruder. . . . Messrs. Beale, Riggs, Rogers, and myself quartered at the Fort; the men encamped two miles below on Utah Creek, in a beautiful grove of cottonwoods. A tent was sent to them, and with fresh bread and meat they were soon rendered perfectly comfortable. There was excellent pasturage around their encampment, on which the mules soon forgot the hard marches they had made since leaving Westport. . . .

> As it was found impossible to obtain here the men and animals that we required, and that it would be necessary to go to Taos, and perhaps to Santa Fe, for this purpose, Mr. Beale and Major Blake left for the former place on the morning after our arrival at the fort. . . . During our detention at Fort Massachusetts, I took frequent rides into the mountains on each side of it.[5]

When Beale returned he brought a guide and a muleteer, cousins who each bore the name Felipe Archilete. The guide was distinguished by the nickname "Peg-leg," given to him after an injury in an Indian battle, which cost him a limb. He not only knew the Rockies well, but he also was skilled in speaking the Ute language. Despite his lameness he was well qualified to substitute for Antoine Leroux, whom Beale had been unable to secure for a guide, as originally hoped. While at the fort Beale also hired Patrick Dolan, a soldier whose tour of duty had expired, and discharged one Mexican who had traveled with the party from Westport.

On June 15 the expedition resumed its march. Six miles from Fort Massachusetts they crossed Robidoux's wagon road. Passing through the valley they encountered wet ground, in which some of the mules became mired. The mules also showed a troublesome inclination to try to return to the fort. When Rogers and Heap decided to go back to the fort for an additional bit of supply, they hired another muleteer, Juan Lente, and also bought a mule for him.

While Heap took care of these errands, the main group had crossed the Rio Grande, where they encountered Ute Indians hunting for wild horses. The Indians camped with the expedition that night and parted on friendly terms the next morning after sharing breakfast. Beale's group then headed north toward Saguache Creek. Heap's journal describes their route:

> We crossed a fine brook of clear and cool water—the Rio de la Garita, which rises in the Sahwatch mountains, and flowing east, discharges itself into a large lagoon at the base of the Sierra Mojada, in the northern part of the valley of San Luis. . . . In ten miles from the Rio Garita, we came to an abundant spring, surrounded by good grass, where we rested for a moment to drink [at Russell Spring]. . . . At the spring we found a trail leading to the Sahwatch valley. . . .
>
> The valley of the Sahwatch has two entrances from that of the San Luis. The one which we selected, on account of its being the nearest, is called by the Spaniards El Rincon del Sahwatch ["the corner of the Sahwatch"], as it forms a cut-off into Sahwatch valley proper. The main entrance is a few miles farther on. We went three miles up the Rincon, and encamped at sunset at a spring of excellent water, where our mules found fine pasturage. . . .
>
> Mosquitos allowed us little rest. . . . For two and a half miles our course was west by north; we then turned to the northward over some steep hills, and upon reaching their summit obtained a glorious view of the valley of the Sahwatch. [The "Rincon" seems to be Tracy Canyon.][6]

They reached "the celebrated COOCHETOPE PASS" on June 18. Heap observed that this pass and Carnero Pass were the two routes most frequently used by Indians traveling to and from the San Luis Valley. A military post strategically placed between the two in Saguache Valley would do much to hold the Indians in check, he pointed out.[7] He had an opportunity to examine Carnero Pass two weeks later when he and "Peg-leg" returned to Taos to replenish supplies lost in an accident. Since the Puerto del Carnero, or "Mountain Sheep Pass," was known only by Indians and Mexicans trading with them, Heap was pleased to have this observation firsthand.[8] However, because he repeatedly described this route as being about a mile from Cochetopa Pass, it must be assumed that he did not mean a route along Carnero Creek but the route over today's North Cochetopa Pass.[9]

They also inspected an alternate route from the upper end of the Saguache Valley to the San Luis Valley. They ascended a narrow valley and then turning east came down a series of almost level valleys until they reached Carnero Creek, which flowed through a gap. Heap describes the trip down Carnero Creek thus:

> Half a mile below this gap there is another, and a quarter of a mile farther a third; the passage through them is level, whilst the trail around them is steep and stony. In the afternoon, we went through the first gap, made a circuit around the second, as it was much obstructed with trees and bushes, and, leaving the third on our left, rode over some low hills, and five miles from [the first gap] crossed the Garita. We were once more in San Luis Valley. . . . We encamped on the Rio Grande del Norte, as the sun was setting behind the pass in the Sierra de San Juan, at the head of the Del Norte . . . the one in which Colonel Fremont met with so terrible a disaster. . . . From the plains this pass appears to be more practicable than either the Carnero or the Coochetope; but it can be traversed only by mules, and by them only from the middle of August until the first snow falls.[10]

This information gathered by Heap was more complete than any yet provided, but it was not published before two other surveys covered much of the same country. The first was sponsored by the government and the second by Benton again. One can easily understand the pressure to locate a route for transcontinental transportation. In the 1850s the fastest means of reaching the California gold fields from the East was by steamboat with a land crossing of Panama, a thirty-day trip at best.

Beale scarcely had begun his trip to California when Captain John Williams Gunnison of the Topographical Engineers undertook an army reconnaissance of the central route. His orders from the United States War Department were to survey a line through the Rockies near the headwaters of the Rio Grande. Benton tried to get his son-in-law, Frémont, appointed to lead this survey, perhaps because of rumors that this exploration was intended to prove the impracticability of the central route. Regardless of such supposed conniving, Gunnison was a reasonable choice since he had some previous experience in the West, surveying in Utah.[11]

Gunnison's survey was not planned to be fast-paced. He left Westport in June 1853 with thirty-one men and several wagons loaded with supplies and provisions. In the party were Lieutenant E. G. Beckwith, Gunnison's assistant; Sheppard Homans, astronomer; R. H. Kern, artist and topographer; and botanist Frederick Creutzfeldt, who with Kern accompanied Frémont in 1848-49.

They approached the San Luis Valley by the Huerfano, after losing some time by following the Apishapa in error. Crossing Sangre de Cristo Pass with the wagons caused another delay of four days while the road was cleared of overgrowth. In addition to this pass, other possible routes into the valley were surveyed before the party left the area, but Sangre de Cristo was the only one recommended by Gunnison for a railroad.[12]

As Beale's party had done also, the Gunnison expedition lay over for a few days at Fort Massachusetts. While repairs were made on wagons, Gunnison went south to Taos and engaged Antoine Leroux to guide him through the mountains. Then, while the wagons and most of the men headed west, Gunnison and a few others went north through the valley. In this small party was Sheppard Homans, for whom Homans Park near Poncha Pass was named. Poncha Pass itself was surveyed and named Gunnison Pass, a title that never gained common usage. Turning back to join the main group, the men surveyed the entire area around "Coo-che-to-pa Pass."[13] However, the official report did not recommend this key pass for the rail route.[14] In fact, the failure of this army survey to recommend a suitable route through the San Juans became a major cause of the ultimate defeat of Benton's dream.

Tragedy awaited Gunnison's expedition when it continued west. Near the southwest corner of the present state of Utah, a small reconnaissance party was attacked by Indians. Eight men were killed, among them Gunnison, Kern, and Creutzfeldt.[15] Lieutenant Beckwith was then charged with the responsibility of completing the survey and preparing the official reports.[16]

The third survey for the central route in 1853 had to be abandoned in Utah. This expedition was led by Frémont, whom Benton sent west with private financing after the army survey was given to Gunnison. As in 1848 Frémont entered the San Luis Valley through Medano Pass from the Wet Mountain Valley, but he also examined Roubidoux Pass. Ascending Cochetopa Pass, he observed that trees had been cut for a wagon road. There was snow on the pass, and as the party descended toward the Gunnison River, some of Frémont's recipes for cooking mule meat over tallow candles had to be put to use again. When Frémont reached Utah his old enemies—snow, cold, and hunger—defeated him again. One man died and all supplies had to be abandoned.[17] Frémont's fifth expedition concluded the search for the proposed central route to the Pacific, and the Pathfinder's career as an explorer was finished.

Travel adventures staged in the San Luis Valley in the 1850s still were not concluded, though. In 1857, at the time of the Mountain Meadows Massacre in southern Utah, trouble between the Mormons and the United States government reached a crisis. Colonel Albert Sidney Johnston was sent to quell the rebelliousness of the "Saints," but his supply train was so harassed by Mormons as it crossed Wyoming that Johnston had to send for additional supplies and help before reaching Salt Lake City. From Fort Scott, a temporary post built after the Mormons destroyed Fort Bridger, Captain Randolph B. Marcy was ordered to Fort Union in New Mexico for reinforcements. Marcy's expedition became another of the harrowing tales of winter travel in the mountains.

Marcy set out on November 27, 1857, with forty soldiers, twenty-five mounted men, packers, and guides. Jim Baker, a fur trapper of earlier times, accompanied as interpreter. Tom Goodale was the party's official guide. With Tom came his Indian wife and her pet pony. Sixty mules were trailed along to carry provisions on the return from New Mexico.[18]

By way of Brown's Hole and the Roan Plateau of northwestern Colorado, the party arrived in the Gunnison country and headed for Cochetopa Pass. Already they had been in deep snow for two weeks, and half of their food was gone. As the snow depth increased in the approaches to the pass, the men packed a trail by crawling on hands and knees, inching forward. Otherwise, they sank to their waists in snow. Progress was so slow that provisions were exhausted before the men reached the summit of Cochetopa. Tom Goodale's squaw wept as her pony was killed to be eaten. The next meal was an old mule, which could go no farther. Mule meat was the menu for the next two weeks. Sprinkled with a little gunpowder, it tasted almost as good as if seasoned with salt and pepper. At one point they missed the correct route, but one of the Mexicans got them back on the trail to "that Mecca of our most ardent aspirations"—Cochetopa Pass.[19]

With the San Luis Valley in sight at last, Marcy sent two Mexicans with three mules to Fort Massachusetts for help. Eleven days later the Mexicans met the main group on the west edge of the San Luis Valley. With them came fresh horses, food, and a jug of brandy. Overcome with good cheer, some of the men became intoxicated, while their captain, as diplomatic a leader as he was courageous, looked the other way. Four days later, on January 18, 1858, the men arrived at Fort Massachusetts. From there they proceeded to Taos and Fort Union.[20]

On his return, Marcy did not recross the San Luis Valley but traveled up the east side of the mountains. He was escorted by Colonel William Wing Loring, who was conducting reinforcements to Colonel Johnston. They reached Johnston in June. Loring then returned to Fort Union by way of Camp Floyd, Utah.[21] En route they crossed Cochetopa Pass. So the "Buffalo Pass" of the Indians, the proposed line for a central railroad, became a wagon road. For a few years after this expedition the route was known as "Loring's Trail."[22]

Loring kept a journal during this journey, but it was a perfunctory job of reporting. He was concerned with undramatic subjects such as soil conditions and the availability of water, grass, and wood for fuel, which might avert hardship or tragedy for future travelers. With particular interest he noted the speckled trout found in the waters of Carnero Creek and the Rio Grande. On September 6, Loring's party passed Fort Garland, just built to replace Fort Massachusetts and named for General John Garland, commander at Fort Union. The grass near Fort Garland was "excellent," Loring reported.[23]

The year 1858 saw the last of the early explorations that passed through the San Luis Valley. The valley had been undergoing many changes during the 1850s, and even greater events would take place in the following decade. Explorers' mule trains were soon forgotten.

Peaks of the Culebra Range soar behind a crumbling adobe house at Los Fuertos.

VIII

"In Voices of Gladness"

Sun-baked plazas, flat-roofed adobe homes with hollyhocks and squash and peach trees growing in grassless yards, irrigation ditches lining unpaved streets, crosses crowning church spires and desolate cemeteries, stores built of adobe, schools built of adobe. These could belong to Spanish-speaking communities anywhere in Old Mexico, West Texas, New Mexico, Arizona, Southern California, or even the San Luis Valley of Colorado.

The first permanent settlements in what is now Colorado were in the San Luis Valley, and they are towns such as these. The pioneer builders of homes and tillers of fields came from the area of Taos, Santa Fe, and Abiquiu. Some of these first settlers were of Spanish blood, some were *metizos* of mixed Spanish and Indian blood, and some were Indians who joined the villagers, adopting their language and names. Whoever they were, they shared not only language but also poverty, and they still do in many cases.

More than a century since their founding, these settlements in the San Luis Valley retain the look, the sound, even the flavor of their origins. To Anglo visitors the towns appear so foreign that it is difficult to recall that they were begun after the United States possessed the San Luis Valley and the rest of New Mexico. Although they are on land originally granted by the Mexican government to some of its subjects, the settlements actually have been under American rule since their inception.

Efforts to colonize in the valley were begun several years before the United States took possession of New Mexico, but Indians drove out the would-be settlers again and again with the same harassment experienced by the people of Rio Colorado, a few miles south of the valley. The first attempt to colonize in the San Luis Valley was on the Conejos River. Land for the colony was granted in 1833, this grant being one of several made by the new government of Mexico after the rebellion of 1821. The intent was to encourage the settling of remote areas of New Mexico. Some of these grants carried a taint of political favoritism; but the grant on the Conejos, made to a group of citizens rather conspicuously lacking in economic or social influence, seems to have been one of the exceptions. The land was conveyed to fifty families on the condition that they effect a settlement on the grant, but hostile Navajos prevented them from fulfilling this obligation. The best the grantees could do was to herd sheep there in 1840 and 1841.[1]

In a move to reestablish a claim to the grant, Seledon Valdes and other grantees or their heirs petitioned in 1842 for a revalidation of the grant. At this point the history of the first grant in Colorado becomes entangled, apparently forever, in bureaucratic red tape. According to the later testimony of Valdes's son, the petitioners sent the original documents of 1833 to Juan Andres Archuleta, prefect of the First District of New Mexico, who secured the governor's somewhat ambiguous permission to grant a renewal. Archuleta subsequently ordered that the grantees again be given possession of the land, but the original papers ascertaining the grant of 1833 disappeared during these transactions. In October 1842 Cornelio Vigil, justice of the peace court at Taos, went to the site called San Francisco de Padua on the Conejos River and formally gave the tract to eighty-four families from Taos, El Rito, Rio Arriba, Rio Colorado, Abiquiu, and other villages in northern New Mexico. Most of these people were descendants of or substitutes for original grantees who had died since 1833. The grant was made in the names of Julian Gallegos and Antonio Martines, who thus were accorded particular respect by the others.

The proclamation granting the Conejos tract in 1842 incorporated the following provisions, which were customary in Mexican land grants:

The tract aforesaid shall be cultivated and

never abandoned, and he that shall not cultivate his land within twelve years or that shall not reside upon it will forfeit his right; and the land that had been assigned to him will be given to another person—that the pastures and watering places shall be in common for all the inhabitants—that said land is donated to the grantees to be well cultivated and for the pasturing of all kinds of live stock, and therefore, owing to the exposed frontier situation of the place, the grantees must keep themselves equipped with firearms and bows and arrows in which they must pass review as well at the time of their settlement there as at any time the Alcalde [mayor] or Justice of the Peace in authority over them may deem proper to examine them—the grantees being fully notified that, after the lapse of twelve years after the act of possession, all the arms they may then have must indispensably be firearms in good condition, under the penalty that whoever shall fail in this requirement shall forfeit his right in the said grant—that the towns they may build shall be well walled around and fortified—and in the mean time the settlers must move upon said tract and build their shanties there for the protection of their families.[2]

To signify their compliance and joy, the new owners of the grant "plucked up grass, cast stones and exclaimed in voices of gladness, saying 'Long live the sovereignty of our Mexican nation!'"[3]

The boundaries of this large grant were described as extending north to La Garita Mountains, east to the Rio Grande, south to San Antonio Peak, and west to Sierra Montosa. Each family was to be allotted a long, narrow strip of land for cultivation. These plots, about five hundred feet wide, eventually filled most of the irrigable land between San Antonio River and La Jara Creek. As stipulated in the proclamation, pastures and watering places would be held in common, and roads in and out of town would be public.

During the 1840s and early 1850s the grantees attempted three or four times to settle on their land and to plant crops of wheat and corn, but each time Indian threats drove the grantees out, thereby preventing them from establishing the required permanent homes. Instead, the farmers returned with their harvests to winter in their old homes in New Mexico. This intermittent tenure, coupled with the loss of the original decree of 1833, caused the United States government to disallow the grant in the 1860s, although New Mexico's first governor under American jurisdic-

tion, Charles Bent, assured the grantees in 1846 that "they may by virtue of their former right . . . go to settle on the Conejos River if they choose to do so."[4]

Rather than impeding settlement of the New Mexican land grants, the fledgling American regime was encouraging it, at least at local levels. An explanation might be that those in authority sometimes were the same individuals who held grants. William Gilpin, first governor of Colorado Territory, once stated that members of Frémont's expedition of 1843-44 had planted the seeds of a scheme whereby New Mexican merchants petitioned for grants in their own names but took in associates who were not citizens of Mexico, as original grantees were required to be.[5] Himself a member of the Frémont expedition to which he referred, Gilpin was not known as a modest man or even a zealous adherent to literal truth; but in this case one is inclined to believe him, for he was linked closely with New Mexican land-grant history.

In 1843 and 1844 four land grants were made in what now is Colorado. The grantees in these instances were quite unlike the *peones* at Conejos. One of the new doles was the Beaubien-Miranda, later known as the Maxwell. It lay partly in Colorado and partly in New Mexico. Another of the new grants was the Sangre de Cristo in the southeastern portion of the San Luis Valley. The Sangre de Cristo Grant contained more than a million acres and was the largest privately held piece of land ever to exist in what is now Colorado.[6] Its size exceeded even the well-known King Ranch in Texas.

Some owners of the four grants authorized in 1843 and 1844 were naturalized citizens who had come to New Mexico from Canada and Missouri in the 1820s with the fur trade. For example, one of the grantees for the Sangre de Cristo was Stephen Luis Lee, formerly a fur-trade man who had become more successful as a distiller of "Taos Lightning." He also was sheriff of Taos County and brother-in-law of "Don Carlos" Beaubien.

"Don Carlos" was the father of thirteen-year-old Narciso Beaubien, the other grantee of the Sangre de Cristo. One might wonder why Don Carlos himself was not the grantee, instead of his young son, until it is understood that the elder Beaubien was co-owner of the Beaubien-Miranda Grant, which approximately equaled the size of the Sangre de Cristo. A French-Canadian who had come to New Mexico in the early 1820s, Beaubien had married a wealthy señorita, changed his given name from Charles to Carlos,

Charles H. Beaubien was a French-Canadian who acquired the title
"Don Carlos," Mexican citizenship, and land grants totaling about
two million acres. *Denver Public Library, Western History
Department photo.*

adopted citizenship in Mexico, and soon was operating a prosperous business in Taos.

During the Taos Rebellion in 1847 both Lee and Narciso Beaubien were killed. Through this tragedy "Don Carlos" came into possession of the Sangre de Cristo Grant. Narciso's share was inherited directly by his father, while Lee's estate was administered by Joseph Pley, an associate of Beaubien. In the spring of 1848 the latter purchased Lee's half of the Sangre de Cristo Grant for $100. In addition to the deaths of his son and brother-in-law, the Taos Rebellion had caused the loss of Beaubien's partner in the Beaubien-Miranda Grant when he took flight into Old Mexico during the uprising. Consequently, Don Carlos found himself in full control of both grants, which totaled about two million acres. Since he also had been appointed judge of the northern district of New Mexico, in which jurisdiction these two grants lay, Beaubien had a free hand in the role of feudal baron.[7]

His two grants were separated by the Culebra Range of the Sangre de Cristos. The Sangre de Cristo Grant, with which we are concerned in this history, lay on the east side of the Rio Grande, beginning one Spanish league above the mouth of Trinchera Creek, from which point the boundary ran straight northeast to the summit of "Sierra Madre," or Blanca Peak. From there the boundary followed the spine of the Sangre de Cristos southward along the Culebra Range to take in the headwaters of Costilla Creek and then ran generally northwest to meet the Rio Grande.

After the granting of the Sangre de Cristo tract in 1844, no settlement was attempted on it until 1848. When the San Luis Valley was visited in 1846 and 1847 by Barclay, Ruxton, and the Mormon brigade, they found no towns there. In 1848 George Gold (or Gould) attempted to establish a colony at or near the present town of Costilla, New Mexico. Gold was a mountain man who had headquartered in Taos after giving up trapping. When he undertook his enterprise on the Costilla, it was without the blessing of Don Carlos, who quickly banished the trespassers from his grant.[8] The settlement was gone when Frémont retreated through the valley in January 1849 and found the most northerly settlers at Rio Colorado.

Later in 1849, however, the first permanent settlement was made in the San Luis Valley. With Beaubien's encouragement several families built rude shelters on Costilla Creek where Garcia, Colorado, now is located, less than a mile from the present town of Costilla, New Mexico. In 1849 the village that became Garcia was called Plaza de los Manzanares, deriving its name from

two brothers, surnamed Manzanares, who had come from El Rito among the original settlers.[9] The name was changed when two brothers, Guillermo and Agipito Garcia, petitioned for and obtained a post office a few years later.

These early colonizers faced not only the formidable task of scratching out enough food for survival but also the continual threat of marauding Indians. This hazard surely came as no surprise, for raids were commonplace occurrences in all the rural areas of northern New Mexico, until, following the Mexican War, United States military forces made concerted efforts to halt these activities. Several punitive expeditions were undertaken, especially against the Utes and the Navajos. During the winter of 1847-48 one of these campaigns, led by Colonel Benjamin Beall and guided by Kit Carson, engaged Apaches east of Sangre de Cristo Pass, and two chiefs were taken captive. In March 1849 Lieutenant J. H. Whittlesey conducted another expedition through the San Luis Valley with Antoine Leroux as guide. This contingent attacked a Ute camp about fifteen miles north of Rio Colorado. It has been suggested that avengers of this battle were responsible for the murder of "Old Bill" Williams and Dr. Benjamin Kern, when they returned to the San Juans to recover Frémont's equipment.[10]

Despite this tragic event, the army's Indian campaigns succeeded in convincing the Utes that they should agree to a treaty with the United States, whereby the tribe recognized—on paper, at least—the authority of the government in Washington for the first time. The Indians agreed to release both American and Mexican captives, to return stolen goods, and to permit free passage through their lands.

Encouraged by the Utes' acceptance of this treaty, more New Mexicans set forth in 1850 to colonize Beaubien's Sangre de Cristo Grant. At Costilla a cluster of *jacales* appeared among the cottonwoods. These temporary, crude huts were built by setting logs upright and chinking them with mud. During the next year, 1851, Costilla achieved the status of a village with modest importance when three merchants from Taos opened a store there.[11] This first business enterprise passed into the ownership of F. W. Posthoff and next Ferdinand Meyer, a German immigrant who had worked for Posthoff in Taos previously. Meyer was to occupy a central role in the life of Costilla for many years and was to become known throughout the region after he opened other stores in San Luis, Conejos, Fort Garland, Del Norte, and elsewhere. In Costilla another store opened under the ownership of Louis Cohn, who

Weeds now crowd the once-lively plaza at Costilla, New Mexico. *Photo by Thomas J. Noel.*

soon moved his business to San Luis.[12]

The communities at Manzanares and Costilla both were built on a plan which was typical of later settlements. The colonizers erected their homes around a central plaza, or square, and prominent lots were reserved for future religious or government buildings. Several plazas, all with different names often made up a closely knit neighborhood, and considerable historical confusion results from the proliferation of names for these little complexes. For example, several small plazas appeared along Costilla Creek east of Ute Peak — Plaza de Arriba, Plaza del Media, Placita ("Little Plaza") de Los Madriles, Placita de Los Cordovas, Plaza de Los Chalifas, and, of course, Plaza de Los Manzanares.[13] Some of these plazas are known today by the names of later occupants, some have variant spellings, some are impossible to locate, and all are so close together that they usually have been called collectively "Costilla."

A second cluster of plazas was begun on the Sangre de Cristo Grant at Culebra Creek in 1850. The first settlement here was attempted at San Pedro, about three-fourths mile south of the present town of San Luis.[14] The first colonizers to come to this area included Juan Salazar, Antonio Jose Martines, Julian Gallegos, and Benacio Jaquez, according to the reminiscences of Salazar's son Antonio. These first-comers were driven out by Indians, but two returned with a larger group in the spring of 1851 to make a second effort to establish homes. In the party were Juan Salazar, Benacio Jaquez, Faustin Medina, Mariano Pacheco, Dario Gallegos, Juan Ignacio Jaquez, Ramon Rivera, Antonio Jose Vallejos, Juan Angel Vigil, and Jose Hilario Valdes. During the autumn of 1851 Indians killed Rivera, Vigil, and Vallejos.[15] After this attack the men left the valley for the winter, but they returned again the next spring to stay.

When they returned one of their first undertakings was the digging of an acequia to irrigate their wheat, beans, corn, and vegetable gardens. Although ditch rights were not recorded at the time, because water was held in common on the grants, this acequia had the distinction of being the first recorded water right, dating from April

10, 1852, when Colorado required filing of such data. It was called the San Luis People's Ditch.

The Culebra settlers laid out their farms in long, narrow strips, anywhere from fifty-five feet to one thousand feet long, depending on the size and importance of the families receiving the plots.[16] The farmers lived in plazas and went to their fields by day. On the east side of town, Beaubien gave the people a public pasture, called a *vega*, of nearly nine hundred acres. This combination of privately and publicly owned land was usual in New Mexican communities.

Beaubien also set up rules for the conduct of the colony at San Luis. The settlers were charged with the responsibility of keeping their town clean and orderly. Providing for its future growth, he required newcomers to obtain permission to live in the town by applying to the district judge—Beaubien himself—or to the justice of the peace, and a dwelling or a lot could be purchased by paying its value to the church.[17] Despite this nominal encouragement of religion, San Luis did not have its own priest for several years.

As early as 1852 there were two plazas on the Culebra—San Luis and San Pedro, although they did not actually go by those names. San Pedro, at the junction of Culebra and Vallejos creeks, was known for several years as Upper Culebra or Plaza Arriba, while San Luis was called Culebra or San Luis de Culebra. In 1853 San Acacio was settled downstream, and it was called Lower Culebra or Plaza Abajo.[18] Los Fuertos, also called Vallejos, was established at about the same time. Its name referred to its log cabins, designed to serve as fortresses to protect the villagers in the event of Indian attack.

As each plaza was built, irrigation ditches were dug. While the ditch at San Luis was being dug, another was under construction for San Pedro. The San Pedro Ditch has Colorado's second recorded water rights, dating from April 1852. The third was the Acequia Madre Ditch, taking its water from Costilla Creek and recorded in the name of Ferdinand Meyer in 1853. The Montez Ditch on Rito Seco dates from August 1853, followed by the Vallejos Ditch on Vallejos Creek. Manzanares Ditch, dug in 1854, and Acequiacita Ditch, in 1855, both took water from Costilla Creek.[19]

The history of Colorado's water rights provides one of the few sources of recorded information about these early towns. Unfortunately, church records for marriages, baptisms, and burials do not begin until 1854, when priests from Taos and Arroyo Hondo first visited the grant to perform religious rites. Oral reports handed down by descendants of early settlers often are vague or conflicting. For instance, it has been said that San Pablo was settled as early as 1849 by Antonio Jose Vallejos on the pie-shaped piece of land lying between Culebra and Vallejos creeks, across the Culebra from San Pedro's location. According to one report, San Pablo was attacked by Indians and Antonio was killed, after which the plaza was reoccupied by Antonio's brother and others.[20] It seems probable that this information has been confused with the settlement of 1851, when Antonio Vallejos also is said to have been killed. Because of such conflicting accounts much of the early history of the San Luis Valley may never be known accurately. The problem is compounded by the desire of several plazas to be called first, and certainly all of these rivals are worthy of recognition.

Although Indian depredations continued, new settlers arrived in the valley each year. In 1854 two more villages were started near San Luis. These were Chama, upstream from San Pedro on Culebra Creek, and San Francisco on San Francisco Creek.[21] The latter plaza subsequently was called La Valley or was immediately adjacent to another plaza by that name.

On the west side of the valley colonization was finally taking hold at the same time. The first permanent settlement on the Conejos Grant was made in August 1854, ending the long period when farmers and sheepherders stayed on the grant only during the summers. In 1854 Jose Maria Jaquez led a group of colonizers from El Llanito to the Conejos River. They came with wooden ox carts, horses, and burros, and chose a spot on the north side of the Conejos and lived there that summer. They called this place El Cedro Redondo, meaning "the round cedar." Meanwhile, in August a larger group of approximately fifty families arrived about four miles downstream. This party was from Abiquiu and was under the leadership of Lafayette Head. The settlement that they built on the north side of the Conejos River was called Plaza de Guadalupe. In October it received a boost in its population when the people at El Cedro Redondo decided to move their homes down to the larger colony.[22] Thus, Guadalupe became the first permanent settlement on the Conejos Grant, and it was just in time to fulfill the requirement that the grant be settled within twelve years after the decree of 1842.

As in the Costilla and Culebra Creek areas, other colonizers soon built several plazas on the

Guadalupe, as it appeared in the 1870s.

Conejos Grant. Servilleta appeared two miles east of Guadalupe and was named for the village from which its founders came.[23] Mogote, also settled in 1854, was about six miles west of Guadalupe and was named for nearby volcanic hills, called *mogotes*, meaning either "stacks of corn" or "horns of animals," both of which they resemble.

Irrigation ditches also appeared quickly. In 1855 the Guadalupe Main Ditch and Head's Mill and Irrigation Ditch were dug. Others followed on all of the neighboring tributaries of the Rio Grande. Individual farm plots were allotted to families living on the grant with tracts running north and south between San Antonio and La Jara creeks.

Although the people who settled the Conejos Grant were a mixed group, Lafayette Head was like none of the others. Already coming up in the world as an important citizen in New Mexico before he came to the valley, he soon emerged as one of the most influential pioneers of the San Luis Valley. Coming from Missouri, he first had seen

Santa Fe with the Army of the West during the Mexican War. Shortly after the province was occupied, he moved to Abiquiu, where he operated a store, became a United States marshal, and with the help of his friend Kit Carson was appointed Indian agent. In 1853 he was elected to the New Mexico legislature, in which he also served later as a member representing Conejos. Undoubtedly, his public image was helped by his having a Spanish wife, whose dowry had been as pleasantly plump as her girth became. "Uncle Lafe," as he was known when his hair had turned to snow, became the patriarch of a little empire on the Conejos.

But most of the settlers of the Conejos Grant were poor when they came, and so they remained. They were faced with creating their primitive shelters, providing enough food for their families, and defending themselves against Indians. Still, they preferred to remain, for most of these people had little hope except their stake in this new land. Many were peons, who as young boys had been placed by their fathers in the service of wealthy

Above, the old plaza at Conejos was called "Fort Head" in honor of Indian Agent Lafayette Head; *left,* Lafayette Head, or "Uncle Lafe" as he was called, was the patriarch of the Conejos settlement.

families. When their period of servitude expired, they became free men; but frequently they incurred indebtedness to their patrons for goods acquired, sometimes at inflated value, during the period of peonage, and so their economic freedom was not promised. Furthermore, the colonists on the grant faced possible fines if they did abandon the settlements, as the people at Ojo Caliente learned when they requested permission to leave their homes because of Indian hostilities.

Also among the settlers were people of mixed blood, the progeny of Spaniards and Indians. Intermarriage had been common in the 1700s and 1800s, especially with *genizaros,* Indians who had been captives of other tribes and who had been ransomed by the Spanish government and given citizenship. For this dispensation the *genizaros* agreed to adopt Christianity and the ways of civi-

Spanish of the royal court prevailed. Only slight traces of Mexican elements of speech found their way into the language spoken in New Mexico, and even Indians assimilated into the communities used a courtly Castilian dialect. The isolation of the northern settlements around Taos and Abiquiu and in the San Luis Valley protected the language from change into the twentieth century in remote villages and farms.[24]

While some Indians had become thoroughly integrated into Spanish life, many bands continued to harass the outlying settlements. When Fort Massachusetts was built in 1852, raids were deterred only slightly. The northernmost of a string of military forts along the Rio Grande from Texas through New Mexico, Fort Massachusetts was nearly fifty miles from the settlements on Culebra and Costilla creeks, and it was also

At Conejos the Ute agency and Lafayette Head's family shared the long building at left.

lization. They also served the New Mexican province by settling outlying colonies, such as Abiquiu, where they acted as a buffer against hostile Indians. The *genizaros* of Abiquiu spoke Spanish and intermingled freely with the Hispanic settlers there. Most likely, some of the colonizers of the Conejos Grant who came with Lafayette Head from Abiquiu were descendants of the *genizaros.*

Language presented no barrier between settlers in the northern colonies for all spoke Spanish. Although two and a half centuries had elapsed since the *conquistadores* had entered New Mexico, the mother tongue of the conquerors had remained not only dominant but also remarkably pure. Some of the original Spaniards who occupied the New World spoke Andalusian, Galician, or Spanish-Portuguese dialects, but Castilian

several miles off the Sangre de Cristo Pass trail, which the army intended to protect.

The fort was authorized in March 1852 and was ready for occupation by June.[25] The name of the outpost was almost as inappropriate as its location, but it probably pleased Colonel Edwin V. Sumner, commander of the Ninth Military Department who ordered the fort's construction and whose home state was Massachusetts. Regardless of its strategic faults, the fort could take pride in itself as a symbol of civilization, to which nothing else in the entire area compared. Where else could surveyors and military expeditions find such comforts as an officers' quarters, a hospital, a kitchen, a blacksmith shop, and a stock of provisions?[26] Certainly not in the villages to the south. Heap described the advantages and disadvantages of the place when he visited it in June 1853:

This post is situated in a narrow gorge through which the Utah [Ute Creek] rushes until it joins the Trinchera, and is a quadrangular stockade of pine log pickets, inclosing comfortable quarters for one hundred and fifty men, cavalry and infantry. Lofty and precipitous mountains surround it on three sides; and although the situation may be suitable for a grazing farm on account of the pasturage, and the abundance of good timber may render this a convenient point for a military station, it is too removed from the general track of Indians to be of much service in protecting the settlements in San Luis valley from their insults and ravages. The Utahs, who infest the Sahwatch mountains, enter San Luis valley by the Carnero and Coochetope Passes from the westward, and by those of Del Puncha [Poncha], Del Medino, and Del Mosque [Mosca] from the northward and northeastward, and a post established at the head of the valley of San Luis would be more effective in keeping these marauders in check, as it would there be able to prevent, if necessary, their descending into the valley in large numbers, and completely cut off their retreat with their booty. . . .

The cavalry at Fort Massachusetts numbered seventy-five men, of whom forty-five were mounted. Though their horses were excellently groomed and stabled, and kept in high condition on corn, at six dollars a bushel, they would soon break down in pursuit of Indians mounted on horses fed on grass. . . . Of this fact the officers at the fort were perfectly sensible, and regretted that they were not better prepared for any sudden emergency. . . .

I replenished our provisions from the sutler's store, and had a small supply of biscuits baked; a bullock which I purchased from the quartermaster was cut up and jerked by the Delaware, and the mules were reshod, and a supply of spare shoes and nails obtained. They were completely rested, and in even better condition than when we started from Westport; after a general overhauling of the camp equipage by the men, everything was put in order for resuming our journey.[27]

Because of difficulty in obtaining sufficient provisions for the fort's own use through the winter, the stockade was unoccupied except for a few guards from October 1853 until April 1854. By the time that the fort was manned again, under the command of Lieutenant Colonel Horace Brooks, the importance of keeping troops in the valley was clear. During the spring of 1854 Indians had raided villages along the Rio Grande, even south of Taos. The San Luis Valley served as the main route for the Indians in these depredations. One band was pursued in May by cavalry

guided by Kit Carson across Mosca Pass, while Fort Massachusetts established its value as a place where troops could organize their maneuvers. The expedition succeeded in catching up with the Indians near Raton Pass.[28]

This punitive expedition in the spring of 1854 was the forerunner of greater trouble with the Indians. During the summer of 1854 a smallpox epidemic among the Muache Utes was blamed by the tribe on contaminated goods distributed to them by the United States government. In retaliation the Muaches, led by Chief Blanco and joined by Jicarilla Apaches, massacred the settlers of Pueblo on Christmas Day, while the occupants of the trading fort were celebrating the holiday with "Taos Lightning." From there the Indians moved into the San Luis Valley, killed some settlers at Costilla, and drove off the plaza's livestock.

As a result of these crimes, another punitive expedition was organized in Taos. Ceran St. Vrain recruited volunteers, and Kit Carson joined again as guide. By early February 1855 Colonel Thomas T. Fauntleroy arrived from Fort Union to lead the troops north to Fort Massachusetts, which itself was under threat of attack. Brush was cleared away, extra fortifications were put up, and guards were posted. The attack did not come, though. Instead, Colonel Fauntleroy traced the enemy to the Saguache Valley, where corpses of smallpox victims were found in the snow. Shortly after this discovery the troops saw about 150 Utes and Jicarilla Apaches coming down Cochetopa Pass toward them. Not realizing the strength of their opposition, consisting of four companies, the Indians drew up for a fight. They were routed quickly. Two chiefs and six warriors had been killed, while on the American side only two men were wounded. The next day, leaving wagons and artillery under guard, the main command tracked the Indians through the mountains to Poncha Pass, while about 150 other men moved into the Wet Mountain Valley to join other troops who were there. North of Poncha Pass the main body engaged a large band of Indians on March 23. Some were killed and a few prisoners were taken before the Indians scattered. Again they were pursued, this time into the Wet Mountain Valley, where another battle and rout took place. Colonel Fauntleroy and his men then returned to Fort Massachusetts by way of Mosca Pass to obtain supplies.

After a rest the men set out again in late April. This time some of the volunteers crossed the Sangre de Cristos to campaign against the Apaches while others went to the southwest portion of the San Luis Valley. In the meantime Colonel Fauntleroy's regulars were tracking the Utes again into Poncha Pass. A night march across the pass brought the troops to a Ute encampment near the main trail. Despite having marched continuously since leaving Fort Massachusetts, the Americans attacked. Twenty-five minutes later the battle was over. Forty Indians had been killed, many more were wounded, and six children had been taken prisoner. All of the Indians' plunder was either loaded up or burned. Without rest the troops headed toward Cochetopa Pass, where they met about eighty Utes in a series of skirmishes. From there the victorious command retired to a campsite on La Garita Creek for a much needed rest before returning to Fort Massachusetts and Taos, their mission against the Indians completed.[29]

While these events were taking place, another incident had occurred at Guadalupe. There Indians had surrounded the plaza and run off most of the settlers' stock, which had been herded into the plaza at night for protection.[30] Later when the Utes attacked the village again, Lafayette Head led the settlers in a fight, which took place on the fields east of town. The battle lasted from dawn until noon, when the Utes withdrew after their leader, Chief Kaniache, was severely wounded by "Major" Head.

After these victories won by military troops, by volunteers, and by the settlers themselves, a period of comparative peace followed the spring of 1855. Promised a new treaty, the Utes and Jicarilla Apaches were not a major threat to colonists in the valley thereafter. Although the Muache Utes still retained a tenuous claim to the northern end of the valley, roving Utes never again would dispute the occupation of land in the southern end.

Following the Indian campaign in 1855 the settlers on the Conejos and Sangre de Cristo grants at last thought that they had something about which to exclaim "in voices of gladness." They replaced their stolen stock while neighbors arrived in steadily growing numbers. Little communities proliferated with log *jacales* and *fuertes* being replaced by more permanent, flat-roofed adobes. Although the threat from Indians had diminished, homes still were built around the traditional plaza.[31] Such sophistications as windows still were often absent, or at least very small to withstand the onslaughts of summer heat and winter cold as much as Indian arrows. When windows were provided, they were simply large pieces of mica or, more often, sheepskin parchment. Earthen floors were covered with rag rugs

woven in strips, called *jerga*, but furniture was an almost unknown luxury for most people. Beds were mattresses laid out upon the floor at night and rolled out of the way during the day's activity.[32]

Almost entirely dependent on their own resources, the settlers spun and wove fabric for clothing, bedding, and rugs from the wool of their own sheep and goats. They also raised some cattle, hogs, and chickens but relied mainly on a vegetarian diet. Their crops consisted chiefly of corn, oats, wheat, barley, beans, peas, lentils, potatoes, and chili peppers. Of these, corn was the one crop that could be depended on to survive.

Farming implements and techniques were primitive but reliable. Most plows were simple pine stocks, twisted and bent, to which plowshares were attached with leather thongs. The same oxen that pulled the plows, pulled two-wheeled, wooden *carretas*, or carts, to carry the crops. Sweating under the hot sun, the settlers and their oxen dug ditches to bring water to the fields, and eleven of these were completed by 1855 with nine more added by 1857.

In the first years corn had to be ground by hand in Indian-type *metates*, shallow stone basins with small, stone, hand grinders. Thus, it was an event of major importance when Maria Jaquez built the first flour mill in the entire valley in 1856. This mill was located about two and a half miles east of Guadalupe on the south side of the Conejos River, and it served all of the plazas in the southwestern part of the valley for a brief period. As in other mills built shortly, native lava stone was used for the burrs to grind a rather coarse meal. The flour was not separated from the bran.[33] Of such was the staff of life.

Man does not live by bread alone, but the early settlers of the San Luis Valley did not have much religious care in the first few years either. Since most New Mexicans were Catholic, the need of a formally organized parish with a resident priest to perform rites was keenly felt by many. Conejos was the first settlement to have a church. When Lafayette Head moved his household from Guadalupe to the south side of the river in 1856, the center of community life moved with him. In Guadalupe the people had met in a small *jacal* on Sundays to recite the Rosary and a litany and to sing a few hymns, but in Conejos the building of an adobe chapel was undertaken at once. Though still incomplete, this structure was used by the Reverend P. Gabriel Ussel when he visited the plaza and offered the first Mass in the newly created mission of Conejos in 1856. In 1857 Father Jose Miguel Vigil visited the mission and

The adobe church at Conejos in the 1870s.

dedicated the still unfinished church to Our Lady of Guadalupe. This was the first church not only in the valley but also in all of present-day Colorado. The parish itself was organized in June 1858, the same year in which a convent opened, and was served by Father P. Montano from 1858 until 1860, when he was replaced by Father Vigil. In 1860 the adobe church of modest proportions was completed, and a rectory was built. Both were blessed by the famed bishop of Santa Fe, John Baptiste Lamy, in 1863.[34]

Catholic worship soon became organized formally throughout the valley. In 1859 a small chapel was donated to the people of San Luis by the Dario Gallegos family, and in the same year another was built at San Pedro. Records for these outlying areas were kept at the parish in Conejos. At one time these records showed twenty-five villages and placitas to have been included in the parish.[35] Such records provide one of the few sources of information about the valley's growth in the early years.

After 1860 this parish became part of the Colorado mission administered by the Reverend Joseph P. Machebeuf. The clergy serving this area, including Lamy and Machebeuf in the hierarchy, came from the French secular priesthood and from Italian Jesuits as a result of changes in the church of New Mexico after the Mexican War, a change that was not popular among Spanish-speaking parishioners. After 1868, when Colorado's Catholic churches were separated from New Mexico and administered with Utah's parishes, the San Luis Valley's churches underwent further cultural estrangement.

From the outset the San Luis Valley's spiritual leaders found themselves in competition with a deeply rooted religious organization called *La Hermandad de Nuestro Padre Jesús,* or *Los Hermanos Penitentes.* The Penitentes were most active in northern New Mexico and southern Colorado from 1850 to 1890. They were not a new brotherhood but one which had existed since the sixteenth century in Spain and was transplanted with the *conquistadores.* The order took root firmly in northern New Mexico, where, because of isolation from the centers of population, settlers rarely saw a priest.[36] Not always were the Penitentes a response to an absence of traditional religion, though. For instance, at Chama, settled in 1859 on San Francisco Creek, four miles southeast of San Luis, there was a large Penitente organization despite the presence of nearby Catholic chapels in both San Luis and San Pedro.

The Jaquez Grocery in San Luis occupies one of the first church buildings in the town.

Like this small church near Jarosa, many chapels are found in the rural countryside of the San Luis Valley, where neighboring farmers once gathered. *Photo by Thomas J. Noel.*

Penitentes gathered in meetinghouses such as this one in Costilla County. *Photo by Thomas J. Noel.*

The brothers were—and still are, for that matter—Catholic laymen. Their most conspicuous characteristic was their means for expiating sin. Among these customs were self-flagellation, standing on cacti, placing stones in their shoes, and being bound to wooden crosses. The brotherhood's meeting houses, called *moradas*, which were built adjacent to many of the villages of New Mexico, are still to be found in Costilla, Alamosa, Conejos, and Saguache counties in Colorado, but the old *moradas* seem like the gathering places of a secret, underground society. Partly because of such extreme practices as flagellation and cross-carrying, pressure from the church and from the civil government was brought against the movement. One of the first opponents was Bishop Lamy, who directed that Penitentes be denied the Catholic sacraments. As late as the mid-1880s the church still felt that the brotherhood was so active that additional bans were issued.[37]

The colonists of the San Luis Valley demonstrated their independence in other aspects of life, also. Just as they believed that witches could possess one's soul—and almost every village had

some old crone who was suspected of being a witch—the settlements also had persons who were designated as faith-healers, capable of curing the ill. When faith alone was inadequate, various maladies were treated with folk medicines derived from plants and minerals of the surrounding countryside. Such medicines were prepared and administered by a *médica,* a local woman who nursed the villagers. Many families still use some of nature's medicines, which are more affordable than a druggist's.[38] Babies were delivered with the help not of a physician but of a *partera,* or midwife. It is small wonder that such self-sufficient people also relied on their own methods of healing their souls as they were able to do within the brotherhood of the Penitentes.

More traditional religious observances contrasted with the somber activities of the Penitentes. Everyone, young and old, took part in happy, colorful festivals celebrating Christmas, saints' days, weddings, and so on. In addition to the services conducted by priests, the villagers had gaudy processions, evening services illuminated by bonfires, and religious plays such as *Los Pastores* during the Christmas season. Dances

Penitentes' crosses lie behind a morada in Saguache County. *Photo by George C. Simmons.*

Inflammatory descriptions of Penitente activities were used to stir up opposition to the brotherhood in the late 1800s. This sketch from Darley's *Passionists of the Southwest* shows men being dragged to death. *Denver Public Library, Western History Department photo.*

and sports events were part of the religious festivals, too. The gaiety and color of these occasions provided a much-needed change from the usual routine of a drab, hand-to-mouth existence.

Another welcome diversion was going to the store. Until 1857, when Dario Gallegos opened his retail business in San Luis, going to the store meant a trip to Costilla, but Gallegos's mercantile house changed the way of life in the Culebra plazas. He had green coffee, unrefined sugar, corn meal, dried fruit, salt, peas, chocolate, tobacco, matches, and yard goods. His total inventory when he opened shop had cost him only $452, but it must have seemed like a miracle to the local folk who came to ogle the stock, select a small purchase, and chat with the neighbors. Gallegos's business, conducted in a forty-by-twenty-foot building, was so brisk that he began to send wagons to Missouri in 1858 to bring merchandise for his store. The first trip took eleven months, and the second failed when Indians raided the wagons on the plains near present-day La Junta.[39]

Gallegos's store succeeded despite this setback, perhaps because he was an integral part of the community and knew his customers' needs and problems. People with little cash could exchange eggs and produce for such items as coffee and sugar. Gallegos himself had arrived in San Luis in 1851. When Antonio Salazar married Dario's daughter in 1874, the pioneer roots of the family and the business were sunk even deeper, for Salazar's father was one of the men who had attempted a colony in 1850 at San Luis. He had been killed by Indians soon afterward, and young Antonio became a sheepherder. Later Antonio worked for Ferd Meyer in Costilla, and Ferd taught the boy to read and write. The Gallegos store was bought out by the Salazar family after Dario Gallegos's death, and it still is in operation, although the original adobe building burned in 1895.

When gold was discovered in Colorado in 1858, a few enterprising people recognized that more money could be made from prospectors than from

Los Pastores processions still mark the Christmas season in the San Luis Valley.

This long, adobe building housed the store which belonged to the Gallegos and Salazar families in San Luis. After this store burned in the 1880s, it was replaced by another which still stands.

prospecting. Two such men were H. E. Easterday and Ceran St. Vrain, who were operating a mill and freighting and mercantile businesses in Taos. Recognizing a growing need for flour in the mining country, they decided to build a new mill in the San Luis Valley near the farms of that area.

When journalist Albert D. Richardson traveled through the valley in the autumn of 1859, he noted the exceptional yield of corn and wheat that had been raised under irrigation. While visiting in the home of F. W. Posthoff in Costilla, Richardson examined the mill at that plaza. He observed that it was the usual Mexican type, grinding only very coarse, unbolted flour. In the early months of the gold rush this type of flour was all that was available for shipment to Denver or the mines. Easterday and St. Vrain intended that their mill would be capable of producing more finely ground flour which Americans preferred.

Easterday oversaw the construction of the new mill at San Luis and remained there as resident manager of its operation. By April 1860 Easterday was advertising American Mill Flour in Denver's *Rocky Mountain News.* From Costilla and the area around Amalia, New Mexico, from Vallejos and San Pedro, the farmers were hauling

their grain to the new mill. This business and increased traffic on the road running north from Costilla, by a route where Sanchez Reservoir now is located, helped establish San Luis as the dominant Spanish-speaking town in the southeastern part of the valley.

On April 7, 1860, Easterday sent his partner, Ceran St. Vrain, an order from the "San Luis Mills," in which he requested goods to stock a store that he was building. He pointed out that the town's name, hitherto Culebra, was being changed to San Luis and that a post office was being requested. In the same letter he asked St. Vrain to "buy us a good strong negro woman that can do all kinds of house work, and bring or send her with the wagons."[40] Because of the hubbub of activity around the place, Mrs. Easterday needed help in the house, he explained.

Although the color of Mrs. Easterday's servant probably excited some interest, the arrival of a slave in the San Luis Valley would not have seemed exceptional. The people there were accustomed to social and economic systems which created widely divergent classes. As one example, public education was unknown in the early settlements except among the *ricos,* the comparatively well-to-do families, where schooling was provided in private homes. This distinction alone helped to perpetuate social and economic differences into the future. Slaves in a household also perpetuated the system, by lending status and providing help with the work.

Acquisition of Indian servants began in New Mexico with the first *conquistadores* and *padres*. Besides the servants acquired for government, military, and church officials, other Indians who were captured in battle were donated to loyal citizens. By the 1700s slave traders were in full operation, obtaining Indian women and children from raiders and distributing them frequently by lot. From 1700 to 1760 alone, eight hundred Apaches were placed in Spanish homes as servants. They were baptized into the Catholic faith and given Spanish names in the process, but they were not given full status as family members.[41]

By the mid-nineteenth century the slave trade still was flourishing in towns all along the Rio Grande with Taos being one of the principal markets. Most of the captives at that time were Navajo children.[42] The Ute Indian agent at Abiquiu, Albert Pfeiffer, reported in 1858 that Utes

Juan Carson was an Apache who became a servant in the home of Kit Carson after Mrs. Carson bought the child from his Ute captors.

and Apaches were at the agency in large numbers awaiting the arrival of New Mexicans from the area of Taos who were to join them in a campaign against the Navajos. When this force returned to Abiquiu after their expedition, they had with them twenty-one small Navajo girls, as well as about fifty to seventy-five horses, another valuable trade commodity.[43] The Utes normally exchanged captives, deerskins, venison, and buffalo for horses at Abiquiu. It was also fairly common for the poorer New Mexican men to conduct their own raids against Indians to acquire captives, since a slave might be sold for as much as $500. Perhaps some New Mexicans felt justified in capturing Indians in retaliation for the theft of Spanish boys, who were taken to Indian camps and given the chores of "squaw work."

Among the early settlers of the San Luis Valley were many Indian slaves, or "servants." In homes blessed with these Indians, the señoras and their daughters were spared the menial tasks that were the normal lot of the poorer women of the valley. In the Gallegos household, for instance, an Indian named Guadalupe was the cook, and in the manner of cooks anywhere, she ruled the entire family quite efficiently. The Salazar family also had its "Tia," a Navajo who was accepted as payment for goods at the Gallegos-Salazar store.

Indian slaves were not confined to any one area of the San Luis Valley and were found in households of the Conejos plazas as well as in the Culebra and Costilla Creek villages. In 1865, when Lafayette Head was required as Indian agent to submit a list of Indian captives in service in the valley, he named eighty-eight in Conejos County. Several of these were described as having been purchased within the San Luis Valley. Surprisingly, many were Utes. Whatever the tribe, the majority of the slaves had been acquired during the early 1860s and were quite young—under ten years old—indicating that the slave trade was still being carried on vigorously in the valley as late as the Civil War. In Costilla County, where Head also reported the census of slaves, sixty-five were counted. Their descriptions generally compared with those in Conejos County, except that an even higher percentage had been purchased as late as the 1860s. More of the slaves in Costilla County were bought from Mexicans than was the case on the western side of the valley, where the majority were traded or bought from Indians.[44]

When the Indian slaves were given their freedoms as a result of the Civil War, most left the families whom they were serving. Some remained, though, among them being five who appeared before the Costilla County clerk to declare that they wished to remain and that they enjoyed all legal freedoms within the households where they lived.[45]

Although the end of the slave trade thwarted the ambitions of a few traders and settlers, the development of the valley was not significantly affected. What mattered more in the long run would be the availability of land and the enterprise of newcomers who wanted it.

Through the 1850s new plazas built by Spanish-speaking people had proliferated. Different from most of these settlements was the village near Fort Garland, the fort built in 1858 by the army to replace short-lived Fort Massachusetts. At the new location of the military post, Mexican adobes soon appeared. Their builders were attracted by opportunities to raise garden produce to sell to the fort, by a few jobs that could be picked up there, and by the social life that was sure to be lively wherever American soldiers and Spanish *señoritas* met.

Other more typical Spanish-speaking settlements also took place north of the fort. At the western base of Sierra Blanca, Zapata was settled in 1864 by former residents of Taos Valley. The people of Zapata herded sheep and sold mutton to the fort.

Across the valley, settlement extended north of La Jara Creek into the outlying portions of the Conejos Grant after 1858 and 1859. In one group of these settlers was Jesus Valdez, a member of the rescue party from Rio Colorado that had been sent to assist Frémont's expedition in 1849. Valdez and Luis Montoya settled on San Francisco Creek near the present town of Del Norte, while others, including Domacio Espinoza, Crescencio Torrez, J. Mateo Romero, and Susano Trujillo, continued north to La Garita Creek. The original settlement of La Garita was west of the present townsite. *La Garita* means "the lookout point" or "the sentinel," perhaps referring to a column near the head of Saguache Creek, an elevated point above La Garita and Carnero creeks from which Indians are said to have sent smoke signals, or possibly referring to any one of a number of lookouts found in the buttes northwest of Del Norte. Soon after, Jose Damian Espinoza, Julian J. Espinoza, and Santiago Manchego of the same party settled on Carnero Creek at the mouth of the canyon, where Utes had an important camping ground. With this group of settlers were hundreds of head of sheep, cattle, and other farm animals. Ditches were dug in a short time to divert water. Although this settlement was established on land assured by treaty to belong to the Utes, the Indians tolerated the newcomers for the first year or two.[46]

Also in the spring of 1859 fourteen families came from Santa Fe, Ojo Caliente, and the Conejos area with fourteen wagons and a herd of milk goats to build a plaza near present-day Del Norte.[47] The name of this settlement was La Loma de San Jose, *La Loma* referring to the rise of ground on which it was located. Around this plaza a confusing array of other plazas was spawned in the mid-1860s. Prominent among these were Seven-Mile, or Valdez, Plaza and Lucero Plaza. The latter was about four miles upstream on the Rio Grande from today's Monte Vista. The founders of Lucero Plaza were a few families from Santa Fe who came in 1859 but were driven out by a hard winter and Indian threats. A larger group, led by Manuel Lucero, a member of the original party, returned in 1865 to farm and to establish a permanent settlement.[48]

The Silvas, who were the leading family in the district, induced Jesus Maria Alarid to join them in the new colony to teach the catechism and secular subjects to their children. In addition, the Silvas brought a Ute servant child, Juan.

As other plazas fanned out around La Loma de San Jose, the area became laced with irrigation ditches. First of these was the Silva Ditch, followed by some forty others within a decade. As evidence of their assumptions regarding their legal right to settle in this area, these colonists called the entire region La Garita District of the Conejos Land Grant.

As a result of this persistent movement to make new homes in the San Luis Valley, Spanish-speaking settlers had by the early 1860s transformed the valley into an area typical of rural northern New Mexico, with small plazas dotting most of the land which could be irrigated easily. The valley at last seemed to have fulfilled its role as a frontier for the expansion of Spanish New Mexico, however belatedly.

Fort Garland in 1860.

Blanca Peak looms behind the abandoned buildings of Fort Garland.

IX

"A Matter of Grace"

By the late 1850s, with settlement in the valley accelerating and the rush to the gold fields of the Rocky Mountains under way, the presence of Indians, however peaceful some of them might be, was an obstacle to expansion that would not long be tolerated. Because Indians still roamed through the valley and the Central Rockies as a whole, they were fated to become witnesses, opponents, and victims in turn while the invasion of their homelands took place. Waves and ripples of antagonism were felt in the San Luis Valley as settlers, itinerant miners, promoters, and government officials all increased the pressure to contain and finally to remove the Indians from the region.

During the Civil War years Indians posed more problems in the San Luis Valley than did the war between the states. Some of this unrest may have been inspired by Confederate agents, attempting to divert Union energy into Indian warfare, as has been suspected of some Indian troubles elsewhere in the West. More obvious as a cause was the flagrant self-interest of miners and various promoters in direct conflict with the Indians' interests. Meanwhile inadequate resources of the United States Bureau of Indian Affairs compounded the red men's grievances. Many of these complaints were heard in the San Luis Valley, because a major Ute agency was located there in the 1860s, but often the relationship between Indian and agent was little understood by anyone involved.

For example, in March 1861 T. C. Wetmore of Canon City went on a prospecting trip to the San Juan Mountains. Upon his return he fired off a letter to the commissioner of Indian affairs in Washington, advising him that he had found the richest mining districts in the new Territory of Colorado full of Navajos and Utes, with whom, he claimed, the United States had no treaty. With an

eye to the season when miners would be able to enter the mountains, Wetmore asserted that it was imperative to have a treaty before June 1. He thought that an appropriate treaty could be negotiated for three or five thousand dollars by a special agent, and, of course, Wetmore volunteered to be that agent for a small salary.[1] He apparently had no understanding that these Indians already were assigned to agencies and that an agent had no power to negotiate treaties anyway. Furthermore, Wetmore erred in the belief that no treaty existed, for there had been one since 1849. This misunderstanding was shared by many miners and land speculators in the West, who contended that nomadic tribes had no valid claims to land. This attitude permitted them to violate existing treaties without a qualm of conscience.

An important influence in maintaining a tenuous peace between the Indians and the settlers or miners was Fort Garland. When the fort was built to replace Fort Massachusetts in 1858, its chief purpose was to protect northern New Mexico from Indian attack. By leasing a site for the fort from the Sangre de Cristo Grant for twenty-five years, the army was able for the first time to gain an effective position from which to guard the roads running east, south, southwest, west, and northwest in its vicinity.

Named for General John Garland, commander of the Department of New Mexico, the new post could boast a proper parade ground, but the buildings surrounding it were less than impressive. They consisted of nine long, low structures built of native adobe brick to serve as barracks and officers' quarters. These mud buildings were heated by open fireplaces, which probably offered little warmth in the bitter winters of the valley. Outside this compound were several other adobe buildings—a hospital, stables, shops, laundry, commissary, bakery, and trading post. The journal kept by Colonel William Wing Loring during his expedition in 1858 noted that the site also had access to both good grass for grazing and wood for fuel.[2]

In 1860 the troops who built this post were replaced by the Tenth Infantry under the command of Major E. R. S. Canby. After the Civil War broke out in 1861, most of the Tenth's men were sent to theaters of action. In New Mexico they participated in the defeat of a Confederate thrust at Valverde, which was the closest that fighting came to Colorado soil during the war. In the meantime Fort Garland was manned by volunteers.[3] A regiment of two hundred volunteers was organized in the San Luis Valley for this purpose, and it included many Spanish-speaking settlers.

Although the Indian agency was not located at the fort, it inevitably became involved with Indian problems. Formerly under the administration of the War Department, Indian agencies logically had been located near army posts in many cases. Perhaps because of these past associations Fort Garland's commanders often found themselves listening to the grievances of the Indians.

Until 1860 Utes, Navajos, and Apaches in northern New Mexico, including the San Luis Valley, were assigned to agencies at Abiquiu and Taos, where Albert Pfeiffer and Kit Carson, respectively, were agents. On August 25, 1860, another agency for the Tabeguache Utes was established at Conejos with Lafayette Head as agent. His first budget reveals something of the agency's operations. Besides his own salary of $520, agency expenses were budgeted for $1,000, with another $170 requested for Head's "interpreter sometime." A year later semiannual expenses had risen to $750 for Head's salary, $250 for the "interpreter sometime," and $3,600 to $4,600 for "contingencies." The increased costs resulted from the unexpectedly large number of Utes—about two thousand—who had appeared at the agency during its first months of operation.[4]

When the Territory of Colorado was created in 1861, Head's agency came under the authority of Colorado's territorial governor, who was ex officio superintendent of Indian affairs in the territory. The first governor and superintendent was William Gilpin, ardent advocate of mining in the San Juan Mountains. Apparently foreseeing no conflict of interests, he also espoused the reservation system for Indians. His argument for adopting reservations was that money to buy provisions for Indians was scarce, due to the Civil War, and the Indians could hunt for their own food if they had enough land, eliminating the need to give them costly provisions. Otherwise, the hungry Indians would be forced to plunder and fight.

Head's Indians already were complaining that they were starving. They had lost their hunting grounds, and Head was not distributing rations fairly, they charged. Gilpin came to Head's defense, pointing out to the secretary of the interior that Head had been forced to purchase supplies on his own credit to provide rations for the Utes. Since Gilpin himself soon was removed from office for irregularities in attempting to pay the costs of Colorado Volunteers in the war, it is understandable that he sympathized with the agent's problem. Gilpin described Head as "a most efficient and competent officer, a sincere Republican, and friend of the Administration and greatly respected by the Mexican population, whose language he speaks with fluency."[5]

Be that as it may, the Utes contended that Head's interpreter could not speak Ute and that the agency still was not providing them with sufficient food in 1862, when a delegation went to Fort Garland in protest.[6] Head denied their accusations again and asserted that the Utes' problems would be solved if they were given a reservation in western Colorado, where they could hunt and provide for their own needs.

Besides the problem of food, which caused begging and thefts, the mere presence of the Indians in the valley made the settlers nervous. In 1861 citizens of the Conejos area traveled to Denver to present facts to Governor Gilpin about their fears of intertribal warfare. The *Rocky Mountain News* reported that "an alliance has been formed between the [Arapahos] and four [other tribes], to make war upon the Utahs the coming season. A bloody contest is expected, and the settlers . . . fear that one party or the other may encroach upon the white settlements. The delegation now in the city is composed wholly of Mexicans. They are a fine looking and well informed set of men, very gentlemanly and prepossessing in their appearance and bearing."[7]

Sometime in the early years of settlement on the Conejos, the colonists had witnessed one such battle, which took place between the Utes and Kiowas. The battle ground was a small, conical hill afterwards called *El Cerrito de Los Kiowas*, and it was about twelve miles east of Conejos. The fight occurred when a small band of Kiowas, worked up to a frenzy of courage by "Taos Lightning," attacked an encampment of about two hundred Utes. The Utes' leader was killed. The

William Gilpin, who was the first governor of the Territory of
Colorado, was deeply involved in the development of the Sangre de
Cristo Grant and the Baca Grant No. 4.

avenging Utes found the main group of Kiowas on the hill that now bears their name. Surrounded, the Kiowas took refuge behind a hastily built breastwork of lava rock from which they fought off the Utes for several hours. Only after more than sixty Indians were killed did the battle end, with the Utes victorious.[8]

When John Evans replaced Gilpin as territorial governor in the spring of 1862, Evans also subscribed to reservations as the solution to such problems. Furthermore, he believed that the Indian Bureau's policy to convert nomadic Indians to farming had special merit for Colorado, where Utes occupied some of the best mining land. Head took a few Utes to Washington in 1862 to impress them with the wisdom of the Great White Father, but actual change of procedure for dealing with the Utes was slow in coming. With a firm proposal in hand at last, Governor Evans went to Conejos in October 1863 to meet with the Utes and their agent. At this council were representatives from the Tabeguache, Capote, and Weminuche bands of the Ute Indians, but only the Tabeguaches were present in sufficient numbers to negotiate. The Muache band entirely refused to attend.

Under Chief Ouray the Tabeguaches agreed to the treaty offered by Evans.[9] It gave this one band an immense reservation of about 5,785,000 acres on the Western Slope, with the Muaches being urged to join the Tabeguaches on the reservation at a later time if they chose to sign a treaty. Although the reservation was to be open to mining, railroads, and military posts, the Indians were granted relative freedom on the land. They were promised $20,000 in trade goods, annual provisions for ten years, five stallions with which to improve their horse herds, cattle, sheep, implements, and a blacksmith. To remove the other bands farther from white settlements, the Capote and Weminuche Utes were persuaded to accept an agency in southwestern Colorado. Although this Treaty of 1863 was ratified by the United States Senate in March 1864, several changes were incorporated, generally reducing annuities.

Unfortunately, the treaty did not remove the Indians either from mind or from sight. Head continued as agent for the Tabeguaches, and the agency remained on the Conejos. In fact, the agency was improved somewhat in 1865 when Head built a new rambling adobe on higher ground above the floodplain of the Conejos. The Muaches also were still very much on the scene. In 1864 and 1865 they conducted several raids east of the Sangre de Cristos. Hoping to avert an Indian war, Ouray finally captured the Muache chief and turned him over to Kit Carson.

Carson had become the best-known Indian fighter in the West. Though small in stature, he towered over friends and foes in courage and reliability. After distinguishing himself in service during the Mexican War, he had decided to settle down to domesticity and ranching at Taos, but he was called upon repeatedly to resume the role of Indian fighter, particularly in campaigns against the Navajos and the Apaches. From 1853 to 1858 he was the agent at Taos for the Capote band of Utes. In 1855 he participated in Fauntleroy's campaign against the Tabeguache Utes, who afterward were also assigned to Carson's agency at Taos. When the Civil War broke out in 1861, he helped organize the 1st Regiment of New Mexico Volunteers, and as their commander in several campaigns against Indians in Arizona, New Mexico, and Texas, he rose to the rank of brigadier general. Among these campaigns are two that are especially well known—the roundup of hundreds of Apaches and Navajos for their removal to Bosque Redondo and the Battle of Adobe Walls. During the roundup of Navajos at Canyon de Chelly, Carson was assisted by his long-time friend Albert Pfeiffer.

In 1866 Kit Carson took command at Fort Garland, but his tenure there was brief for his health was failing. A year later he resigned, and in 1868 he died. His year in the San Luis Valley was a reasonably happy one, in which Kit was able to round out his career while enjoying the presence of his wife Josefa and their children. He loved the valley, and he was near his old associates from Taos. Above all, he was fully competent in his work, both in his dealings with his men and with the Utes.[10]

Shortly after assuming command of Fort Garland, Kit Carson wrote in a report that the fort's location was one "of great beauty and remarkable Salubrity" for both man and beast, but the settlers were not so fortunate as the troops, for their safety still was constantly threatened by the presence of Indians.[11] At the time there were in the valley three bands of Utes, numbering 800 warriors, and one band of Jicarilla Apaches, numbering 250, all of whom were supposed to be contained by Carson's command of 60 men. He recommended that the fort be enlarged and strengthened.[12]

In December of 1866 Carson reported to the territorial governor, then Alexander Cummings, that the Tabeguaches were complaining to him about unfulfilled promises of food and provisions. They were near starvation and could not be ex-

When a delegation of Ute Indians and government officials from Colorado went to Washington in 1868, they were photographed by Brady. Well-known Indians in this group are Piah, second from left, and Captain Jack, center. Chief Ouray is fourth from right. Governor A. C. Hunt is to the left of Captain Jack, while Lafayette Head is seventh from the right side of the photograph.

pected to remain peaceful under such conditions.[13] Cummings was not the sort of man to be swayed easily by sympathy for Indians, but in June 1867 the arrival of about five hundred discontented Utes in Denver made an impression on the territorial government as well as the general populace. It was agreed that a new treaty would be drawn up for the Utes and that a stop would be put to the distribution of moldy flour and other inferior food at Conejos. In the meantime, when Governor A. Cameron Hunt succeeded Cummings, it was suggested with renewed vigor that all of the Utes should be consolidated on one reservation and converted at once to farming and stock-raising to solve the problems.[14]

In 1868 the new treaty was negotiated after a pilgrimage of officials and Indians to Niagara Falls and Washington. All Utes were placed on a reservation in southern and western Colorado in an area totaling one-third of the Territory of Colorado. The Utes were promised 160 acres per family, seeds, farm implements, cows, school, sawmills, smithies—everything they could possibly need to become good Midwestern farmers. Unallotted land would provide more than adequate hunting ground.[15]

Two new agencies were to be set up for the vast reservation. One, on the White River near the present town of Meeker, would be maintained for northern bands of Utes, while another on Los Pinos Creek would take care of the southern bands. This latter agency was only about fifty miles northwest of Saguache, across Cochetopa Pass, and it still kept many Indians too close to the white settlements for comfort. It did, however, terminate the agency in Conejos and took

away the right of Utes to wander about the San Luis Valley.

A few incidents occurred in the valley even after the establishment of the Los Pinos Agency. In 1869 a Ute was rumored to have been killed by a white man in the mountains. Ouray and two hundred tribesmen came down to the valley and pitched camp on a mesa north of Saguache. A massacre was expected momentarily, but the fortuitous reappearance of the "dead" Indian saved the village.

Almost as soon as the Treaty of 1868 was ratified, Colorado's settlers and politicians were expressing their dissatisfaction with its terms. The latest of the many territorial governors, Edward M. McCook, asserted that he was unable "to comprehend the reasons which induced the Colorado officials and the general Government to enter into a treaty setting apart one third of the whole area of Colorado for the exclusive use and occupation of the Ute nation. ... I do not believe in donating to these indolent savages the best portion of my Territory."[16]

Predictably, the days of the Treaty of 1868 were numbered. On the whole, Ouray tried to keep the Tabeguaches in check, giving the white people as little irritation as possible. The other bands were not so sagacious, though, and many minor incidents provoked the settlers, thereby justifying in the eyes of the whites a repudiation of the terms of the treaty. The Brunot Treaty of 1873, consequently, removed a large portion of the San Juan Mountains from the reservation and opened that land up to mining and settlement. This treaty also moved the Los Pinos Agency to a more remote, and thus better, location. Although

Ute tepees pitched at the Los Pinos Agency.

it retained its former name, the agency was established on the Uncompahgre River, near the present town of Montrose. The Utes under Ouray were thereafter called the Uncompahgre Utes.

Changes effected by the new treaty should not have mattered much to the Indians, Colorado's citizens argued, because the "savages" were supposed to have settled down on their 160-acre parcels of land to get some farming done. Agent Nathan Meeker at White River especially was determined that his Indians should stop their wandering around and raise some crops. To reinforce his point of view, he ordered the Indians to give up their horse races, and he withheld rations from recalcitrant subjects. Some of his Indians finally rose up against the agency in 1879 and killed Meeker himself. A general rebellion was feared.

Among the troops sent out to quell the expected war and to rescue white women who had been kidnapped from the agency were units of cavalry from Fort Garland. Among the regular troops stationed at the fort in the 1870s were companies of the Ninth and Tenth Regiments of U.S. Cavalry. These regiments included blacks who were accepted for regular duty after the Civil War, and they served at several western forts during the Indian wars. Some were with the troops sent to western Colorado from Fort Garland after the Meeker Massacre.

Fortunately, the expected war did not develop. Ouray helped maintain peace by assisting in the rescue of the kidnapped women, but Colorado's citizens now had enough evidence to force the complete removal of the Utes from all of the state except a small corner in the southwest. Despite the futile protests of a few humanitarians, all of the northern and most of the southern bands were sent to a reservation in Utah, and the Western Slope was opened up to mining and agriculture. Perhaps it was a blessing that Ouray did not live to see the exodus of his people from their home land. He died in 1880, the year before the Utes left Colorado.

The gradual usurpation of Indian land in Colorado had its legal tradition in the courts of the United States, where Indian titles to land did not stand up against the government except as "a matter of grace."[17] Clearly, the Utes had run out of "grace" at the Meeker Massacre.

Long after the Indians were gone from the San Luis Valley, there remained many white settlers whose lives had been closely associated with them. One of these was Albert Pfeiffer, an adopted Ute whose death in 1881 coincided symbolically with the removal of his red friends from western Colorado.

Pfeiffer, the son of a Lutheran pastor, immigrated from Europe to the United States as a young man, arriving in St. Louis in 1844. He came to New Mexico at an undetermined time and married into a Mexican family at Abiquiu, where his inlaws operated a trading post. Pfeiffer became the Indian agent. During the Ute troubles in the mid-1850s, he joined the volunteers under Ceran St. Vrain and Kit Carson in the campaigns in the San Luis Valley. During the Civil War he again served under Carson as a volunteer in Indian campaigns in the Southwest. Also, he is known to have led volunteers from Fort Garland in an action to protect settlers in the Embargo Creek area of the San Luis Valley when Indians raided there in 1862.[18]

While Pfeiffer was stationed at Fort McRae in New Mexico in 1863, a band of Apaches attacked a group of soldiers and civilian women at a spring near the fort. Among them were Pfeiffer, his wife, and her servant girl. Mrs. Pfeiffer, her servant, and two soldiers were killed, and Pfeiffer was wounded. Perhaps some of the dramatic stories about Pfeiffer chasing the Indians across the desert have been exaggerated, but the deep hatred of Apaches and their allies, the Navajos, which he harbored afterward was not.[19]

He and Kit Carson remained loyal friends. Kit was familiar with Pfeiffer's habit of assuaging his grief in alcohol, and Kit worried about this in letters which he wrote to Pfeiffer. In 1866 Pfeiffer came to Fort Garland when Kit took command there. After Kit's resignation Pfeiffer stayed in the area and moved onto a ranch near South Fork. He did little ranching, though. Instead, he often went off to join Ouray's band of Tabeguaches, who had adopted him, in their frequent fights with the Navajos. On one occasion he volunteered to represent the Utes in a hand-to-hand duel with a Navajo to determine possession of the prized hot springs at Pagosa. Pfeiffer won. When he died in 1881, marking in another way the end of an era, this brave but sad man was buried on the north side of the Rio Grande at South Fork.

Chokecherries, a staple in the diet of Indians and Spanish-speaking settlers, are native to the San Luis Valley.

X

"Do You Want to Work for Wages or the First Day's Brandings?"

Major changes in patterns of settlement occurred in the San Luis Valley in the 1860s. Causes of these changes were publicity attending the gold rush, a change in territorial jurisdiction, enactment of legislation to enable homesteading, and the presence of Civil War veterans who were eager to farm and develop the territory.

It was 260 years after Don Juan de Oñate took possession of New Mexico "from the leaves of the trees in the forest to the stones and sands of the river" that the Pikes Peak gold rush began, and Colorado was occupied by Americans as it never had been by Spaniards. Major William Gilpin was one of the foremost promoters who fostered this development.

After he traveled west with Frémont in 1843, Gilpin became acquainted with present-day Colorado during his return from the Northwest in 1844, traveling alone with a Mexican guide. On that trip he passed through the San Juan Mountains and, probably, the San Luis Valley.[1] Deeper familiarity with the Southwest resulted from his service in the Navajo campaigns after the Mexican War. At this time Gilpin was stationed at Abiquiu.[2]

When the fifty-niners headed across the prairie for Pikes Peak and the mines near Cherry Creek, they had a variety of hastily put-together guidebooks, one of which included a speech delivered by Gilpin in 1858 in Kansas City. In it he extolled the "veritable arcana" of "metaliferous elements" to be found in the San Juans and the La Plata Mountains. "It is manifest with what ease the pioneers, already engaged in mining at the entrance of the Bayou Salado [South Park], will in another season, ascend through it to the Cordellera, surmount its crests and descend into the Bayou San Luis. They will develop at every step,

gold in new and increasing abundance. Besides, access is equally facile by the Huerfano, an affluent of the Arkansas coming down from the Spanish Peak, 100 miles farther to the south. From New Mexico, the approach is by ascending the Rio Bravo del Norte. The snowy battlement of the Sierra San Juan form the western wall of the Bayou San Luis."[3]

In other articles Gilpin urged investors from Missouri and the East Coast to put their money into the Bayou San Luis, or "San Luis Park," although he himself seems not to have had money invested there as yet.[4] His verbosity about the Rocky Mountains' future made him so well known in Missouri that he was boosted into the office of governor of the Territory of Colorado, when it was created in 1861.

Guidebooks which appeared early in the gold rush provided not only a wealth of words about the mines but also a handful of maps, each promoting one or another route to Colorado. Referring to his partisans in Missouri as "the Central people," Gilpin ardently espoused the central route between St. Louis and San Francisco, which would cross the San Luis Valley. Other equally ardent promoters backed the Smoky Hill and the Platte River routes to Denver and the mines near it, discounting the central route and the potentials of southern Colorado jealously. William N. Byers, who became editor of Denver's pioneer *Rocky Mountain News*, coauthored one of the guides favoring the northern interests—*Handbook to the Gold Fields of Nebraska and Kansas*. When interest in the San Juan mines appeared from time to time among Denverites, Byers saved no printers' ink in advising that the San Juan mines were a humbug.

Nevertheless, through the autumn of 1860

newspapers of Denver, Canon City, and Santa Fe persistently printed articles about the mines to the southwest. Many of these were in the form of letters from prospectors and agents with unnamed interests. The *Rocky Mountain News* itself carried accounts about a circuitous reconnaissance into western Colorado under the leadership of Richard Sopris. During their return to Denver via the San Luis Valley, this party reported that rich placer diggings had been located near Fort Garland and that hundreds of prospectors had flocked there in the summer of 1860. Sopris, however, did not think that these mines would fulfill their original promise, especially since Indians were said to have threatened the safety of the prospectors.[5] A "Capt. McKee, with a company of thirty-six men . . . had been as far South as the tributaries of the Rio-del-Norte," and they had found the entire region to be gold-bearing.[6]

Perhaps these good prospects were indirectly responsible for an ill-fated expedition near Fort Garland the next spring. One hundred and twenty men from Denver paid D. K. Reeder two dollars each for filing fees on a gulch four miles north of the fort. Gold was not found and, after a vote cast by those in camp, "Reeder was publicly whipped with fifty lashes and sent west."[7]

During the autumn and winter of 1860-61 several parties left the Denver area to try their luck in the San Juans. Some of these crossed the San Luis Valley and made it better known as a result. The best-known expedition was led by Charles Baker, usually called incorrectly the "discoverer" of the San Juan mines. Regardless of his imprecise place in mining history, he did attract a large amount of attention. He also attracted a large group of prospectors as followers, and with some of them came their wives and children. Baker's expedition to the San Juans left Denver in December 1860 and took a customary route down the east side of the Front Range to the Huerfano, across Sangre de Cristo Pass, and through the San Luis Valley. Because of the season they left the valley not by one of the passes to the west but by traveling south from Conejos to Ojo Caliente. At the Chama River they turned northwest on the Spanish Trail to Abiquiu and eventually to the Animas River and Baker's Park, later the location of Silverton.

As detractors of the San Juan mines had prophesied, such a journey in winter was not easy. The Baker group encountered so much snow on Sangre de Cristo Pass that they were forced to cut trees to supply food for their stock, and they lost twelve yoke of oxen. After a rest at Fort Garland, they suffered additional losses between the fort and Conejos when a howling windstorm scattered their livestock. When the party finally straggled into Conejos, a fandango was in progress. Some may have felt better after that. Others probably felt worse. At any rate, the road was easier south of the Conejos River, for the expedition now was traveling a well-used route.

Soon after this ill-starred expedition reached their destination in the San Juans, its members became demoralized, fell into factions, and decided to abandon the enterprise. When they split up, going in three different directions, a Denver-bound contingent left Baker's Park by way of Stony Pass and the headwaters of the Rio Grande. Wagon Wheel Gap between South Fork and Creede takes its name from pieces of broken equipment later found at this location, supposedly left by these members of the Baker expedition during their difficult journey.[8]

In the meantime, major political changes were taking place, and these had a profound effect on the future of the San Luis Valley. Denver and part of present-day Colorado had been in Kansas Territory, the San Luis Valley and southern Colorado had been in New Mexico Territory, and much of the land west of the Continental Divide had been in Utah Territory according to political divisions made after the Mexican War. On February 26, 1861, the Territory of Colorado was established by Congress with its boundaries almost identical to today's State of Colorado. The exception was the southern boundary, which was drawn along the thirty-seventh parallel, almost but not quite where the state line lies today. For the San Luis Valley the most important effect of the creation of the new territory was that most of the valley henceforth would be in Colorado, although the arbitrary division placed the southern end in New Mexico. The political separation of most of the Spanish-speaking people in the valley produced a dichotomy of interest which has never been resolved satisfactorily.

With the establishment of the new territory, counties were delineated in 1861. No longer was the valley going to be a huge, neglected outrider of Taos County, New Mexico. Instead, the section north of the new territorial boundary—by far the larger part of the valley—was divided into two Colorado counties, which automatically were supposed to share Colorado's interests. Costilla County contained the eastern and northern portions of the valley. Guadalupe County encompassed the western side of the valley, north to the

Rio Grande. Guadalupe had its own enormous outrider that took in a long strip across southwestern Colorado all the way to Utah. The name of this county was changed after seven days to Conejos County.

County seats, designated on a temporary basis in 1861, were San Miguel in Costilla County and Guadalupe in Conejos County. The exact location of San Miguel is a mystery, as it was never listed as a station attached to the Catholic mission or as a post office. At any rate, when Costilla County was formally organized in 1863, San Luis was the county seat.[9] Similarly, in Conejos County, Guadalupe lost its title as county seat in 1863 to the newer, smaller settlement of Conejos on the south side of the river.[10]

Headquarters for a few Anglo settlers, Conejos had for its principal booster Lafayette Head. Head ran his Indian agency there, and after his new house was built in 1865, the town could boast the finest home in the entire valley. Nevertheless, old Guadalupe, a mile northeast of Conejos, remained larger and was incorporated in 1869, several years before Conejos took this step. Servilletta, meanwhile, overshadowed both towns in population for a time, but it was destined to fade into obscurity.

Guadalupe was bypassed again when Conejos became the post office in 1862. At the same time three other post offices were established in the valley in Costilla County. These were at San Luis, Fort Garland, and Costilla.[11] Ferd Meyer was postmaster at Costilla, which was then in Colorado Territory.

To have been one of this burgeoning territory's first legislators would, of course, have been a great honor and responsibility. The San Luis Valley's first two territorial representatives both were Spanish surnamed—José Victor Garcia and Jesus M. Barela—while the first member of the council (equivalent to the senate) was Colonel John M. Francisco. Francisco, despite his name, was no relation to his Hispano neighbors, for he hailed from Virginia and Missouri. At one time he operated the suttler's store at Fort Garland. In 1861 he settled in the valley of La Veta, east of Sangre de Cristo Pass at the foot of the Spanish Peaks, where he could keep in close touch with his fellow sympathizers in the Confederate cause, who were influential south of Pueblo.[12]

Transportation quickly became a major concern in the new territory. Perhaps the political station of Francisco helped him and his Unionist friend Lafayette Head to obtain permits to build and to operate two ferries across the Rio Grande.

These permits, granted in 1861, were for La Loma on the old Conejos Road and for a point near Fort Garland north of La Sauces, or La Sauses, on the road between the fort and Conejos. In the same year a third permit for a ferry was granted to Garcia, one of the valley's representatives, and his partner for an operation at the mouth of the Culebra on the Rio Grande, the place being called Paso del Puerto. These three ferries were intended to aid the throngs of settlers and prospectors expected momentarily. Regardless of the extent of their use, the ferries certainly did better than a proposed steamboat. One promoter estimated that the Rio Grande as it flowed through the valley was "sufficiently large to float a Missouri River steamboat."[13]

Rates for the use of the ferries were high, but they were comparable with tolls charged elsewhere in the territory for ferries and toll roads. At La Loma, for instance, a wagon with two horses, mules, or oxen was charged two dollars, while a buggy with a single horse or mule cost half as much. Rates for loose stock were five or ten cents per head, depending on the size.[14]

Whether Francisco and Head operated the ferry at La Sauses is unknown, but a ferry was in business there in 1863 called Stewart's Crossing. Taking advantage of the business from military personnel, prospectors, settlers, and merchants who used this cutoff across the valley, a trading post also operated under the name of Stewart's Crossing.[15]

During the early 1860s the Military Express ran through the valley, linking Fort Garland and Canon City, where it connected with the "Pony Line" from Denver. J. B. Doyle and Company, who operated elsewhere in Colorado, ran the Military Express.[16] After the war ended, a toll road was built by the Denver and San Luis Valley Wagon Road Company to operate between Denver and the valley. This line crossed South Park and Poncha Pass and ran through the San Luis Valley on the Conejos Road as far as the Conejos Indian Agency and Los Pinos, the latter being located near the border between Colorado and New Mexico.[17] These were the pioneer wagon roads authorized by the territorial legislature.

With the end of the war, settlement in the valley accelerated. The passage of the Homestead Act in 1862, together with the Indian Treaty of 1863, had opened up most of the San Luis Valley, including the Conejos Grant where colonial claims were under legal dispute. Some of the new settlements on the valley's grants continued to be made by people from New Mexico. On the west side, between the Alamosa and La Jara rivers, Capulin, meaning "chokecherries," was established in 1867 by people from Ojo Caliente, and La Jara was settled on the south side of the latter stream at about the same time. Plazas around La Loma expanded to the north, while Ortiz and San Antonio began to prosper in the corner of the valley south of Conejos. To the east Ojito on Trinchera Creek and to the north Rito Alto appeared. Nearly every stream within the San Luis Valley had at least one settlement of Spanish-speaking people.

Many of those who began to take up claims at this time were veterans of military service, particularly soldiers who had served at Fort Garland. They were issued script, which they could use when they filed homestead claims. This arrangement permitted the permanent settlement of many immigrants from Germany and other northern European countries, who had served the Union cause. Among the veterans who became pioneers of the San Luis Valley were Henry Backus, who settled northwest of present-day Alamosa; Peter Hansen, south of the same town; James Schultz, near Stewart's Crossing; and Mark Biedell, on La Garita Creek.[18] A group of men from Company One Colorado Volunteers settled on Kerber Creek after 1865. Among these were Captain Charles Kerber, a Lieutenant Walters, and George Neidhardt. The Loren Jenks family from Pueblo also joined this settlement.[19] A former resident of Costilla who had helped recruit men from the valley for the Union Army, Captain Charles Deus, returned to live, but a series of financial losses forced him to leave.

During 1866 the area around Saguache was homesteaded. Led by Nathan Russell, representing Fred Walsen (later of Walsenburg) and Christian Stollsteimer (later of Durango), this group homesteaded the bottomlands along Saguache Creek. Natural arroyos were used to convey water to crops until the arroyos were converted into proper irrigation ditches. The first of these was the "Nathan Russell arolla."[20] Spanish-surnamed laborers worked the fields and dug the ditches.

The principal crop in this area was wheat, hand-sickled and often threshed by sheep. Flour was very much in demand in the new territory, and in 1860 prospectors sometimes had been unable to buy any. In 1861, despite the existence of Easterday's new mill at San Luis, flour could not be had at Francisco's store at Fort Garland or anywhere else in the San Luis Valley.[21] In the next few years pack trains from New Mexico transported food to Colorado's settlements, as additional strain was

put on provisions after the Treaty of 1863 required that rations be distributed to the Indians. What was left for the Indians was likely to be the moldy, wormy flour that the mills could sell only to Indian agents or to the army. In his report of June 1866 Kit Carson complained that flour shipped to Fort Garland was spoiled. Because of this demand for agricultural products in the booming Territory of Colorado, the lush northern end of the San Luis Valley around Saguache was quickly homesteaded and put to the plow after the war.

One of the settlers who went there to raise wheat was Otto Mears. Mears was a Russian Jew who began life in his adopted home land by serving in the Union Army for three years, part of his military duty being under Kit Carson in the Navajo campaigns. After Mears's discharge in August 1864, he took a job as a clerk in a Santa Fe store and soon entered into a partnership in a retail store there. Next Mears moved to the Conejos, where he opened a general merchandise store in the old town of Guadalupe. He also went into partnership with Lafayette Head in building both a sawmill and a gristmill. Because the local Mexican farmers could not produce enough grain for the gristmill, Mears moved again in 1866— this time to Saguache to raise wheat for the Conejos mill and to open another store. During the next year he brought in a mower, a reaper, and a threshing machine for his crops, this machinery being the first such implements in the valley.[22]

Mears's well-known friendship with Chief Ouray began with a business arrangement, when Mears got a contract to supply food rations to the Utes.[23] This relationship eventuated in Mears's becoming a commissioner for the Brunot Treaty and his accompanying a delegation of Utes to Washington.

When the government's price for flour dropped, Mears sought new markets in the Upper Arkansas River Valley, and thus he entered another career as road builder. Finding the Poncha Pass road to the Arkansas River in unsatisfactory condition for freighting, he chartered a toll road across the pass and built a new wagon road. The success of this undertaking in 1867 was repeated in 1871, when he built another toll road across Cochetopa Pass.[24] This road led to the Los Pinos Indian Agency and another store that Mears owned there. His road continued west to Lake City, a supply town that Mears founded for the San Juan mining country. These were the beginnings of the network of toll roads and later rail-

Otto Mears of Saguache—a very big man in a very small package.

roads which established Mears's reputation as "the pathfinder of the San Juans."

Clearly, Saguache had become the home of an energetic empire builder, and Mears had neighbors—Spanish-speaking, Anglo, and northern European—who seem to have been inspired by his example. They were intensely conscious of the importance of the northern end of the valley, and the idea of riding all the way to San Luis to transact county business was both bothersome and demeaning. To overcome this problem, in December

1866 the County of Saguache was carved from that part of Costilla County which lay north of the Sangre de Cristo Grant. After the Brunot Treaty in 1873 Saguache County also encompassed a large area of land across the Continental Divide, previously in the Ute reservation.

One of Saguache County's first officials was Otto Mears, who served as county treasurer. Another influential citizen who held various county offices during his lifetime and who is credited with drawing up the legislative bill to create the county was John Lawrence. Lacking the advantages of much formal education, Lawrence grew up as an orphan in St. Louis and came west in 1859 to make his way as a miner and muleskinner. In 1860 he prospected in the San Luis Valley and returned in 1861 with Nathan Russell and E. R. Harris to settle at Conejos.[25]

In February 1867 Lawrence set out from Conejos to join his friends who already were at Saguache. He recorded the events of this journey, as well as the next forty years of his life, in a diary.[26] Although his spelling was unorthodox, it was as consistent as were his other habits.

As reported by Lawrence, this trip to Saguache presents considerable insight into life in the valley at that time. Lawrence started out with two ox teams, a team of horses, wheat, oats, provisions, and some farm tools. Sylvestre Larux, or Leroux, who accompanied Lawrence, took along lumber and a workbench. Langino Velte, Juan de Jesus Manchez, and Jose Antonio Moran went with them to farm on shares. Working for the party were two Navajo Indian boys, Andres and Gabriel Woodson, who belonged to Lawrence's partner, James B. Woodson. A young herder, Jose Andres Chaves, completed the party. They drove a herd of cattle belonging to Woodson and en route delivered a few head of stock to the Luceros on the Rio Grande and to other ranchers on Carnero Creek. In later years the settlers at Saguache continued to have frequent business with the people around La Loma and La Garita.

Upon his arrival at Saguache, Lawrence spent his first day paying calls on his neighbors and old acquaintances—Nathan Russell, E. R. Harris, Otto Mears, Fred Walsen, and John Greilig. He spent the second day establishing the Saguache cemetery. When he went over to a Mexican camp to visit a family he had known at Conejos, he found that an old man in their outfit had died. The usual procedures of a proper burial did not seem to be on anyone's mind, so Lawrence took charge of affairs. First he got Harris to build a coffin, for which Lawrence and Mears donated the lumber. Then they chose a site on a "nole" south of the river for the burying ground and gave "the first man claiming the name of a white man a deacent burial."

During his long life in Saguache Lawrence was to be state representative, county assessor, county judge, and for twenty-five years a member of the school board. He tried his hand at road building, constructing a toll road five miles west of town, paralleling the government road that had been built farther north.[27] He raised wheat, which he sold to the Ute Indian Agency, and he raised sheep, which he eventually willed to his Mexican workers. He was not the first settler in Saguache, nor was his town the first in the area. (It was, in fact, the third settlement in the immediate vicinity, one of the others being called Milton.) Nevertheless, Lawrence earned the title "Father of Saguache" through his long life of devotion to his community.

Besides Lawrence's diary, another source of information on early-day Saguache is the account of an itinerant preacher. When the Reverend John L. Dyer visited the town in 1867 to hold Methodist services, he found few Protestants. He had incurred the anger of a priest at Fort Garland, in fact, by invading the predominantly Catholic flock there. Nevertheless, at Saguache Dyer "held a two days' meeting at the house of Mr. Ashley, a family from Kentucky. . . . On Sunday the power of God came down, and nearly all were in tears. The lady of the house broke out in a grand shout, the first ever raised in the San Luis Valley. . . . We had there a foreigner, I think of Jewish descent. [Otto Mears, probably.] He sat near the door, and looked first at the door, then at me, and then at the scene among the seekers. A man by the name of Fullerton, and a Mr Woodson, who had Mexican wines [wives?], were present. . . .

"A severe hail storm beat their crops into the ground. Indians were more numerous than white men. Old Chief San Juan came along, and expressed great sorrow at their loss. For him it meant, no biscuits this year."[28]

Leaving Saguache, Dyer continued north toward Poncha Pass. Although his detailed description of the valley did not continue, he at least mentioned finding a settlement as he approached the pass in Homan's Park. This area originally was settled by Mexicans, and in the late 1860s the population grew to about one hundred, many of the newcomers being German-born veterans of the Civil War. They eventually bought up or otherwise gained control of most of the land and water rights in this section of the valley and raised cattle and sheep there. The settlement to

which Dyer referred may have been the town called Philadelphia.[29]

Population trends in the valley were reflected in the creation of post offices, and a list of these issued in 1868 reveals the gradual movement into the northern half. Saguache had a post office with Nathan Russell as postmaster. Another was located at La Loma. Still, the center of the valley's population remained around Conejos with almost six thousand people scattered among twenty-five placitas at that time.

Farms along the Rio Grande became another Anglo and northern European foothold around Conejos. Cattle raising was the principal activity on these farms, with most of the original livestock being purchased from Mexican ranchers on the Conejos River. One of the newcomers here was Peter Hansen, Union Army veteran, who began raising cattle on a homestead near the mouth of the Conejos. His cattle watered in the Rio Grande, summer and winter. In winter this meant chopping holes in the ice, a chore reserved for Hansen's young son William. Mrs. Hansen sold butter to neighbors.

It was not an easy nor a glamorous life for the pioneers in the San Luis Valley, but it could be an honorable one. When William Hansen became sixteen years old, his father asked, "Willie, do you want to work for wages or for the first day's branding of Heifer calves?"[30] Willie chose the calves and became one of the valley's most successful ranchers.

Although land and water rights were not yet causes of overt conflict between original colonists and homesteaders, these problems would arise later. When settlers from New Mexico first diverted water into their irrigation ditches on the land grants, the farmers had no need to register their rights. Later, when attempts were made to do so as required by law in Colorado, the original farmers discovered that claims had been filed already for these ditch rights by such newcomers as Mark Biedell or Russell Green. Contests over grazing rights and land ownership also would occur, especially after the public records in the Saguache County Courthouse burned in 1880. A more indirect reason why the Spanish-speaking colonists found their rights eroded away lay in the failure of the first generation to prepare their children to assume legal and systematic control of the family's property under state law.[31]

Perhaps most significant in ensuing social and economic changes in the valley were the profoundly different attitudes by which the different cultures approached goals. For the Spanish-speaking colonists life was measured by the needs

Sheepherders on the banks of the Rio Grande perpetuate traditions of Spanish-speaking settlers of the San Luis Valley, with the help of modern trucks and trailers.

of the day and the season. For the new breed of pioneers, the day and the season merely marked their progress toward a remarkable array of ambitious aims. The main difference between the young Willie Hansens and their Spanish-speaking playmates was that the Willies knew their options and were being trained to use them.

These adobe ranch buildings were the home of Tom Tobin, who brought in the heads of the Espinosas.

The last legal hanging in Conejos County took place in 1889.

XI

"Bring Their Heads"

With change came disorientation and frustration for many of the San Luis Valley's settlers. In a few instances the reaction was violent.

In 1863 a series of crimes were committed by members of a San Rafael family, the Espinosas, against their enemies-at-large, the newcomers in Colorado Territory. Although the Espinosas' violence has been attributed loosely to a malaise of the mind, it seems quite possible that the family had suffered wrongs perpetrated by Americans and were bent upon avenging these wrongs.

According to one story, while the Espinosas were living in northern New Mexico, Americans had run off their sheep and killed a youngster in the family in an effort to drive them from the land. Soon afterward the Espinosas moved to San Rafael, where two brothers in the family, Vivian and José, turned to what appeared to be run-of-the-mill horse stealing. In the spring of 1863 they branched out and robbed a wagon between Santa Fe and Galisteo, New Mexico. The teamster, from Conejos County, recognized the bandits and alerted authorities.

Volunteers were sent from Fort Garland to the Espinosas' log house at San Rafael, under the pretext of recruiting the brothers for the Union Army. When this invitation was declined, the soldiers made a straightforward move to arrest the pair. The brothers then burst from the house, shooting and killing one soldier, and made their escape.

In the weeks that followed, the fugitives terrorized the back country of southern and central Colorado, in what has been called a "mission" to kill as many Anglos as possible. Their first victim was Judge William Bruce at a sawmill on Hardscrabble Creek near Wetmore, and the second also took place at a sawmill near Fountain. Moving into South Park, they killed at least seven ranchers and miners, while an unknown number of other deaths occurred in the wave of hysteria that these murders precipitated.

Finally a posse from Fairplay tracked Vivian and José to a camp in the rugged terrain below South Park. José was killed there, but Vivian escaped. He next killed two men east of Canon City and, returning to the San Luis Valley, murdered another in Conejos.

After a short stay with his family he set out again, accompanied by a young nephew, toward Sangre de Cristo Pass with the intention of ambushing Governor John Evans who, Espinosa knew, had been in Conejos at Lafayette Head's agency to meet with the Utes. Instead of taking the governor, the Espinosas killed two other men. A couple of days later they attacked a buggy carrying an American man and a Mexican woman to Costilla. The woman was called a "prostitute of an American" and was assaulted, but the man escaped to Fort Garland.[1]

The commander of the fort, Colonel Samuel Tappan, sent for Tom Tobin, who was in residence with squatter's rights on a piece of grazing land about six miles south of the fort. Tobin, who was in Arroyo Hondo at the time of the Taos Rebellion, had drifted up to Costilla with his Mexican wife and was raising cattle and horses. Tobin lived on Trinchera Creek part of each year while his wife and small daughter lived in Costilla with their Navajo servant girl. When summoned by Colonel Tappan to the fort, Tobin was told that he would be rewarded if he could track down the Espinosas and "bring their heads" to the fort. The colonel persuaded Tobin that he should have the protection of some soldiers. Tobin finally agreed to go with a small escort, although he suspected that the soldiers, some of whom were recruits from the Spanish-speaking settlements in the valley, might be as inclined to kill him as the Espinosas.

Near La Veta Pass, Tobin tracked down the murderers and killed both. Taking his instructions literally, he put their heads in a sack and brought them to Colonel Tappan, along with a diary and letters which reported that the Espinosas had killed thirty people during their campaign.[2]

After this event Tobin became a local legend. While friendly to his neighbors and Indians who camped on his ranch, he was taciturn with strangers and angry with Colorado's government, which never fully rewarded him for his capture of the Espinosas.[3] Illiterate himself, he supported schools at Costilla and near his ranch on Trinchera Creek and even became president of a school board. Ferd Meyer bought Tobin's Costilla property when Tobin moved permanently to his Trinchera ranch in 1872, and Meyer helped support Tobin there with monthly payments on that property, too, until Tobin's death in 1904. The family name remained linked with memories of old days when Tobin's daughter Pasquala married a neighbor boy, the son of Tom's old friend Kit Carson.[4]

Had the Espinosa's rampage occurred a few years later, it might have been interpreted as a crusade for justice rather than as a spree of wanton murders, for the rights of Spanish-speaking people on the land grants in the San Luis Valley were becoming disputed issues. However, in 1863 it is unlikely that the full extent of these threats to their rights were fully recognized.

The United States had granted liberty and protection to Mexican citizens living in the Southwest at the conclusion of the Mexican War. Nevertheless, land grants made by the Mexican government required special adjudication. The two grants in the San Luis Valley, being in New Mexico in the 1850s, were assigned in 1854 to the surveyor general of New Mexico, William Pelham, for review. Pelham's report was sent to the General Land Office, then to the secretary of the Department of the Interior, who in turn made a recommendation to Congress for a final decision regarding the validity of the grants.

In 1860 Congress confirmed the Sangre de Cristo Grant, but the Conejos Grant was not considered at that time because no one on the grant had submitted an application as required by the surveyor general. In 1861 the necessary application was made with the names of four settlers in behalf of others living on the grant. Because the original document of 1833 was still missing, the settlers submitted sworn statements of officials who were involved in the granting of possession of 1842.[5] Apparently no action was taken immediately by the surveyor general of New Mexico, and documents regarding the grant were not received in Colorado until 1867, six years after the new territory was created. In 1868 the Conejos Grant was surveyed for the first time by a deputy of Colorado's surveyor general, who noted that a large number of Mexican settlements existed around Conejos, but no other progress seems to have been made by the surveyor general's office.[6]

Meanwhile, the Conejos Grant was being handled as public domain. Spanish-speaking residents already living there were considered squatters with legal rights entitling them to 160 acres each under the Pre-emption Act. Newcomers also were entitled to homestead parcels of land, while the older residents maintained that the land involved was part of the legal grant. Confusion stemming from such situations, which were common to other areas of the Southwest as well, finally led to the establishment of United States courts of private land claims.

When one of these courts opened in Denver in the 1890s, Cresencio Valdes, son of the colonizer Seledon Valdes, petitioned for confirmation of the Conejos Grant and asked that people occupying the grant without consent of the grantees be given notices of eviction or that the grantees be given compensation. In 1900 this petition was dismissed on the grounds that, first, no evidence of the grant of 1833 existed, and, second, the governor of New Mexico had expressed some doubt regarding his own authority to grant possession.[7] The Conejos Grant was null and void, and a great number of clouded land titles, some held by Anglo residents of many years, were settled at last. The embittered heirs of the original settlers had no claim except those of ordinary homesteaders, if, indeed, their land had been filed upon properly.

Because land title had been settled by the confirmation of the Sangre de Cristo Grant in 1860, the way was cleared there for even more complex transactions. After William Gilpin was removed as governor of the Territory of Colorado in 1862, he devoted his full attention to promoting the development of this region and the grant in particular.

In 1853 Charles Beaubien had given away half of his title to the grant in a maneuver, not unknown today, to reduce his taxes if they should be levied on land grants, as the United States government was expected to do. These gifts of convenience were in three shares with one-sixth of the grant going to his son-in-law Lucien Maxwell;

one-sixth to Joseph Pley, who had administered Stephen Luis Lee's estate and who had sold Lee's original half of the grant to Beaubien for $100; and the other one-sixth to James H. Quinn, another business associate.[8] In 1858 Pley sold his share to Ceran St. Vrain for $1,000, thereby enabling St. Vrain and Easterday to open their flour mill and other business interests in San Luis. In 1862 Gilpin bought this one-sixth interest from St. Vrain, giving Gilpin his entree in San Luis Valley real estate.

In fact, Gilpin had more ambitious plans than this purchase implied. His espousal of Colorado's mineral potential was little short of a mania, and he believed that the Sangre de Cristo Mountains could yield untold glittering rewards for anyone who would go after them. The only obstacle to securing those minerals was the land grants within which these mountains lay.[9] Some of the most promising portions of the Culebra Range lay in the Sangre de Cristo Grant, while another group of peaks north of the sand dunes could be reached through the Baca Grant Number Four, which Gilpin was acquiring also.

The Baca Grant was a new tract set aside in the name of the heirs of Luis Maria de Baca in 1860.[10] In 1823 Baca had been granted the very large Vegas Grandes holding around the present town of Las Vegas, New Mexico. When ownership of this land was disputed in later years, the Baca family was permitted by Congress to select five other sites, called "floating grants," each containing 100,000 acres. One of these was Baca Grant Number Four, located on the western side of the Sangre de Cristos around the present site of Crestone.

By early 1862 Gilpin had worked out an agreement to buy this Baca float for the price of thirty cents an acre, or $30,000, to be paid in five annual installments.[11] Gilpin's activities in connection with the Baca Grant and with St. Vrain's share in the Sangre de Cristo Grant soon attracted the attention of Charles Beaubien, who offered Gilpin an irresistible opportunity late in 1862 to buy the half interest in the Sangre de Cristo Grant still owned by Don Carlos for $15,000, or about four cents an acre. Payment was to be complete by March 1863, according to the agreement to purchase.[12] Foregoing further attempts to buy the Baca Grant, Gilpin had difficulty in raising even the cash required for the Sangre de Cristo. Perhaps most citizens at that time were preoccupied with the Civil War, or perhaps they doubted the wisdom of investing money in "Indian-infested" territory. By late

summer of 1863, after traveling from San Francisco to New York in search of backers, Gilpin had his money. By then Charles Beaubien was dead, but the sale was consummated by his heirs. Acquiring the interests of Maxwell and Quinn, also, Gilpin gained control of the entire grant.[13]

By 1865 Gilpin was ready to launch the next stage of his program, marketing the land for a proposed five million dollars. In this campaign he publicized widely a mining appraisal made in the fall of 1864, which proclaimed the mountains within the Sangre de Cristo Grant to be as rich in minerals as the Gregory District itself. Needless to say, the expert who made this appraisal had been hired by Gilpin himself.

To capitalize the sale of the Sangre de Cristo Grant, Gilpin brought in associates who bought about two-thirds interest, the largest of these investors being Morton Fisher of Santa Fe, who gave $162,000 for his share. Others of the diverse group included a cotton manufacturer from Rhode Island and a promoter of Madison Square Garden in New York. Fisher went off to New York, where he set up a corporation for the sale of the grant. He also sent a lawyer to England to establish an office there in hopes of luring European capital, which at that time was being poured into foreign investments. Of greatest consequence in these efforts was that they attracted the attention of an English attorney, William Blackmore, who in turn became the central figure in promoting the sale of the grant.

With these international dealings in the hands of others, Gilpin devoted his frenetic energy to promoting domestic sales. As a real estate broker most of his experience was discouraging. His biographer, Thomas Karnes, recounts an incident in 1865 when Gilpin prepared an elaborate promotion for a group of Philadelphians. Having arrived in Denver by special stage, they were met there by Gilpin, who transferred them to a buckboard and set off to show them his special piece of the Golden West. En route the wagon slid off a mountain road, but, undeterred, Gilpin got his passengers safely to Culebra for a welcoming fandango. The former governor himself led the grand march and outdid himself as a genial host, but the Philadelphians did not buy.[14]

In 1868 Blackmore came to Colorado to see with his own eyes what the Sangre de Cristo Grant had to offer. During his trip across the plains he met geologist Ferdinand V. Hayden and asked him to provide a report on the grant. Hayden's opinions in the resulting report were that the grant contained "immensely valuable" minerals—gold, silver, copper, lead, and iron—and that the land was "by far the finest agricultural district I have seen west of the Missouri River." Hayden's report was included the next year in a booklet published by Blackmore, perhaps with the bombastic assistance of Gilpin, to promote not only the Sangre de Cristo Grant but also other ventures in the West in which Blackmore was interested as a broker.[15]

Blackmore's personal evaluation of the Sangre de Cristo Grant was attuned to the salesman's problems, however. The grant was a white elephant, too large to market in one piece, he concluded. At his suggestion the grant was divided into a northern and a southern portion, to be called respectively the Trinchera and the Costilla estates. While he set about seeking buyers in the Netherlands for stock in the Costilla Estate, Fisher concentrated on selling stock in the other to English investors, their enterprise being organized collectively as the United States Freehold Land and Emigration Company. Of the stocks and bonds initially issued, a Dutch banking firm bought one million dollars of bonds in the Costilla Estate, but at only half their face value. Few other sales were made. The remaining stocks were divided among the promoters with Fisher and Gilpin each receiving $25,000 worth. Hayden, possibly in lieu of payment for his survey and report, received $10,000 in stock. Blackmore and the lawyer who had represented Fisher in England took the lions' share—$575,000 in stock plus a commission of $150,000. Also, Blackmore received 7,500 acres of land on the Trinchera Estate.[16] In a moment of generosity, which it appeared that he could well afford, Blackmore wrote to Hayden, "I have pulled through the 'Colorado matter' and I enclose as a wedding gift to you a Banking draft for 500$."[17]

During 1871 the Freehold Land and Emigration Company made attempts to start development of the Costilla Estate, but the most notable accomplishments seem to have been the personal aggrandizements of the organizers and their colleagues. Gilpin selected a homesite on the Trinchera, and William Blackmore's brother George, who came with a cousin from England to manage that estate, established a ranch and home for himself on the Trinchera, too. On the Costilla Estate, William and Henry Blackmore each chose tracts of 2,500 acres for themselves and gave 2,500 acres to Easterday, miller and surveyor, for surveying the three tracts.

William Blackmore's immediate plans for the Costilla Estate included developing a gold mine, building a reservoir and irrigation system, setting up a model farm to assist the emigrees who were expected to arrive any day to take up farms on the grant, and establishing a new town to be the commercial center of the valley. Unfortunately, the man who was working the gold mine was a swindler, and Newell Squarey who was hired to set up the model farm was little inclined to hard work. Most important, the Spanish-speaking settlers already living on the grant chose not to move out of Blackmore's way.

The Mexican people who had settled on Beaubien's grant were farming their plots of land, had rights to water from streams through their irrigation ditches, and were grazing their livestock and cutting timber on land which they did not own but to which they had right of access during Beaubien's ownership. When the new land company took over, the Mexicans were told that the original settlers would receive quit claim deeds to their property but not timber and grazing rights.[18] Ferd Meyer of Costilla took up the cause of his neighbors and led a public campaign to thwart the developers by means of letters to newspapers and public officials.

Late in 1871, while Meyer was away, Blackmore, Gilpin, and Squarey went to Costilla and made a verbal agreement with the citizens there, followed by a similar meeting at San Luis, whereby the land developers would allow the Mexicans to use water from the company's irrigation system, after the company's own needs were filled. This agreement seemed to bring about a more harmonious state of affairs. Later, when agreements were changed, broken, and generally proven unworkable, the matter of water rights had to be taken to court, where the settlement was in favor of the settlers. However, a reversal by the U.S. Circuit Court at the turn of the century cut the water rights of the Mexicans in half.[19] More than one hundred years after the land company arrived, the question of the Mexican's timber rights still has not been settled.

A further complication stemmed from a survey of the boundary between the territories of Colorado and New Mexico. The thirty-seventh parallel, the boundary established in 1861, was surveyed in 1868 by E. N. Darling, a United States government surveyor, and his survey was accepted in 1869 by the commissioner of the General Land Office. The survey proved that the parallel actually lay just north of Costilla, rather than south of it, and the town of Costilla and neighboring areas of the Costilla Estate, which previously had been in Colorado, were returned to the jurisdiction of New Mexico Territory. As a result, difficulties in obtaining proper legal titles and rights were compounded.

In the quarrel between Blackmore and the Spanish-speaking settlers, Gilpin was caught in the middle. He was resident manager of the Costilla Estate, but he undoubtedly was smarting at having been outmaneuvered by Blackmore in control of the land and the company. At least, he could comfort himself, the local people still referred to the project as "Gilpin's company."

To the former governor's credit, he seemed to have genuine concern for the welfare of the original settlers. In 1866 he had appealed to Father Pierre de Smet in an effort to rally influence for obtaining schools and churches on the Sangre de Cristo Grant. There were six thousand Catholics living there at that time. In addition to the bigger towns there were clusters of people large enough to form new parishes in 1869 at Chama, Ojito de la Trinchera, Rito de los Indios, San Acacio, San Francisco, Sierra Blanca, Trinchera, Zapata, and Placer.[20] When Bishop Lamy sent clergymen to the valley in 1867 to found the new Mission of New Mexico and Colorado, Gilpin offered them land on the grant for their headquarters, but the mission was established instead at Conejos.

In an outright move to block Blackmore's schemes, Gilpin even delayed in turning over titles to land. Beset by well-publicized legal questions regarding titles and water rights, the Costilla Estate's development became stalemated. Few land buyers could be attracted under these circumstances, and the Dutch bankers who might have financed a promotional campaign withheld funds. An economic depression in 1873 dealt another blow.

Hoping to find greater success on the western side of the valley, William Blackmore visited Seledon Valdes in Guadalupe in 1873 and tried to buy out the old settler, who gradually had built up his own holdings by purchasing others' shares in the Conejos Grant.[21] Valdes had no more desire for Anglo intrusion on his grant than did the people of the Sangre de Cristo Grant. In fact, Valdes's neighborhood already was becoming too full of homesteaders and other Anglos who were picking up old Mexican claims for back taxes or by purchase, and Valdes refused to sell to Blackmore.

By 1878 and 1879 the U.S. Freehold Land and Emigration Company was unable to pay its own taxes, and in 1880 the Dutch bankers were forced to redeem the land by paying them. Through the next two decades no significant sales or develop-

ments occurred, and the Spanish-speaking residents on the estate actually were able to continue their ordinary routines with less interference than occurred elsewhere in the valley, while the Dutch bankers wrote off their investment.

Although Blackmore himself enjoyed a brief wave of notoriety as a result of his promotions, he became overworked and overextended with many interests besides the Costilla Estate, and in 1877 he took his own life. His property in the valley was bequeathed to a brother, Humphrey, who in turn gave it to the Boyle brothers. In 1937 the 240,000-acre Trinchera Ranch, with the old Blackmore property as its nucleus, was being advertised as the "largest private estate in Colorado," when it was purchased by Mrs. Ruth McCormick Simms, daughter of Mark Hanna. After her death the ranch was owned by her husband and next by his two nephews. From the surname of these nephews the land became known as the Forbes Ranch and was linked with the *Forbes Magazine* empire.

Thus, a century after Gilpin's extravaganza, part of the old grant again became a package of merchandise for land developers. The Forbes Ranch was being sold by international brokers who offered the public five-acre bits of "the romantic old Southwest." There still remain many Spanish-speaking people on the old grant, and some of them believe that the traditions of the "romantic old Southwest" include such privileges as gathering their firewood where they always have gathered it, whether or not the land belongs to newcomers. A few guns have been fired over this issue. Apparently, the "malaise" of the Espinosas is not entirely dead.

The D&RG's engine, *Kokomo*, with a helper pulls a train past Dump Mountain and across La Veta Pass.

XII

"I Had a Dream"

At the close of the Civil War great energy was turned to another dream of empire, this one built on iron rails. Railroads were deemed the form of transportation best suited to serve the new centers of population in the West, but, just as railroad builders might produce fortunes, they also required large investments. Even while Gilpin's grandiose land speculations were faltering, another dreamer of empire, William Jackson Palmer, caught the attention of Gilpin's backers. Palmer's undertaking, the Denver and Rio Grande Railway, eventually was more successful than the U.S. Freehold and Emigration Company but not without great sacrifice.

Projects such as Palmer's were encouraged by the absence of adequate transportation systems or even provisions for them in the Territory of Colorado. The only means of building roads to new towns, mining districts, and agricultural areas was to charter private enterprises to build toll roads, such as Mears's roads, or to operate ferries, such as those on the Rio Grande. Two of the first toll roads in the new territory had been chartered for the San Luis Valley. The first—the Canon City, Grand River, and San Juan Road Company—was built in the early 1860s. It entered the valley via Poncha Pass and intersected with the military road from Fort Garland to Salt Lake City, which crossed Cochetopa Pass. The second—the San Luis Valley Wagon Road—was built in the latter half of the decade as part of a road linking South Park with the Gunnison country. Actually, both of these were merely improvements on previously existing wagon tracks. In the 1870s additional roads reached the Gunnison Valley and the San Juan country through the San Luis Valley after the Brunot Treaty opened up the area to mining. Otto Mears's Saguache and San Juan Toll Road, built in 1874, heralded this boom.[1]

Mears's home town, Saguache, also figured prominently as a supply town and hostelry for teamsters and travelers heading into the Gunnison region, while Alamosa, Monte Vista, and Del Norte were to receive much of their early importance in connection with the San Juan traffic.

Entrance to the San Luis Valley from the east continued with Sangre de Cristo Pass as the main route, although a shorter but more rugged toll road was built over Mosca Pass in 1871. This newer road boasted a stage station and supply town called Mosca at the foot of the pass, but it failed to compete. Mail came across Sangre de Cristo Pass in a buckboard along with express and a few passengers in the same vehicle. At Fort Garland the wagons turned south to San Luis, Taos, and Santa Fe.

This operation ran under the name the Denver and Santa Fe Stage Line. Billy Jones, one-armed though he was, handled the reins. In 1870 this line was sold to Ben Holladay's Barlow, Sanderson, and Company, the firm that was also operating the Southern Overland Mail and Express as a subsidiary.[2] The Barlow and Sanderson operation was destined to play a prominent role in San Luis Valley transportation for several years until it was supplanted by Palmer's railroad.

It was in early 1870 that William Jackson Palmer, supervisor of surveys of the Kansas Pacific, wrote to Mary "Queen" Mellen, "I had a dream last evening." It was a vision of a railroad built by himself and his friends to link Denver with Mexico City. In the autumn of that year he took the first step toward making this dream a reality by filing for the incorporation of his Denver and Rio Grande Railway. A principal part of his plan was to lay track from Denver to Pueblo, thence up the Arkansas River to Canon City and through the Royal Gorge, over Poncha Pass and through the San Luis Valley to the Rio Grande, which would be followed to Santa Fe and El Paso, Texas. A main branch would push westward to Utah, and provisions for other branches included a line running from near the mouth of Costilla Creek to mines in the Culebra Range and lumber operations on the Maxwell Estate near the top of the range.

Significant among the directors of the corporation were William P. Mellen, wealthy New York attorney who was the father of Palmer's bride "Queen," and Alexander Cameron Hunt, former governor of Colorado Territory who had become a real estate broker. Hunt immediately chartered the Puncha Pass Wagon Road Company and set about buying up land in the San Luis Valley and elsewhere. These acquisitions included the Baca Grant, which, after Gilpin had failed to make good his purchase, had ended up in the hands of the Baca heirs' lawyer, John S. Watts of Santa Fe, in payment for his legal services.

Meanwhile, Dr. William Bell, a British physician and close business associate of Palmer, went to England to seek financing for the railroad. There he contacted William Blackmore with whom Mellen also was acquainted. Through these connections Blackmore soon became involved in selling D&RG bonds to the same Dutch bankers who had underwritten the U.S. Freehold Land and Emigration Company. Their investment in the railroad was encouraged by assurances that track would be laid into the valley promptly and would provide the transportation needed for large-scale development of the Costilla Estate. Also, the land company would be relieved of the burden of building its own rail facility, a possibility that had been authorized by Congress at the time of incorporation of the land company.[3]

Construction of a narrow-gauged roadbed from Denver got underway quickly, and service reached Colorado Springs and Pueblo before financial problems forced a delay during the Panic of 1873, which tightened money from both American and European investors. While D&RG construction was halted, the threat of another railroad's building into south-central Colorado and New Mexico was emerging in the form of the better-financed Atchison, Topeka, and Santa Fe. As a last-ditch move to capture the important traffic to Santa Fe, Palmer was forced to change his construction priorities, and he began to build south from Pueblo toward Trinidad and Raton Pass in 1876, the year in which the AT&SF reached Pueblo.

This shift in the D&RG's routes was pushed, too, by investors in the U.S. Freehold Land and Emigration Company, who hoped to bolster their enterprise's lagging development by luring the railroad over La Veta Pass and through the Trinchera Estate. The Spanish Range Railway Company was incorporated to build into the valley from Cucharas Junction to Fort Garland by way of the town of La Veta and Sangre de Cristo Creek. Although incorporated by D&RG people, this line bore a different name because of the continuing financial problems of the original corporation.[4]

These economic problems plagued the operation as track was being put down and towns were being laid out along the new route. By June 1876 La Veta town was end of track and then Veta Pass, just south of Sangre de Cristo Pass. Fifty to one hundred wagons of freight, meanwhile, were rolling toward the San Juan mines every day as the iron rails inched laboriously across the pass. Slowly the construction crews worked their way down the mountain, building a station about two miles from the summit and calling this point Sangre de Cristo. Then Placer at a mining camp five miles below Sangre de Cristo station was reached with a meal station established there. Sierra was another station near this point. By June 1877 Garland City, thirteen miles west of Placer and six miles northeast of Fort Garland, was finally reached.

A typical, temporary end-of-track town, Garland City consisted of about one hundred buildings, including Perry's Hotel, which were hauled in and tacked up during the first two weeks of the town's existence. Such construction had to be quick, for the place lasted only until rails moved on to Alamosa within a year.[5] Hordes of people jostled through the rickety town, and wagons and teams filled the corrals. A dancing bear chained near one of the saloons added to the circus-like atmosphere. A post office functioned for eleven months until the town pushed on. When the population moved, all that was left was a few piles of rusty tin cans and broken liquor bottles, and the lonely graves of victims of a smallpox epidemic which had swept through the camp during the one winter of its life. The buildings were moved west, just as they had come in from other end-of-track places such as Cucharas Junction and La Veta.

Each mile of construction had carried the company deeper into financial trouble on the gamble that it soon would reap enough revenue to salvage not only its own future but also that of the U.S. Freehold Land and Emigration Company. To assist the beleaguered railroad, the Freehold corporation agreed in December 1876 to quit claim to Palmer an undivided half interest in

After Fort Garland's military reservation was abandoned, the town of Fort Garland was settled around the Denver and Rio Grande's station. Beneath snowy summits of Blanca Peak the towers of the town's Catholic church rise.

the Trinchera Estate and to deed to the railroad company a right of way, not to exceed fifty feet on either side of the track, plus an aggregate of six acres for depots.[6] Despite this help the railroad's hope of pushing west to Alamosa and a terminus closer to the booming San Juan mines was doomed to wait another year while additional financing was sought. The railroad defaulted on paying interests and stock dividends. The U.S. Freehold Land and Emigration Company defaulted on payment of taxes, and the property reverted to the Dutch bankers. And in the wake of these troubles and alcoholism William Blackmore took his life. Palmer's dream had become a nightmare.

It is to the credit of General Palmer that he continued to struggle to save the railroad, pressing toward whatever centers of traffic might help to recoup those who had backed the project. The plucky little Philadelphian had an equally loyal following of friends from the East Coast and England who had joined him in making Colorado Springs their home, and several of these neighbors were investors and officers in the D&RG. One of them was William S. Jackson—banker, treasurer of the railroad company, and husband of popular authoress Helen Hunt Jackson, or "H.H." as she inscribed many of her writings. Rallying to the cause of the railroad, she penned an ecstatic description of a journey to the San Luis Valley over the new rails, and this piece of thinly disguised public relations appeared as a chapter in her *Bits of Travel at Home* in 1878. Others with no vested interest in the railroad company added to the fame of the new narrow-gauge with such jingles as:

It doubles in, it doubles out,
Leaving the traveler still in doubt,
Whether the engine on the track
Is going on or coming back!

The first target for D&RG rails when the line was able to resume building beyond Garland City was Alamosa, centrally located to serve agricultural and mining interests of the surrounding country and destined to become the hub of future railroad activity in the valley. Although the new town on the Rio Grande was called "Rio Bravo" in its infancy, it was platted as the Alamosa Town Company by A. C. Hunt in May 1878. The railroad reached the village scarcely two months later. In addition to the customary array of tents, claim cabins, and saloons, Hunt erected a two-story headquarters building for the railroad at the corner of Sixth Street and Hunt Avenue. This frame structure later housed the Bank of San Juan on the main floor and a hotel upstairs. As the town's position as the commercial center of the valley quickly became fact, the first bank was joined by another—the First National Bank—and mills, stores, and other business operations located there. Two freight companies—Field and Hill, and F. S. Struby and Company—ran general stores as well as doing their main business, which was hauling mining supplies from the railroad to the San Juans. Two newspapers soon were available. One was the *Independent Journal*, which formerly had been published elsewhere as the *Colorado Independent*, and the other was the *Alamosa News*.[7] By the early 1880s the fast-growing community also had a school and a Presbyterian church.

This success in establishing a strategic foothold in south-central Colorado lulled Palmer into the short-lived confidence that he could beat competitors for the southern and western traffic. However, the Atchison, Topeka and Santa Fe put up such a contest for the routes over Raton Pass and through the Royal Gorge that the D&RG was forced to concentrate on those problems instead of its original goals. Again the D&RG's expansion through the valley was stymied, this time for two years but almost forever.

In the meantime, Barlow and Sanderson's mail, express, and passenger services continued to skim much of the cream from the bustling activity of the area. The termini for the stage and wagon line had moved west with each new end of track, from La Veta to La Veta Pass to Garland City to Alamosa. Wherever the track ended, the Barlow and Sanderson operation set up its offices and met incoming passengers and freight, exchanging them with sacks of ore to be shipped on the railroad to mills. In addition to the main stations there were way stations for the stage line, also. Before the railroad reached Alamosa, the stage stopped at Fort Garland and at Washington Springs before reaching the Rio Grande. From there the line continued west to Del Norte and Lake City, and the mail road from Saguache to Lake City also was used. A stage made the run across Mosca Pass to Silver Cliff with a link running south to Costilla by way of Zapata. A hack also made a round trip once a week from Sangre de Cristo north through San Isabel, Rio Alto, Cotton Creek, and Bismark to Villa Grove, where it met the line over Poncha Pass. On the west side of the valley a line ran south from Alamosa to Conejos and Santa Fe, while another post road linked Del Norte and Conejos via Piedra. Mail

In the early 1960s narrow-gauge equipment still could be seen in Alamosa's railroad yards, where three rails accommodated trains of either gauge.

As soon as the railroad arrived in Alamosa, stores opened to supply the central portion of the San Luis Valley. The town is the valley's commercial center today and has the largest population.

O. T. Davis's view of his home town, Alamosa, in 1906 shows the old Colorado state highway bridge.

also ran between Conejos and Pagosa Springs on mountain trails.

With mail and express traffic ranging over so many lonely miles, at least a few holdups were bound to occur. They took place mostly around Del Norte, where ore and payrolls for the mines were most likely to be shipped. On the road between Del Norte and Lake City a holdup occurred beyond Antelope Springs station. After wounding the stage driver, the highwaymen got away with their loot, but a posse from Del Norte captured them. The bandits were two brothers named Le Roy. In true Wild West style, the local citizens strung them up in a cottonwood tree.[8] Not long afterward the Allison gang was implicated in a stage robbery at Venable, a station northeast of the present town of Monte Vista. The sheriff of Conejos County became a local hero when he brought in these men, including Clay Allison himself according to stories told in the valley.

All of the stage stations were located twelve miles apart, and each had a stock tender who was supposed to keep the teams in top shape and to hitch up a fresh team to incoming stages. West of Alamosa there was Riverside Station on the north side of the river.[9] The next was Venable, or Venerable, where a rather slovenly stock tender called "Swede" held forth. One night a stage carrying only the driver and an under-sheriff from Del Norte was held up. In the darkness the driver concealed the mail pouch and some valuable express with a rug, while the lawman lost his own money, watch, and six-shooter. The driver recognized the bandit's voice as being Swede's, but the stock herder never was caught. He disappeared from the valley.[10]

During the battle between the railroads, while D&RG construction again was halted in the valley, the line was leased to the AT&SF, which raised freight rates and allowed trackage and rolling stock to deteriorate. In 1880 a compromise agreement was reached. The D&RG line was returned to its owners, who would be permitted to build west toward Leadville through the Royal Gorge while the AT&SF would be allowed to build south over Raton Pass. The D&RG also was to be allowed a southern extension into New Mexico from Alamosa to Espanola, a point midway between Conejos and Santa Fe. This apparently illogical goal was actually part of a practical plan, for the D&RG people incorporated the Texas, Santa Fe, and Northern Railway to complete the link from Espanola to Santa Fe, when the time came.

As soon as the compromise agreement was made, the D&RG headed down the valley from Alamosa to construct both the New Mexico extension and a San Juan extension from Antonito to Chama, New Mexico. South of Alamosa the roadbed crossed the La Jara Creek, and here was built La Jara Station, downstream from the old Spanish town of that name. Bypassing established settlements was common practice in railroad construction, both because it was easier to acquire unoccupied land and because the railroad could then create its own town company and sell lots. In the case of La Jara, the new town gained a post office and eventually became incorporated in 1895, while the old Spanish settlement faded into obscurity. In later years sidings were added at Estrella and Romeo, but for the time being, La Jara was the only station between Alamosa and Antonito.

Antonito was built about a mile south of Conejos. While Conejos, the county seat and church center for the entire southwest portion of the valley, was left to struggle along as best it might, the new railroad town became the principal community of the area and the division point for the two railroad extensions. In late 1880 a post office called San Antonio was established in the new town, but the name was changed to Antonito in only two months, perhaps to avoid confusion with the other settlement of that name a few miles up the San Antonio River. Antonito soon had a depot built of lava stone, a section house, a bunk house, a sawmill, numerous saloons and gambling houses, a hotel, a newspaper, stores, and three churches—Catholic, Presbyterian, and Methodist—vying for the degenerate souls of the local railroad men. While railroad construction continued south and west, the workmen sought comfort in an entertainment capital of sorts in Antonito with its unusually high selection of bars and painted ladies lounging in the open doorways of their shacks.

South of Antonito stations were built in New Mexico at Palmillo, Vulcano, Tres Piedres, Caliente, Embudo, Chamito, and Espanola. Although various railroads were projected to Taos, including one which would have run through Costilla, no rails ever reached that town. Instead, stages connected with the D&RG at Tres Piedres and Taos Junction on the west side of the Rio Grande. Despite its nickname, "The Chili Line," the railroad carried little traffic in New Mexico, and most of its business was seasonal shipments of livestock, wool, and lumber, as well as mineral products from the Antonito area. Even after the

The extension of the Denver and Rio Grande south of Alamosa helped the economy of agricultural towns such as La Jara.

D&RG acquired the link between Espanola and Santa Fe, traffic to and from the New Mexican capital rarely chose the D&RG route but preferred the standard-gauged service of the AT&SF by way of Lamy and Raton Pass. A third rail, installed between Alamosa and Antonito after 1900, permitted some mixed trains, but on the whole service and equipment were below par, and the line below Antonito was dismantled in the 1940s.[11]

By the time that rails reached Antonito, grading was already in progress for the San Juan extension, and track-laying began in early 1881. The rush to complete this route over Cumbres Pass was due to the importance of reaching Durango and the Silverton country. The right of way for the San Juan extension was south of the old Parkview and Conejos Toll Road, which also crossed Cumbres Pass. The road passed through Mogote and Mesitas, taking a much more direct route than could the railroad, forced to climb in and out of Colorado by way of Whiplash Curve and Toltec Gorge because of the grade. These obstacles to construction soon proved to have some compensation when tourists came to ride the narrow-gauge to see the spectacular scenery

along the line. A lunch stop was provided at Osier before the train reached the station at Cumbres and began its slow descent to Lobato and Chama, New Mexico.

Long after the mining bonanzas of southwestern Colorado had found other, more direct transportation, the Cumbres Pass line continued to serve local passengers, agriculture, and lumber operations. Not until 1951 did regular passenger service terminate. When tracks were about to be pulled up in the late 1960s, rail buffs rallied to save the line. The states of Colorado and New Mexico cooperated in purchasing the line and leasing it as a tourist attraction, now called the Cumbres & Toltec Scenic Railroad. Running between Antonito and Chama during the summer and early autumn, steam engines still huff and puff through at least one corner of the San Luis Valley.

When the D&RG completed the New Mexico and San Juan extension, it turned its attention to building west from Alamosa to Del Norte in 1881 to pick up at last the lucrative traffic for the mines of that area. The railroad built on the south side of the Rio Grande and bypassed already existing villages as usual. A station was built at

Above—The Denver and Rio Grande reached Durango and the mining regions around Silverton by crossing Cumbres Pass, elevation 10,015 feet. The depot fell into disrepair when the D&RG anticipated abandoning the line. Below—A snowshed was needed on Cumbres Pass to protect the tracks for all-weather traffic between Durango and Antonito. Now the line is used in summer only, when the Cumbres and Toltec Scenic Railroad runs excursion trains.

The D&RG's extension to North Creede followed the route of the Rio Grande
through Wagon Wheel Gap, where tourists disembarked for holidays.

Del Norte opposite the old plaza of La Loma del Norte, and stations at South Fork and Wagon Wheel Gap followed. The extension from South Fork to Wagon Wheel Gap was abandoned in 1889 because of the high cost of maintenance for the small amount of revenue it produced. Just two years later mining boomed at Creede beyond the gap, and the line had to be extended again.

When tracks first were laid to Del Norte, a water tank was built at a point called Lariat. There was nothing else at Lariat besides the tank until a red-haired woman, Mrs. Lillian L. Taylor, stepped from the train one day in 1881. She decided to set up a shanty beside the tank and to use it for a home and a store. A few days later, as the story goes, a Mrs. Silsbee, mother of Mrs. Taylor, boarded the train at Alamosa and asked the conductor to let her off where the "red-haired woman" had disembarked.[12] Thereafter they both ran the store. After Mrs. Taylor married Charles Fassett, a neighboring rancher and mine investor, the growing business, which became the largest department store in Monte Vista and for miles around, was called the L. L. Fassett Store. For a time the mother-and-daughter team also ran a post office called Lariat.

When a town was staked out at the water tank in 1884, it was not a typical railroad town, for this enterprise was based on agriculture. The Empire Farm Company was building up its land holdings, while the Empire Canal Company was developing irrigation systems. The owners of these operations platted the new town at Lariat. The place was renamed Henry in honor of Denverite T. C. Henry, who was at the head of the corporation developing the area. T. C. Henry obviously intended that his namesake would display more decorum than other new towns along the railroad, for the town's first public event was a Sunday School meeting, followed quickly by the organization of a public school that met in the same building used for religious gatherings. No saloons were allowed within the town.

The good intentions of this outpost of civilization soon attracted the attention of the Travelers' Insurance Company, which invested in further development. The insurance company promoted an addition on the west side of Henry and donated land for a real school building, which was completed in 1886. When hotels, mills, and a railroad depot began going up there, the Fassetts decided to move their store into the new community, too. In 1886 the town was renamed Monte Vista, and it was incorporated that autumn. Its character remained unchanged. "No Eastern town," the D&RG boasted in a promotional booklet, "is more law-abiding or has a higher moral tone. No gambling dens or liquor saloons have ever existed in Monte Vista."

The railroad extension over Poncha Pass into the San Luis Valley also was forged in 1881, a year of great accomplishment for the D&RG. An early proposal had placed the railroad's route on the east side of San Luis Creek. This line was supposed to connect with the main route from La Veta Pass at a point just east of Washington Springs. By the time that work began on the Poncha Pass line, the D&RG's resources had been stretched to the limit, though. Consequently, the best that the railroad could do in 1881 was to reach the iron mines at Orient southeast of Villa Grove. To serve the ore trains crossing Poncha Pass, the railroad also put in a shop and water tank at Alder, on Round Hill as the railroad called it, about twelve miles north of Villa Grove.

Only in 1890 did the D&RG continue building south from Villa Grove. Two developments prompted this rather belated extension—agricultural promotion in the area and a problem in railroad operation. The D&RG had converted its main line south of Pueblo to standard-gauged tracks. As a result, the San Luis Valley's rails were stranded unless a link was made with the narrow-gauge line that came through the Royal Gorge.

When the D&RG finally built south from Villa Grove, it ran down the west side of San Luis Creek and connected with the line from La Veta Pass at Alamosa. Much of this route consisted of fifty-three miles of straight trackage—the fifth longest stretch of uncurved rails in the United States. Along this strip the D&RG anticipated large revenues from farm centers at a number of points. One of these was Moffat, a town named for one of Colorado's foremost citizens and railroad promoters, who at the time was president of the D&RG. Moffat, which also became a post office in 1890, was a stock-shipping center and a division point for a branch to the Cottonwood mill and the Crestone Estate, formerly known as the Baca Grant Number Four. The station at Moffat had been promoted, in fact, by George H.

Moffat was a rail center serving mines around Crestone to the east and farms around Saguache to the west.

"By jove! If the railroad raises its freight rates and the farmers raise the price of wheat, we'll raise our interest on loans, too."

Adams, president of the Crestone Estate, and by Otto Mears of Saguache. Adams operated a livery stable that conveyed passengers and freight from the railroad to either Crestone or Saguache across the valley. Later a railroad spur into Crestone became a logical addition when mining boomed there.

South of Moffat the next station was La Garita, a confusing designation since this rail point lay on the east side of the valley while the old Mexican town of that name was almost due west on the opposite side of the valley. Gibson, or Dune as it was sometimes called, was south of La Garita station. Gibson, or Dune, had a post office until 1895. South of this station was Hooper, which, until the D&RG took over, had been called Garrison, the name of a local merchant. This place had a post office with each name in succession. Supposedly, Garrison's name was changed because it was easily confused with Gunnison, but the D&RG's passenger agent, Major Hooper, undoubtedly preferred the new designation. South of Garrison, or Hooper, was Mosca, or Streator as it formerly was called. Mosca became

a post office in 1890. And south of Mosca, or Streator, was Alamosa, the hub of the D&RG's tracks and influence in the San Luis Valley.

To complete the story of railroad building in the valley, one must include two lines of a later period, neither of which belonged to the D&RG system. One was the San Luis Southern, later called the San Luis Valley Southern. This road operated between Blanca and agricultural areas developed on the Costilla Estate. Completed in 1910 to San Acacio, the San Luis Valley Southern was planned to reach Taos and even Santa Fe, but an extension through Mesita to Jarosa was its limit, and even the line between San Acacio and Jarosa was short-lived.

The other independent line was the San Luis Central, built from Monte Visa to Center in 1913. Popularly known as the "Peavine," this shortline hauled sugar beets, lettuce, and other produce from the agricultural "center" of the valley to the D&RG's tracks at Monte Vista. The San Luis Central still operates seasonally, but the other line's rails were removed in 1958 with the exception of a mile and a half of track between the

Spring's warming sun shines down on a weathered barn near Moffat, but winter still hovers over the jagged peaks of the Sangre de Cristos.

Rolling stock and chamiso vie for their claims to the San Luis Valley Southern's right of way, near Blanca.

The San Luis Valley Southern's station at San Acacio was photographed in 1910 by O. T. Davis of Alamosa, a well-known photographer who recorded the valley's life diligently.

D&RG and a shipping facility at Blanca.

Thus, the San Luis Valley became laced with a network of railroad tracks, almost but not quite entirely the projects of the Denver and Rio Grande. One extension that perhaps should have run through the valley, but did not, was the D&RG line to the Gunnison area from the Arkansas River Valley. This line was constructed over Marshall Pass, northwest of Poncha Pass, a route that proved to be too high for efficient all-season use, and it was dismantled ultimately. The oft-touted choice of a route via Cochetopa Pass, an option never taken up by any railroad, might have been, after all, a more satisfactory location for a transcontinental railroad through Colorado. But this is a matter for hindsight.

What did occur was a gradual need to standard-gauge the D&RG trackage. The line over La Veta Pass, where lumbering and a box factory helped perpetuate a town for several years, was standard-gauged to Alamosa and North Creede. The line to Antonito was double-gauged, too. Finally the narrow-gauge tracks were removed from La Veta Pass, and the Poncha Pass line was dismantled.

Although the narrow-gauge scenic railroad over Cumbres Pass remains as a nostalgic reminder of a former time, change escapes no one, not even railroad builders with dreams of empire in their heads. Meanwhile, dreams of empire created from mineral wealth were dancing in the heads of other men around the San Luis Valley.

On South Mountain the Summitville District boomed in the 1870s and 1880s, and the reverberations were felt twenty-seven miles down the mountain in Del Norte. This photograph of Summitville was made in 1938, when the camp still was active.

XIII

"Thirty-six Saloons and Seven Dance-Halls"

From the first *conquistadores* looking for Cibola and Quivera to the last tattered miners working for wages, the silvery mountains ringing the San Luis Valley have beckoned and often taunted those who sought minerals there. The stubborn hope of striking pay dirt has survived for nearly four hundred years through the fact that a few did find gold. And if not gold, silver. Or if not silver, maybe lead, iron, copper, or even uranium.

When early Spanish explorers came seeking mines in the Sangre de Cristos, they reported finding some gold between Culebra and Trinchera creeks. Much later William Gilpin was sure that the Culebra Range would yield a bonanza. Although some gold-bearing ore was located near Rito Seco, east of San Luis, this area's only commercially important mineral was galena. The district, in fact, was called Plomo, which is the Spanish word for lead.[1]

A little farther north soldiers stationed at Fort Massachusetts and Fort Garland had heard and repeated legends about Spanish gold, and the men often spent their time off poking around the slopes of Blanca Peak and panning the gravel in the streambeds. With the opening of the rush to the Rockies, the soldiers were joined by a few prospectors, such as the unsuccessful Reeder expedition in the spring of 1861. After Hayden's optimistic report was published in 1869, the soldiers began to take their pastimes even more seriously, concentrating on a placer called "Officers' Bar" at the confluence of Placer and Grayback creeks. A little settlement called Placer grew up near the workings, and it was joined by another town called Russell, which had a post office by 1876. In 1877 the owners of the Trinchera Estate, hoping that at last they might recoup some of their losses in the property, ordered the squatters out of the area and surveyed claims for future development as the Grayback Mountain Mining District.[2]

The town of Russell survived as a station on the D&RG, and eventually a short spur ran from the railroad at Russell to Grayback.[3] Placer's life also continued, for it was only two miles from a large mine that opened up in the early 1880s on Grayback Mountain, or Iron Mountain as it was renamed. Owned by the Colorado Coal and Iron Company, this mine produced iron and some silver, and the Trinchera Estate received royalties from the operation. For a while there was a smelter furnace at Placer, but activity died after only two or three years. Only a little gold was taken from the district, despite the working of a few mines with such legend-provoking names as the "Hidden Treasure."[4]

Although the Culebra Range and Blanca Peak never fulfilled the exaggerated promises of either the Spaniards or William Gilpin, their prophesies for the San Juans materialized. After a few preliminary expeditions in the early 1860s, prospecting in the San Juans was thwarted by Indian troubles and Indian treaties. By the late 1860s, after the first big discoveries around Silverton, the tide of prospectors no longer could be stemmed. The first major strike near the San Luis Valley came shortly on South Mountain at Summit, or the Summitville District as it became known. As mining developed in this area, most of the metal was gold, but silver and copper also were produced.

The story of the strike here was like many of the other booms in the mountains of Colorado. After the first discoveries in the summer of 1870—made by James and William Wightman, Sylvester Reese, E. Baker, and Cary French—most of the prospectors who joined them left in the fall, because the district, lying at an elevation over eleven thousand feet, was too high and inaccessible for working in the winter. With the spring thaws came waves of new prospectors. In 1873 the richest mine, the Little Annie, was discovered, and it produced anywhere from $80 to $2,000 per ton for several years. As other mines also opened, a stamp mill went into operation in 1875.[5] By 1876 the permanent population of Summit was about five hundred, and the town could boast of having plenty of stores and saloons, as well as a post office, the name of which was changed to Summitville in 1880. The rough toll road from Del Norte, twenty-seven miles away, could be negotiated by a hack in summer, but in the winter mail and other supplies came in by saddle horses, pack trains, or skis.

In the summer of 1886 a mine superintendent set off on this road with a gold brick for shipment to the Denver mint. Two gunmen, a miner and an accomplice from Monte Vista, waylaid the rig. A shot was fired and the team bolted, upsetting the carriage. The man with the gold brick played dead and saved his valuable cargo as a result. Later one of the gunmen was tracked down and arrested, but he escaped from jail. When a posse found him hiding in the mountains, he was shot.[6]

Always locations in a good district were claimed quickly, and latecomers or those who had lost out fanned into the surrounding area in search of other promising sites. The first new camp near the Summitville District sprang up in 1874 at Jasper, at an elevation about two thousand feet lower than Summit. The new camp was on the Alamosa River. The principal mine here was the Miser, which produced gold, although the original strike was at a silver mine, called the Perry. A partner in the development of the Perry Mine was Alva Adams, who became governor of Colorado.[7] Both of these mines were on Cornwall Mountain. The area, in fact, was called the Jasper-Cornwall District. A miner named John Cornwall ran a post office, called Cornwall, from 1879 until 1882, when it was moved to nearby Jasper and renamed.

Production at Jasper warranted a stamp mill quite early. Despite the bad name the district earned when the developers of the Sanger Mine swindled their investors, the camp survived longer than many others. The post office at Jasper operated until 1910, for example, although a branch of the L. L. Fassett Store of Monte Vista, which opened at Jasper in 1900, pulled out by 1905.[8]

Another important camp in this region was at Stunner. Stunner was above Jasper on the Alamosa River and about six miles below Summit, or Summitville as it now was called. Actually, Stunner was preceded by a nearby camp called Blainvale, which had postal service in 1882 and 1884, but this post office moved to Loyton in the fall of 1884 for one month. That this post office closed after only one month indicates that the mines probably were not very active at that time. When service resumed in 1886, the place was called Stunner. This time the post office remained open until 1894 with a brief resumption in 1913-1914.[9]

Four miles south of Stunner was Platoro, taking its name from the rich silver and gold ores found there. Although the first mines are said to have been opened up in the early 1880s, no postal service was initiated before 1888. The first mine in this district, called the Mammoth Mine, has continued to produce in recent years, but the best mines were those that opened about 1890. These were very rich silver producers. The success of these finds resulted in the building of a toll road via the Conejos River in 1891 to permit all-weather shipments.[10] However, the silver soon played out. A rich body of gold was discovered at the Gilmore Mine on Klondyke Mountain in 1913.[11] Although this operation, too, lasted only a couple of years, it inspired a brief renewal of mining at Stunner and Jasper, as well as the revival of Platoro.

While mining in the 1880s and 1890s was keeping the camps lively northeast of Antonito, mineral production amounted to little in the San Juans to the south. The one exception was the Good Hope Mining District about thirty miles southwest of Antonito. Crofutt's *Gripsack Guide* reported that this camp was producing a little low-grade gold and had two stamp mills.

The discovery of gold and silver in the Summitville District had stimulated prospecting all around the San Luis Valley, but even more significant were the new silver mines at Leadville, which drew thousands of people to Colorado in the late 1870s. Prospectors spilled over Poncha Pass from the Upper Arkansas River into the San Luis Valley in the wake of this invasion. Prospecting around Kerber Creek west of Villa Grove resulted in the discovery of a good mine at Exchequer in 1880. This initiated the discovery of a number of other mines that comprised the Kerber Creek Mining District.

When Captain Charles Kerber homesteaded near Villa Grove in the 1860s, he bestowed his name on Kerber Creek, which flowed past his home near the end of its journey from the Cochetopa Hills to San Luis Creek. A few other homesteads were taken up along the creek in the 1870s, and, inevitably, a little prospecting was done. Miners heading for the Gunnison area noticed a few traces of minerals, but no claims were actually filed. The most important of these omissions was the bypassing of the Rawley float.

The first strike in the Kerber Creek area to prompt a stampede of prospectors into the region was the Exchequer, located in 1880. The next discovery was about a mile below it at the Bonanza Mine, which kicked off a boom all along Kerber Creek. South of the instant town of Bonanza, which sprang up sixteen miles west of Villa Grove, another strike was made at what became known as Sedgwick. Sedgwick's fame soon escalated when the only brewery in the area was built there, and the stream so honored by its presence was called Brewery Creek. Kerber City, which appeared on the north side of Kerber Creek, opposite Sedgwick, was a mere collection of tents and cabins, compared to Bonanza and Sedgwick, both of which got post offices in 1880.[12]

One mile above Bonanza, Rawley Creek flows into Kerber Creek, and just above that junction Squirrel Creek flows into Kerber Creek. Exchequer was on Squirrel Creek and spread into Sawmill Creek. Its population, too, called for a post office by 1881. Beyond Exchequer was a little silver-mining camp called Bonito that bloomed just long enough to have its own post office also from 1881 to 1883, and two miles farther was Spook City. To the southwest of Bonanza a few miles lay a handful of mines on Ford Creek.

The hub of all these camps was Bonanza with a population of nearly fifteen hundred in the flush of its youth. However, as Anne Ellis commented in her classic book *The Life of an Ordinary Woman,* "In speaking of population you didn't count people, anyway, you counted saloons and dance-halls. There were thirty-six saloons and seven dance-halls."[13] For that matter, Sedgwick was holding its own as an entertainment capital. With a population of only 650, it had a billiard hall, a bowling alley, two hotels, and two dance halls—plus the brewery.

Mining camps such as these, crowded into narrow mountain gulches, had a ready but much-abused source of water. In fact, the livery stable at Bonanza straddled Copper Creek so that watering the stock was a simple task. Various small gulches in the district also provided the only convenient place to dispose of mine tailings

and mill wastes. As a result of this pollution, disputes arose between miners and the ranchers who lived below, both in the early days and more recently, regarding the poisoning of Kerber Creek. Anne Ellis, who lived in Exchequer as a child, also recalled warnings about drinking the creek water. She was told that it would give her "tyford fever" and that dead cattle had been found in the creek downstream.[14] She also could remember, years later, only three bathtubs in Bonanza, regardless of its proximity to water. One of these was in the back room of Billy Hannigan's barber shop, where only men or "fancy women" ever went. The second was a sitz bath, belonging to a saloon keeper who occasionally lent it out to his special friends. The third was a Turkish bath that sometimes was pressed into service to sober up a miner who had overindulged.

Despite the absence of the finer things such as bathtubs or even a church, Bonanza had a newspaper, the *Enterprise,* later replaced by the *Bee.* The town was incorporated and had a justice of the peace court, presided over by an English accountant, Hubert Pool, who also dispensed free legal advice to his neighbors. Oxford-educated though he was, Pool found Bonanza to his liking and remained there until his death during the influenza epidemic in 1918. Both he and Anne Ellis are buried in the Exchequer cemetery.

Transportation to and from the booming district was improved when the Denver and Rio Grande crossed Poncha Pass to Villa Grove in 1881. A stage line and ore wagons from the mines connected with the railroad via a toll road, which Otto Mears built as soon as mining took hold at Bonanza. Although some people coming in from the north used a short cut to the camp from Alder, the vast majority used the toll road. The residents seem not to have resented the fee they had to pay to get in and out of town but were grateful to Mears for their good road. Mears built another road above Bonanza across the mountains to reach Shirley on the D&RG's Marshall Pass line, but this operation did not survive long.[15] Bonanza itself was situated at about ten thousand feet above sea level, and the route across the mountains was too high for successful use. Nevertheless, an aerial tramway carried ore from the Rawley Mine to the railroad at Shirley, seven miles north of Bonanza, in the 1920s and 1930s.[16]

Among the speculators who rushed to see Bonanza was former President Ulysses S. Grant. When he toured the mines of Colorado in 1880, looking for promising investments, his party

Bonanza, the home of thirty-six saloons and seven dance-halls.

camped at Sedgwick for several days. Mrs. Ellis reports, "Grant offered forty thousand dollars for the Bonanza Mine, which was promptly refused— for by now the owners were charging one dollar per head just to look at this hole down only a few feet. Grant also offered one hundred and sixty thousand for the Exchequer."[17] The Exchequer's appeal was some very rich silver-copper ore, but the Bonanza turned out to be a producer of only low-grade silver-bearing lead ore.

While not good enough to make fortunes, the Bonanza worked for many years and was promising enough to attract leasers. About the turn of the century it was leased by Mark Biedell, one of the Fort Garland veterans who had remained in the valley. He built a concentrating mill in Bonanza for the mine.

In the first half century ten times as much value in silver as in gold was produced by the Kerber Creek Mining District, but the gold mines often kept the camp going. After the price of silver dropped in 1882, most of Bonanza's miners drifted away, and the devaluation in 1893 was a devastating blow to all silver camps. In the meantime the Empress Josephine Mine, located in 1880, and the St. Louis Mine, which is thought to strike the same body of gold ore, kept miners employed for many years when most silver mines

were closed. A supervisor who became known as the "father of Bonanza" because of his concern for his neighbors' welfare was John E. Ashley of the St. Louis Mine.

Despite the benefits to the community of the Empress Josephine and the St. Louis mines, in the long run the silver-bearing Rawley Mine has outstripped all others in the camp. Having been bypassed by its first discoverer, the Rawley was filed on in 1880, and it went into production in 1882. After the turn of the century it was developed extensively by a series of leasers representing eastern companies. One of these built a large concentrating mill, an aerial tramway, and electric facilities with power lines coming from Alamosa ninety miles away. For a few years ore concentrated in this mill was shipped out over the tramway to the D&RG, which freighted the ore to Leadville for smelting. Primarily because of the expansion of the Rawley Mine, Bonanza's population was large enough to require a school. In the same decade a fire destroyed most of the town, and it never was rebuilt.

The Rawley Mine, however, kept going, and others in the area, such as the Empress Josephine, have worked from time to time since World War II. The quietness which has descended on Kerber Creek belies the scale of operations still

104

going on underground, where electric locomotives move ore trains that once required dozens of men and burros. To all appearances Bonanza, which once had nineteen mills and four smelters and hundreds of families, is now little more than a ghost town.

As might be expected, the mountains lying between the Summitville and Kerber Creek Mining districts received their share of hopeful attention, but no major districts developed here. Mark Biedell promoted some of the activity in this area. When Summitville boomed, he had given up farming and moved to Del Norte where he could make faster money as a merchant in the supply town. He probably grub-staked some of the prospectors who located some mines in the 1880s southwest of Saguache around Biedell and Carnero creeks. The principal mines were the Esperanza, which has been worked off and on for nearly a century since its discovery in 1883, and the Buckhorn Mines. For a year activity at the latter warranted a post office, called Biedell, which moved to Carnero in 1884 for a two-year tenure. Mail came in from Green, as the La Garita post office then was called.[18] Carnero also had a few small mines, but its chief reason for being a ripple in the mining boom was that it lay on the stage route between Saguache and Del Norte. Also in this area was a camp called Belleview, which may have lasted only for a year—1883—when it had a newspaper called the *Crystal Hill Pilot.*

In the more remote mountains to the west, where the ghosts of the Frémont expedition lingered, a few prospects in the Embargo and Wannamaker Creek areas resulted in the establishment of a gold camp called Sky City. The Sky City Mine was a mile and a half upstream on Wannamaker Creek from its junction with the South Fork of Saguache Creek.[19] The owner of this mine was Senator Thomas Bowen, who kept it working into the 1900s and built a mill for processing ore. Bowen had obtained the Little Annie Mine at Summitville and invested in various other mining properties. A post office called Bowenton, operating in Rio Grande County from 1881 until 1884, may have been another camp in which he was interested. To the north of these mines in the La Garita Mountains a camp called Iris was located near Cochetopa Pass.

One can imagine the frustration of William Gilpin when the San Juan mines revealed the riches he had prophesied, while the Sangre de Cristos in which he was involved financially refused to yield minerals in significant quantity.

During the years, squatters gradually had entered the Baca Grant Number Four. By 1872 there were post offices at San Isabel, Rio Alto, and Cristonie (Crestone). In the mid-1870s the D&RG group leased the grant to investors, one of whom, George H. Adams, became manager of the estate. Thereafter settlement was more systematic, but farming and ranching, not mining, were the chief activities. The town of Cottonwood was established on Cotton Creek in 1876, and irrigation ditches were dug.[20]

As events turned out, Gilpin's luck was changing. In 1877 he bought the Baca Grant from the financially straitened D&RG group. Although the grant still was leased, he owned the mineral rights and was to receive royalties on profits from mining on the grant. In the spring of 1880 gold in paying quantities at last was found on the west side of the Sangre de Cristos. The area around Burnt Creek was the scene of the first big discoveries. Prospectors flocked in, investors in Philadelphia built a concentrating mill, George Adams and A. H. Major opened a store in an old adobe building, and Crestone received a post office.

The town also had a bar, of course. At the grand opening free drinks and lunches drew a crowd, and a grateful sheepherder partook so freely of this bounty that he died. The next day Windy Bill, a local dignitary, delivered a eulogy for the sheepherder: "To Juan's veracity, all bear testimony; to his capacity, sad to relate, there was a limit."[21]

A short-lived camp with a post office called Tetons existed north of Crestone in 1880 and 1881. The name came from three jagged peaks north of Music Peak. These summits and a stream that flowed from them were called Trois Tetons by early settlers.[22] The names probably were bestowed by trappers who left several French titles on landmarks. In this case the suggestive French words were replaced with proper, English names—Crestone Peak, Crestone Needle, and Kit Carson Peak.

During the mining boom the little town of Cottonwood also blossomed into a sizeable camp. Its mines produced gold, silver, copper, lead, and iron. For a while a stamp mill owned by Tom Bowen operated here.

For Gilpin the good news was that he was able to sell the Baca Grant to George Adams and others for $350,000 in 1886. Not so lucky were the squatters and miners on the grant, all of whom were evicted by the new owners. In the territories of the West when mines were discovered, the rights of their owners were protected by a system that had evolved. Mining districts were created to facilitate the recording of mine claims, to provide local laws and justice, and to administer civil needs of the miners in the districts. After Colorado achieved statehood, the legality of mine ownership in such districts was confirmed. However, on a land grant an entirely different condition existed. Mining districts were not legal there unless a grant's owners organized them. As a result, miners on the Baca Grant had no legal choice but to leave.

About 1890 the new owners of the grant attempted additional mining on the property, taking advantage of workings and equipment developed by the evicted miners. Cottonwood's population again swelled to about one thousand, and smaller camps sprang up along the edge of the towering mountains at Julia City, Spanish, Lucky, Pole Creek, and Music City.

A thriving new town in 1892 was Duncan, which grew to about four thousand when miners thronged to gold camps after the collapse of silver in 1893. Some investors in Duncan's mines were Alamosa businessmen. Duncan had all the amenities—a school and a store, a tavern and telephones, a barber and a post office—everything, in short, except George Adams's permission to stay there. After much litigation and another sale of the grant, questions about titles and rights were settled in favor of the grant's owners, and Duncan closed shop in 1900.[23]

When the people of Duncan left the grant, they set up a new town called, symbolically, Liberty. Liberty was just outside the grant at the north end of the sand dunes. Although this camp had a stamp mill, its hopes exceeded production. Still, the town struggled along, as evidenced by the presence of a post office from 1900 until 1919 and sporadically thereafter.

When miners at Crestone also received Adams's eviction notices in the late 1880s, they set up another camp, Wilcox, just north of Crestone. About 1890 Crestone again boomed, following new gold discoveries, which repopulated the town. The chief operation was the Cleveland Mine. The building of the D&RG line from Villa Grove to Alamosa facilitated movement of freight between Crestone and the outside world via the new railroad station at Moffat. About 1900 another wave of expansion occurred at the mines, and a rail spur was laid into Crestone from Moffat. During this peak of activity a hotel was built in Crestone, and the neighborhood became a short-lived center of real estate development—a

recurring condition in the San Luis Valley. With a slightly better record for endurance, mining continued off and on for many decades in Crestone.

While gold and silver mines in the twenty-five-mile strip of the mountains around Crestone perennially opened and closed, iron mining nearby proved to be a venture more stable if less glamorous. Near Blanca Peak iron in the Grayback District had attracted the Colorado Coal and Iron Company to invest in mining on the Trinchera Estate. Toward the northern end of the San Luis Valley another source of iron promised an abundance of ore without the necessity of paying royalties to the owners of a land grant.

Limonite deposits in the Sangre de Cristos southeast of Villa Grove had failed to capture the attention of prospectors looking for gold in the 1870s, at what was called the Blake Mining District. No mining was done here until about 1880, when the Colorado Coal and Fuel Company bought about one hundred acres just north of the Valley View Hot Springs and opened the Orient Mine to extract the iron-bearing limonite ore from limestone. By 1880 the town of Orient City had sprung up with two restaurants, a saloon, and other places of business.[24]

Two years later the mine was able to produce 30,000 tons of ore, and after a brief slump in the mid-1880s, its capacity reached over 200,000 tons annually. The ore was shipped to smelters in both Pueblo and Durango.[25] In 1881 the D&RG built a spur from Villa Grove to Hot Springs, the name used by the railroad for its station near Orient.

Orient City grew to about four hundred people with company houses, a school, and even a library officiated over by the barber. The miners themselves represented a cosmopolitan background, including Italian, Northern European, Irish, and, the largest group, Mexican. A resort for the pleasure of the residents of Orient and the general neighborhood developed at Valley View Hot Springs, then called Haumann, apparently a variation of spelling for Homan. Haumann was a post office from 1882 until 1885.

Activity at Orient and Bonanza combined to make Villa Grove a thriving center, a role that continued in dwindling degree as long as trains operated between Salida and Alamosa. In tribute to the railroad's importance, when Villa Grove published its first newspaper in 1891, it was called *The Headlight*. Its owner was a local attorney, S. E. Van Noorden, just as the local saddlery and boot shop was run by the justice of the peace, A. H. Schwackenberg.

Under the control of the Colorado Coal and Iron

In contrast to the ethereal appearance of the valley below, the concrete foundations of the Orient Mine's buildings appear solid and permanent, but the mine closed more than a half century ago.

Iron-bearing limonite ore was shipped to CF&I smelters in Pueblo and Durango by rail with a spur between Villa Grove and Orient City facilitating freight.

The soothing waters of Valley View Hot Springs once gave comfort to miners, worn out either by work or by revelry or by both.

Company's new organization, the Colorado Fuel and Iron Company, the Orient Mine and Orient City survived until 1919, when new mines in Wyoming made the Orient operation obsolete. After its demise the northern end of the valley settled down to a quiet pace with the remnants of mining at Bonanza, ranching, railroading, and occasional outings to Valley View and Mineral Hot Springs.

As each of these discoveries, influxes of population, and, too often, abandonments took place, the valley as a whole was affected by the excitement and the disappointments. In already-existing towns near the mineral districts a wave of prosperity would spark local businesses and create a surplus of jobs, often filled by transient young men or out-of-luck miners. Farmers and ranchers, eager to sell food to the nearby camps, would bristle with energetic ideas about marketable crops and livestock. Road builders and freighters carved deep scars into the mountains, which did not heal when activity in a district ceased.

Nothing in the first two decades of mining in and around the San Luis Valley prepared the local people for Creede, however. Creede was in a class by itself. This camp lay some distance northwest of the valley on Willow Creek near the headwaters of the Rio Grande, but, since much of the traffic to and from this camp came by way of Del Norte and Wagon Wheel Gap, Creede's tumultuous life was of considerable interest in the valley.

Creede blossomed late in Colorado mining history, and one might assume from its legends that no mining was done at Creede until Nicholas Creede discovered the Holy Moses Mine in 1889. In fact, prospecting had taken place there in the 1870s and a few claims, including the Bachelor Mine that later developed into a bonanza, were recorded then. In the mid-1880s a few new prospectors also worked the area. The discovery of the Holy Moses Mine led to the rapid location of several more very rich mines, and by 1890 Creede was booming. Every load of ore coming down the narrow gulches seemed richer than the previous one.

The boom town and its rustic suburbs were

Tiny cottages at Valley View Hot Springs still can be rented by visitors with a taste for history and economy.

jammed into any available niche in the rugged terrain. To keep up with the growth of the mines and the town, a new railroad hauled in trainloads of timbers and lumber as soon as the Rio Grande, seeing a windfall, completed a line into Creede in 1891. Soon false-fronted stores, false-fronted hotels, and false-fronted saloons replaced the tents that had housed local businesses, including Soapy Smith's well-publicized gambling tables and Bob Ford's bar.

Crowded down in the bottom of the valley, the town's one main street was a hive, vibrating with ore wagons, burro trains, muleskinners and miners (relaxing in or taking apart the dance halls according to a moment's mood), painted ladies strolling the boardwalk, children playing on their way from school, housewives trying to cross the muddy street, and a few people even going to the First Congregational Church.

Cy Warman was publishing a newspaper, and in it he printed his well-known lines about the boisterous camp:

> It's day all day in the daytime,
> And there is no night in Creede.

Many investors in the mines were outside businessmen with capital for ambitious development. David Moffat of Denver was notable in attracting such backers. Thomas Bowen was one of the local investors. Ores from Creede were silver, gold, copper, lead, and zinc, a diversity which enabled the mines to survive vacillations in market prices. Mineral production in the Creede Mining District totaled $69.5 million from 1891 through 1966 and another $11.5 million in the next four years alone.[26] Creede may have learned the difference between day and night since Cy Warman's time, but its mines are far from asleep.

In recent years the mines of Creede and the Rawley Mine at Bonanza have been significant sources of precious metals that still provide jobs and income in the San Luis Valley. Otherwise, only brief flurries, such as a short-lived rush at Orean northeast of Zapata and another nearby at the Commodore Mine on Blanca Peak, both about the turn of the century, have kept alive the hope of striking pay dirt.[27]

More often now, such unglamorous materials as sand and gravel or soda are the products of the valley. Volcanic slag from a cinder cone near

Mesita and tuff from the Del Norte area also have been removed, but most important of the volcanic materials has been perlite, mined by Johns-Manville south of Antonito since 1959. Other minerals have been manganese ores from Saguache County, and uranium from that county as well as from the Culebra Range.[28]

Although not a major economic factor, turquoise mines have delighted lovers of Southwestern jewelry with some stones of exceptional quality. Copper miners northwest of Villa Grove discovered the turquoise deposits there in the 1890s, and the Hall Mine became a sporadic but important source of gem-quality material. Closed now, this mine still yielded several hundred pounds of turquoise annually as late as the 1950s. East of Manassa the ancient Indian workings were rediscovered by Israel Pervine King in the 1890s. The King Mine revealed one of the world's largest pockets of turquoise in the 1940s, and one blue-green nugget of superior quality weighed nearly nine pounds. For several years a large portion of Manassa's population owed their livelihoods to mining or cutting turquoise. The Kings continue to work this mine from time to time, shipping material to New Mexico, where members of the same family are dealers.

Probably few residents of the San Luis Valley today would welcome a revisitation by the often hungry, disgruntled prospectors who straggled through the area in the 1860s or by the rowdy miners and muleskinners who infested it in the 1870s, 1880s, and 1890s. Most people even have forgotten the profound effect that mining exerted on the valley, but the patterns of the region's life changed irrevocably during that period, and the results still are evident today.

XIV

"Significant Little Evidences of Refinement"

Shortly after Cary French and his companions found gold on South Mountain in 1870, one of them, who was taking out his rifle to shoot a beaver, accidentally shattered French's leg with a stray bullet. French was taken down to old Loma, where a Mexican woman, Juanita Lobato, cared for him for about three months, but the wound did not heal. Finally Juanita had her son take French to Fort Garland, where the army surgeon took over. From there the recovering prospector went home to Kansas for the winter, but he returned in the early summer of 1871 to rejoin his mining partners. When autumn arrived again, French stayed in the area and promoted the idea of building a new town below the mines as a permanent base for the miners and their families. This town on the south side of the Rio Grande del Norte was to be called Del Norte.[1]

Early the next year Del Norte's development began in earnest with the promise that anyone who built there by May could be a stockholder in the town company. A plat was filed late in 1872, and French, who was elected president of the town company, sent for his family the following year.[2] Meanwhile, George Ingersoll built a much-needed bridge across the river, and the post office that had operated three miles downstream at Loma de San Jose since 1867 moved to Del Norte. A new town called Loma was platted across the river from Del Norte, and it too had a post office from 1873 to 1875. Mark Biedell came down from the La Garita area to open a general store, while Alva Adams, who already had hardware businesses in Colorado Springs and Pueblo, started a branch in Del Norte. By 1875 the United States Land Office was established to keep track of claims which were filed by hundreds of prospectors who milled through the town. As French had hoped, many of them set up permanent homes in Del Norte and its rival additions on the west side and across the river. The settled population grew to 1,500 by 1875, although the town of Del Norte was not incorporated for another ten years.

With freighters and miners thronging to Lake City and Silverton, an improved road was needed. This route was surveyed in 1875 by members of the U.S. Corps of Engineers, who were part of a large program of exploration and surveying directed by Lieutenant George M. Wheeler. The new road from Del Norte was surveyed on the south side of the Rio Grande to Wagon Wheel Gap. At the gap and above it traffic was to cross the river in several places by bridge. A road company took over construction with costs repaid by tolls. A toll gate was maintained at Antelope Park, where this portion of the road ended. Another section was then built to Lake City with separate tolls being collected for it. When rancher Martin Van Buren Wason added yet another pay gate near the entrance to Creede in 1891, he infuriated miners who could not get in and out of town without paying his tolls. Despite such irritating charges, toll roads gave access to remote portions of Colorado for many years, and the old Antelope Park road remained a principal route to San Juan country until 1916, when the Wolf Creek highway opened to automobile traffic.

What everyone needed even more than a toll road in the mid-1870s, however, was the construction of the Denver and Rio Grande Railway line into the San Luis Valley and Del Norte, but the railroad was hamstrung east of the mountains. In the meantime, the task of hauling tons of mining equipment, supplies, and ore in and out of the San Juan mines became a bonanza for freighters. Although some of this load reached the southwest mining country via Saguache and Cochetopa

Above—Before the railroad was completed, wagon trains like this one at Del Norte carried tons of cargo to and from the mines and nearby supply towns. Below—When mines opened in the San Juan Mountains, stage stations and livery stables needed all the hay that the San Luis Valley could produce. This large barn was near a stage station on the Alamosa River route to Jasper and Cornwall.

Pass, Del Norte's streets, billowing with dust in the summer and mucking with mud in the winter, received the majority of the rowdy teamsters. When the Whitsitt Hotel opened in 1875, travelers had their first adequate inn at Del Norte, and just in time, for Barlow and Sanderson established a stage station in town the next year, adding their share of horse-scented confusion to the streets. Forty-some head of horses were pastured in the area to keep the stages rolling.

At Wagon Wheel Gap another stage station and a hotel of sorts opened. In 1878 the more commodious Hot Springs Hotel was built nearby, and it continued to operate for many years as a resort of muscle-sore miners and tourists. In the late 1880s it belonged to the Denver and Rio Grande.[3]

Events of the entire region were reported by the *San Juan Prospector,* a weekly that began publication in 1874 and has continued to keep its presses rolling ever since, although its first owner, Nicholas Lambert, soon found prospecting more enticing than writing about it and sold out. As subsequent newspapers appeard in Del Norte, they were either absorbed into the *Prospector* or left town. Even Summitville had a newspaper in the 1880s, but it lasted only for a year.[4]

To handle the burgeoning amount of county business, Rio Grande County had been created in 1874 with Del Norte as its county seat. With heavy influxes of people and activity elsewhere in the San Juans, other county reorganizations took place, with each new county striving to serve its own economic and political needs, often to the detriment of counties from which the new ones were carved. Rio Grande, Hinsdale, and La Plata counties all were sliced from Conejos County in the same year. At the same time Gunnison County lost a little ground to Hinsdale and Saguache counties. In 1879 a northern prong of Rio Grande County was yielded to Saguache County, but in 1893 both Saguache and Rio Grande as well as Hinsdale lost portions of their jurisdiction—and revenue—to the newly created Mineral County, which had Creede as its county seat.

Politics were important to the towns spawned by the mining boom, especially in Del Norte. Jealousy had existed between advocates of mines around Denver and mines in the San Juans as early as 1860. When the southwestern part of the territory finally proved its worth in the 1870s, a demand arose for a government separate from the control of Denver, and a state to be called San Juan was vociferously promoted. Pueblo joined the campaign in hopes of becoming the capital, but Del Norte, never deterred by modesty, was the leading contender for this honor.

A conspicuous leader in this scheme for statehood was Thomas M. Bowen. Bowen was a man of exceptional talent and energy, as demonstrated by his admission to the bar in Iowa when he was only eighteen and his election to the legislature there when he was twenty-one. After a move to Kansas and service in the Union Army during the Civil War, he went to Arkansas, where he became a state supreme court justice. Next, President Grant appointed him governor of the Territory of Idaho. In 1875, at the ripe old age of forty, he settled in Del Norte, opened a law practice, and espoused the cause of the State of San Juan.[5] Perhaps he even had aspirations to become its governor.

The desire to establish the separate state was aggravated when Colorado was admitted to the Union as a state in 1876, and the majority of its first congressmen and state officials hailed from the northern part of Colorado. The San Juan campaign soon lost some of its momentum when the citizens and the press of Saguache defected. Complete defeat was acknowledged when Pueblo also rejected the scheme. In the meantime, Del Norte's political leaders had gained enough popular support to propel their future careers. Thomas Bowen soon became a state senator and in 1883 was elected to the United States Senate, interrupting his San Juan mining activities for one term of six years in Washington. Democrat Alva Adams also got his start in politics when he went to the state house of representatives in 1876. He was to become governor of Colorado in 1887 when he was only thirty-seven, and he served another term in the same office in the 1890s. Another influential political figure was Charles H. Toll, an attorney from New York State, who moved to Del Norte in 1875. He became county judge the next year, state representative in 1879, and Colorado's attorney general in 1881. His descendants have been some of Colorado's prominent citizens.

In addition to regional politics another issue occupying attention was women's suffrage. Hoping to establish their right to vote in the new state, suffragettes campaigned to win the vote in 1877. When it failed to pass, opposition from the southern counties was singled out as a major cause, the heavy conservative Mexican population there having rejected the issue, it was claimed. Although it is true that these counties voted negatively, the issue would have been defeated by other counties anyway.[6] Perhaps one of

Ranch women in the San Luis Valley did not need "women's lib" to help them find a job.

the revealing results of this election was the polarization of progressive and conservative elements in the state. In this regard the miners and Spanish-speaking people within the San Luis Valley found themselves in opposing political camps, too.

Along with statehood and regional politics came district courts, which for many years were served by elected judges in Colorado. Thomas Bowen was elected district judge in 1876 for the Fourth Judicial District, then encompassing all of the San Luis Valley and the southwestern quarter of the state. To hold court in this far-reaching district, the judge moved his sessions from town to town. Occasionally court met in a large tent when no suitable building was available, as at San Luis. Even a district court, which provided trial by jury, failed to put an end to the well-established practice among some citizens of taking law into their own hands. Vigilantes around Del Norte were especially eager to settle scores with stage robbers or cattle rustlers in frontier style, even after the district court was established.

Nevertheless, it was evident early in Del Norte's life that many of the residents wished to cultivate a law-abiding, sober way of life. Churches were part of that evidence. As early as 1872 a Catholic church was organized in Del Norte, and in later years the headquarters for a parish located there.

In 1874 the Methodists built a log structure between Del Norte and West Del Norte to serve as a meeting place for their brethren in the rival parts of town. When this building was replaced by a stone church in 1876, Susan B. Anthony gave an address at the dedication ceremony, indicating how the Methodists felt about women's suffrage in Del Norte, at least.

The Episcopal bishop for Colorado and Wyoming was the energetic Reverend Franklin Spaulding, who traveled to many towns and mining camps organizing churches in the 1870s. In 1874 he arrived in Del Norte and held services at the little adobe building that housed the county offices. Two years later an Episcopal church in Del Norte was built.

114

Undiscouraged about denominational competition, the Reverend Alexander Darley arrived in Del Norte in 1876 to organize another Protestant church, the Presbyterian, with the supervision of Sheldon Jackson, Spaulding's counterpart in authority and vigor. Darley not only served Del Norte's congregation for the next few years but also energetically organized other groups around the San Luis Valley. In 1882 with the assistance of the Reverend George Darley, Alexander's brother, a handsome church was completed in Del Norte. Senator Thomas Bowen donated a bell for the steeple, and it was generally agreed that this was the most beautiful church in the entire Rocky Mountains, although some might have argued that the little church which George Darley, a skilled carpenter, had built in Lake City was even prettier.[7]

The D&RG's tracks finally had been laid into Del Norte and beyond to Wagon Wheel Gap and Del Norte's city fathers were in an expansive mood when the Presbyterian state synod met there in 1883. George Darley, who had become the pastor at Del Norte, presented a petition to have a Presbyterian college located in this town, which promised to become the center of commerce and culture for the entire San Juan country. The mayor of Del Norte reported that the citizens wanted the college, and local businessmen pledged land and money for it. The Presbyterian parishioners offered their beautiful new church for the school's use. As a result of this barrage of donations and arguments, Del Norte did become the home of the school called the Presbyterian College of the Southwest, which the synod had been expecting to locate in Denver or at least on the Eastern Slope.[8]

By 1884 the institution opened its doors to thirty students, some of whom were Spanish-speaking seminarians training to become missionaries among their own people. A dormitory had been built, an addition for classrooms was attached to the church, and three faculty members arrived from Ohio. However, the ambitions of the school's promoters were greater than the resources actually available for such a project. A main college building, designed on an impressive scale, never was built, although an observatory was set up on Mount Lookout behind town. Under pressure George Darley suffered a nervous breakdown, and in 1893 the uninsured church and college burned, despite the heroic efforts of Del Norte's three fire brigades. By the turn of the century the school had to accept defeat and closed, but the observatory clung to the summit of

The Presbyterian College of the Southwest, never prosperous enough to construct a classroom building, met at Del Norte's Presbyterian church until it burned.

Mount Lookout until 1940, when it blew away in a windstorm.

Despite this ill-starred venture and despite a slump in mining in the mid-1880s, Del Norte's economy had become relatively stable, in large part because of agriculture in the surrounding area. Farming and ranching were encouraged by the markets found in mining camps, especially in Creede in the 1890s. Although two banks moved to Alamosa after the railroad arrived there, two others remained in Del Norte. One of these was Asa Middaugh's Bank of Del Norte that opened in 1881 and became a reliable fixture in town. Middaugh also operated a mercantile company, while the New York Cash Store ran competition. Despite the acute disapproval of some citizens, a large brewery operated on San Francisco Creek, and across the Rio Grande from the freight yards the inevitable red-light district appeared.

At the depot, where Del Norte's town offices now are located, Don Haywood was the agent who kept tons of freight moving. His name was given to a siding between Monte Vista and Del Norte.

The college's observatory on Mt. Lookout was a landmark at Del Norte until the 1940s.

When Del Norte was born as a supply point for the San Juan mines, the town's closest rival was Saguache. Already a county seat and post office by 1867, the town quickly established itself as the principal settlement in the northern end of the valley. Although another community called Milton was located on the south side of Saguache Creek with a school, a church, a hotel, and a store, the land was too marshy and the residents decided to join Saguache on higher ground. Otto Mears, who had married a Saguache girl in 1870, was boosting the area's farms, selling supplies to the Los Pinos Indian Agency, and acting as an arbitrator in opening up the Ute reservation to mining development.

After the Brunot Treaty of 1873, events quickened for both Mears and his town. He instigated the publication of the *Saguache Chronicle* to boom the region, and he and Enos Hotchkiss built a toll road to Lake City. The next year, 1875, Mears established another newspaper at Lake City, which he also had platted, to further his promotion of the area. It was a promising tale of hope and riches, interrupted only momentarily by such events as Alferd Packer's alleged canni-

balism. Packer was brought down to Saguache for safekeeping in the new jail, which today is part of a historical museum.

Saguache was a closely knit community. In 1874 the town company was organized by Mears, David Heimberger, Isaac Gotthelf, Nathan Russell, and others in anticipation of the growth which would accompany developments to the west. Heimberger, the first president of the town company, was the county physician, and in later years he owned the *Chronicle*. Gotthelf, who was justice of the peace, ran a mercantile company that he had opened in 1867 and that still exists in Saguache. He also raised cattle and operated a branch of his store at the Los Pinos Agency, at one time in partnership with Mears. After a few years as a state legislator, Gotthelf founded the Saguache County Bank, with Leopold Mayer as a partner.

Mears continued in the retail business for a while after the Indian agency moved to the Uncompahgre River. Occasionally Indians still came down to his store to trade for tobacco and whiskey at Saguache. Whiskey seems to have been one of the important items at the store, for the

Saguache's first flour mill ground wheat with Spanish-type stones, but another mill soon was producing real American flour.

Saguache's first house had undergone numerous improvements, such as the addition of a tin roof, when the whole family lined up to have their picture taken.

Several prosperous ranches were located along Saguache Creek toward Cochetopa Pass.

local women singled out Mears's establishment on one occasion when their husbands had been overindulging. In Carrie Nation style, the ladies smashed Mears's whiskey barrels, but the wily businessman had the last word. He simply charged the cost of the liquor on their next monthly bills.[9]

For several years Mears's home remained in Saguache at the site of the present courthouse, which was built in 1910. In 1877 he became a naturalized citizen, District Judge Thomas Bowen signing the papers, and in the ensuing decade Mears served in the state house and senate. Increasingly, the building of toll roads and railroads dominated his business life and gave him a legendary reputation as the "path-finder of the San Juan." Later he retired to California, where he died.

By the time that railroads were cutting into staging and freighting, Saguache, like Del Norte, had developed a firm economic base as a supply town for the agricultural neighborhood. Hotels at Saguache provided lodging for travelers heading down the valley toward Del Norte or over Cochetopa Pass for several more years, however. The

Fairview was the first, and the cornerstone of the Saguache Hotel was laid in 1910, a contradiction to stories that President Grant stayed there. Grant did visit Saguache in 1879, however, when an exuberant celebration was staged in his honor.

Saguache was no slacker at enjoying itself, but on the Fourth of July 1879, merriment turned to widespread sorrow. A horse race was staged to highlight the holiday, and the whole town bet heavily on a local favorite that had never lost a race. The winner turned out to be a horse belonging to a traveling man from Kansas, who rode out of Saguache with most of the town's ready cash and a few Indian ponies besides.

On the whole, though, Saguache had a stable character. Small irrigation ditches ran along each street and encouraged cottonwoods to grow quickly, giving the shady streets a settled appearance. There were several churches—Catholic, Methodist, Presbyterian, and Baptist. Baptist evangelizing in the mining camps around Bonanza was carried on with headquarters for the mission in Saguache. Apparently Unitarian meetings also were held here, for Otto Mears's infant daughter was baptized in that church in

The Fourth of July always was a big event in Saguache, and 1912 was no exception.

119

Reflections of the past.

Several of Saguache's handsome buildings were constructed with brick.

Saguache in 1880. Fraternal organizations, such as the Masonic Lodge and Odd Fellows, and ladies' literary groups were active.

If Del Norte had a college of which to boast, Saguache County's schools were a source of considerable pride, too. A public school was organized in Saguache in 1874, Milton already had one previously, and others soon appeared in farm communities, mining camps, and ranch areas throughout the county.

A third contender for importance in the upper half of the San Luis Valley was Alamosa. Difficulty in crossing the Rio Grande kept traffic that was destined south and west concentrated in locations served by ferries—near the Culebra, at La Sauses, and at Loma. Fording the river elsewhere was a tricky affair for heavily loaded wagons because of quicksand and mud.

When Alexander Hunt preceded the Denver and Rio Grande into Alamosa, he first set up camp on the east bank of the river and established a ferry large enough to transport two wagons and their teams. With the arrival of rails into Alamosa in 1878, the Rio Grande ceased being an obstacle to efficient movement of freight. When a small steamboat was launched at Alamosa, it did little either to assist in transportation or to compete with the railroad. While the

railhead remained at Alamosa, an immense quantity of freight was transferred there daily. From the railroad yards ox-drawn wagons rolled south to Santa Fe and west to Del Norte and the San Juans.

In 1878 another wagon road was approved by Congress to give access to the Pagosa Springs area without the long haul by way of Cumbres Pass, which was the customary route for freighters. The new road ran from Fort Garland and Alamosa to Gato Creek, across the mountains to intersect with the road from Tierra Amarilla, and thence to Pagosa Springs and the southwestern corner of the state. It was a difficult, lonely crossing, little used by freighters.

Since Alamosa owed its inception to the railroad, it was only natural that the economy during the first years depended heavily on freighting. Even after rails extended beyond Alamosa and the forwarding of supplies and ore no longer was so important, the D&RG's division offices and shops still contributed in a major way to the local welfare. Offices for telegraph service were here, too, as wires and poles had entered the valley along with rails and ties. The depot now standing in Alamosa is a comparatively recent addition, which was preceded by two others that burned.

The rapidity in which Alamosa became estab-

This well-built brick farmhouse was a few miles from Saguache.

Pioneer buildings in Saguache often possessed pleasing architectural details which set the town apart from its rougher, tougher neighbors in the valley.

lished as a trade center and residential community resulted in the publication of several newspapers during the first few decades of its life. Churches also quickly arrived, the first when the untiring Reverend Alexander Darley sent a building for the Presbyterian church transported on a flatcar from Garland City. Alva Adams set up a hardware store, and two banks moved in from Del Norte.

Alva Adams's cousin, William H. Adams, clerked in the new hardware store, later becoming a rancher in the La Jara area. Billy, as he usually was called, early showed an interest in local politics and became the town treasurer at the age of twenty-two. Next he was mayor for two terms and then a commissioner of Conejos County, until, with all this experience behind him, he moved to the state house of representatives and to the state senate. Before his career was finished he served three terms as governor and was recognized as the elder statesman of Colorado politics. In tribute to his service to the San Luis Valley, his name was given to the state normal school that was established in Alamosa in the 1920s.

For more than three decades Alamosa chafed under the time-consuming inconvenience of handling its county business in Conejos. The northern portion of the valley had become populated primarily by Anglos in the 1870s and 1880s, and the valley's economy had shifted from south to north. Saguache and Del Norte were county seats, so why should not Alamosa enjoy the same status, the local citizens argued. Only after a strenuous political and legal battle was Alamosa County finally created in 1913 from portions of Conejos and Costilla counties. The last of Colorado's sixty-three present counties, Alamosa County was not dignified with its handsome courthouse until another quarter century had passed, because the new county was required to share for several years the bonded indebtedness of Conejos County. Today Alamosa, the "cottonwood grove," is the San Luis Valley's largest city.

While great progress was taking place elsewhere in the valley, one anachronistic symbol of frontier days was crumbling in a lingering twilight. Fort Garland, always out of step with the life of the rest of the valley, had been living on borrowed time after the Ute agency moved west to the Uncompahgre River. In the early 1880s it closed.

For a few years after the Civil War, the facility was staffed again with regular troops and appearances of a military operation were kept up, although a certain amount of hospitable neighborliness was extended to local people in need of assistance. En route to the mines several veterans

of the war found a kind welcome at the fort in the early 1870s. But in exchange for a warm bed, the guests were expected to comport themselves in a manner befitting a military post. When one ill-advised prospector smuggled in some whiskey for himself and the soldiers, he was shackled with irons in the guardhouse with rations of bread and water and then ordered to leave the fort and the entire vicinity as well.

The offending whiskey probably was purchased just south of the fort at the store owned by F. W. Posthoff of Costilla. This establishment did a thriving business in whiskey since it could not be stocked at the fort's commissary. For that matter, Posthoff also ran the commissary and later turned the operation over to his partner Ferd Meyer. In addition to other indispensables, the sutler's store carried a remarkable variety of goods, from patent medicines to buffalo robes, according to William Rideing, who visited Fort Garland with the Wheeler Survey.

From the time of the Beale expedition in 1853, mappers, surveyors, and others under army sponsorship had used first Fort Massachusetts and then Fort Garland as a post at which to rest, reorganize, or resupply. An exception among them was the Hayden parties, because their work was undertaken as civilian operations. When Hayden came to the San Luis Valley in the late 1860s his project was sponsored in part as a government geological survey and in part as a privately financed report, but none of his backing came through the army, unlike most pre-Civil War surveys. When several divisions of Hayden's surveys worked in Colorado again in the 1870s, he had an increased appropriation from Congress to support his work, but it still was entirely civilian. Hayden's topographic crews were in the mountains around the San Luis Valley in 1874, a year when several large forest fires hindered work. Hayden parties did not use Fort Garland.

On the other hand, the survey with which Rideing traveled in 1875 when he stopped at Fort Garland was sponsored by the Corps of Engineers. This vast project was called the United States Geographical Surveys West of the Hundredth Meridian, better known as the Wheeler Survey. Although mapping of topographic features and surveying of roads was included in this program, its great achievements were the determination of latitude, longitude, and altitude by triangulation and other methodical procedures. A Wheeler party came through the San Luis Valley in 1873 en route to the San Juans, and another passed through the Conejos area in 1874.

A journalist who joined the 1875 project at Pueblo, Rideing described Fort Garland as "a rectangular group of adobe buildings, flat-roofed, squat, and altogether dispiriting in their unmitigated ugliness. . . . [The] buildings are increasingly dilapidated."[10]

Despite the stultifying effect of the fort's appearance and isolation, Rideing acknowledged that good discipline was maintained with military pomp accompanying even the dullest routines. Moreover, "the officers contrive to crowd many significant little evidences of refinement into their incommodious quarters, notwithstanding the difficulty of obtaining anything except the necessaries of life. The rooms are in some instances carpeted with buffalo-robes and bearskins, while the walls are adorned with guns and relics of the chase. To members of our expedition coming out of the field, this revelation of domesticity and comfort proved a grateful change from the hardships of an American explorers' camp."[11]

When this division of the survey left Fort Garland, it proceeded southwest to Conejos and thence to the Tierra Amarilla region and the San Juans. Meanwhile, another division worked around the headwaters of Saguache and La Garita creeks. To commemorate the work of these military men and the scientists affiliated with the enterprise, a group of unusual geologic formations northeast of Wagon Wheel Gap, high in the La Garitas, was designated Wheeler National Monument in 1908. It was one of the first areas in the nation set aside as a national monument. Because of its inaccessibility its status later was changed to that of a Geologic Area under the administration of the U.S. Forest Service.

The departure of the Wheeler party from Fort Garland in 1875 marked the close of the fort's role in the exploration of the West. Life at the post quickly resumed its humdrum routine, broken chiefly by the comings and goings of wagon traffic past its gates. With the construction of the Denver and Rio Grande Railway, the soldiers had a new diversion from the usual monotony. The sutler's store and the little settlement of adobe houses outside the fort also shared in this stir of excitement, one of the houses achieving the status of a hotel when it erected a sign over the front door to that effect.

When Helen Hunt Jackson saw the post in 1878, she wrote, "It is not a fort which could resist a siege—not even an attack from a few mounted Indians; it must have been intended simply for barracks."[12] Within a few months even the barracks proved inadequate, when the regular garrison, which usually consisted only of a company of infantry and a troop of cavalry, was increased to nearly fifteen hundred after the Meeker Massacre in northwestern Colorado. Most of these new troops were encamped outside the fort proper. During the negotiations of a new treaty with the Utes, which resulted in their removal from the Uncompahgre area, a large number of these soldiers moved to the Uncompahgre River, Fort Garland's chief function then being a supply depot guarded by a small garrison.

Even that role became unnecessary when the Utes were removed; and, as a result, the fort was abandoned in 1883. The remaining troops were transferred to Fort Lewis near Durango, Colorado, and the military cemetery was moved elsewhere, also. The land reverted to the Trinchera Estate.

Until this abandonment only civilians associated with the fort could live on the military reservation. In adobes near the post after 1883 a few families set up housekeeping. People who had worked in the mess hall stayed and took jobs on the railroad's section gang or tried their hands at farming. A few former soldiers stayed around, some with their Mexican or Indian wives and one running Ferd Meyer's store and the post office.

The fort itself was owned privately and used as a ranch home and headquarters until 1928, when a group of San Luis Valley residents bought it for the purpose of preserving it. This group, organized as the Fort Garland Historical Fair Association, presented the property in 1945 to the State Historical Society of Colorado, which restored the fort and opened it as a museum to the public.

Although the fort's prime is recaptured now in the museum like a moment suspended in time, the fort was, figuratively speaking, a museum piece long before the army abandoned it. When the flag was lowered in the parade ground in 1883, the adobe buildings had been crumbling for several years just as persistently as the old frontier had been disappearing elsewhere in the San Luis Valley. The boom years of the 1870s had altered the way of life as irrevocably as a bachelor's life is changed when his bride decides to start moving the furniture around a little bit. Clearly, the San Luis Valley was becoming domesticated.

125

Little remains of many crossroads settlements, such as Swede's Corner.

XV

"Manassa Was Strong on Religion"

Miner and merchant, road builder and teamster, banker and preacher, soldier and suffragette—these and many more played roles in the changing scene of the San Luis Valley during the 1870s. However, the main characters proved to be not these but the undramatic farmers and ranchers who settled in the valley during this and the ensuing decades.

Development of agriculture progressed rapidly in the San Luis Valley during the 1870s for several reasons. The Homestead Act had encouraged settlement of public lands. The end of the Civil War had provided both the opportunity and the necessity for war veterans and people from ravaged parts of the nation to relocate in the West. National economic distress in the mid-1870s and immigration from Europe swelled the stream of people seeking new beginnings on the frontier. Meanwhile, Colorado's mining boom and urban growth both presented unfilled markets for agricultural products. The San Luis Valley contained land suitable for farms and ranches near some of the mines and towns. Men like Otto Mears and General William Jackson Palmer would overcome the problems of transportation to the more distant markets.

Perhaps when some families arrived in the 1860s they intended merely to create self-sustaining farms, but men like John Lawrence and Nathan Russell with their ranches west of Saguache and Otto Mears with his new-fangled threshing machine clearly had something bigger in mind. At first their Mexican neighbors failed to grasp the implications of the changes going on around them and regarded such things as the threshing machine as foolish because it was wasteful of grain. Although the first mill built in the Saguache area—the Robertson Mill of about 1870 or 1871—was a Spanish type, it soon was succeeded by the Saguache Mill, which could produce the finer flour preferred in the mining communities and in Denver.

Flour was not the only product soon being shipped from the Saguache area. Hay was sold to the mining camps for feed, and many head of cattle, sheep, and horses were raised for sale in these markets. Hogs were fed on locally grown peas, and a dairy ranch, called Rockcliff, operated about fifteen miles west of Saguache. This farm, where a post office was located from 1874 to 1880, and Samuel Hoagland's inn nearby were prominent ranches on the road to Cochetopa Pass.[1]

Although land along Saguache Creek west of the town of Saguache was taken up quickly, newcomers in the 1870s found other locations in the county to the north and east. Villa Grove, called Garibaldi in the early 1870s, was laid out to serve farms and ranches in Homan's Park and along Kerber Creek. Near Bismark, about eight miles southeast of Villa Grove, there were enough settlers to warrant a post office by 1872. A couple of miles south of Bismark another post office known as Cotton Creek opened in 1875 but moved to Mirage in 1895. One of the farmers in this vicinity, DeWitt C. Travis, produced 70,000 pounds of potatoes in 1875 and became the first commercial grower of potatoes in the valley. Farther south on Rio Alto and Sangre de Cristo Creek most of the settlers were Spanish-speaking, engaged in raising sheep and cattle.

In 1877 Saguache County's first fair was organized after a group of local people acquired a piece of land at Saguache for their agricultural exhibition. Among the winners in the horse show, which was staged as part of the fair, was stock belonging to Otto Mears.[2]

Another section of the San Luis Valley that attracted farmers and ranchers was the fertile region above Del Norte. One of the earliest settlers here was an Englishman named Alden, who had acquired the land at Antelope Springs before 1872. At the junction of Willow Creek and the Rio Grande, Martin Van Buren Wason established a ranch in 1871, also. He became an important supplier of horses with his livestock ranging throughout the area above Wagon Wheel Gap. Creede later was located on part of Wason's range, a geographical coincidence that accounted for Wason's determination to collect tolls from those entering the camp. In 1877 Wason, who had earned a reputation among his neighbors as the most rugged of individuals, was married to an English poetess in a ceremony performed by Judge Thomas Bowen. The Wasons reigned over their corner of Colorado for a quarter of a century.

West of Del Norte about two hundred German immigrants undertook a cooperative colony in 1872, but its members became independent farmers within the decade. In this area one of the best-known families was the Edwin Shaws, who arrived in Del Norte in 1873. After operating a hotel there briefly and living on various ranches in the neighborhood, they settled on Shaw Creek twelve miles west of Del Norte, where they ran an inn on the stage line along with their ranch activities.

Northwest of Monte Vista Swedish immigrants took up farms in an area called Swedes' Lane about 1875. North of here on La Garita Creek ranches were acquired by Englishmen, while south between Del Norte and Conejos land was settled during the early 1870s by Middle Westerners from Iowa and Illinois for the most part. Post offices were established during this decade at La Jara, Piedra, and Rio Grande, a town at the junction of La Jara Creek with the Rio Grande. On Rock Creek some of these early settlers were Dunkards from Iowa. The Strip, as the land around Piedra (Rock) Creek and La Jara Creek was called, previously had been known to the Spanish-speaking residents there as Llano Blanco, or the "White Plain," perhaps because of alkaline seeps in the area. Mexican settlement in the area was confined primarily to the neighborhood around Capulin, but these people who considered the land as part of the Conejos Grant also cut hay along La Jara Creek and elsewhere. De-

Clearing a field of greasewood was a four-horse job.

spite their futile objections, titles were conveyed to the Anglo homesteaders. Before long several of the newcomers were persuaded to sell their land to an eastern investment group called the Philadelphia Cattle Company, which ran several thousand head of cattle on the combined holding.[3]

Most of the cattle raised at this time were longhorns from Texas, but few homesteaders attempted to raise cattle on their original tracts, which were too small for grazing. At first several raised wheat, which had been selling for three to six dollars a bushel, but after prices declined in the mid-1870s many of the homesteaders diversified, raising vegetables and poultry and selling milk and butter and eggs. Some sold out to the larger ranchers.

Across the valley on the Sangre de Cristo Grant similar changes were forestalled by legal and financial difficulties which handicapped the U.S. Freehold Land and Emigration Company's sale of land, although the Trinchera Ranch on the northern half of the grant was being developed by the Blackmore family. A few small farmers and ranchers who had sold livestock, hay, and vegetables to Fort Garland also could be found north of the Costilla Estate—Tom Tobin a few miles south of the fort, Charles Newton on Ute Creek, John Williams, and later Kit Carson's son William.

North of the Trinchera Estate in the Zapata area several Mexican families had small farms. They were joined in 1870 by a German immigrant, William H. Meyer and shortly thereafter by Anglo settlers who arrived on Medano Creek with a herd of Texas longhorns.

The Mexican settlers contested the rights of the newcomers by claiming that the land involved was a Mexican grant, dating back to 1820-21 and known as the Springs of the Medano and the Zapato.[4] Papers to support this contention were submitted to the surveyor general in 1874, but the documents were declared to be forgeries and the matter was tabled, allowing a group of investors to obtain title to the Zapata Ranch in 1876. The purchase was made from one of the professed owners of the grant. By 1879 a post office was operating at Zapata.

William Meyer, meanwhile, had established himself in county politics, was elected to the state senate, and became lieutenant governor in 1882. Shortly afterward he bought the abandoned Fort Garland and converted it into a home, office, and warehouse for his sheep and cattle enterprises.

Through the purchase of Mexican farms, the Medano Ranch developed gradually into a large operation belonging to the Dickey brothers. In 1882 their 130,000 acres of fenced range was sold to New York investors, Adee and Durkee, who developed the largest cattle operation in the valley with cattle grazing from Poncha Pass to the Rio Grande and south of it.[5]

Beginning in 1874 a store and post office called Medano Springs were located at what also became the ranch headquarters. This property had been a homestead occupied by the Herard family. They and their neighbors had raised horses near the sand dunes, and their strays may have been the inspiration of legends about wild horses seen on the dunes.[6]

Small ranchers, who remained in the neighborhood and who needed more grazing land than was available after the Medano outfit fenced its property, occasionally rearranged matters by clipping a wire fence here and there. During the 1870s and 1880s cattle rustling was commonplace in the valley, and the Medano and Zapata ranches were especially vulnerable because they were so far from a sheriff's office. These ranches were in Costilla County with the county seat in San Luis and in Saguache County with the county seat in Saguache. Consequently, the town marshal of Alamosa sometimes was summoned to deal with trouble on these big spreads.

North of the Medano Ranch and the sand dunes lay the Baca Grant. During the period from 1878 until 1885, when George H. Adams leased the property from William Gilpin, extensive improvements such as fencing, irrigation ditches, and ranch buildings appeared on the grant. It has been claimed that Adams put in the first barbed-wire fence in the San Luis Valley. Eventually the grant had 150 miles of irrigation ditches and dozens of artesian wells, and the range was stocked with registered Herefords.[7] With mining and ranching combined on the grant, this property became a major asset to its owners, encouraging the sale in 1885 that finally gave Gilpin some profit in his real estate investments.

Adams's interests eventually included the ranches south of the grant, an occurrence that was linked with Mormon colonizing in the San Luis Valley. Prior to the arrival of Mormons around Blanca Peak, enough people had settled in Uracca Canyon south of Zapata Creek to warrant the opening of a school by 1887. Most of the men in these families were tie-cutters for the railroad.[8] In 1889 the Mormon Church bought part of the Zapata Ranch and the following year the Medano Ranch together with the rest of the Zapata Ranch, including the Uracca area. For the next few years this holding was known officially as the

Blanca Branch of the Manassa Ward but unofficially as the Uracca Mormon Church.

Construction began on irrigation canals to tap streams from Medano Creek to South Zapata Creek, but water rights could not be cleared and work on this project stopped. The destitute Mormons, many of whom were impoverished tenant farmers from the Southeastern states, became timber-cutters and sold firewood in Alamosa to feed their families. The enterprise declared bankruptcy, and George Adams was named receiver of the property. In 1900 both the former Mormon land and the Baca Grant were sold to E. L. Sylvester.[9]

Mormons had begun to settle in the valley in the late 1870s and, unlike the Uracca experience, were successful for the most part in establishing farms and communities, although not without overcoming many obstacles.

In 1877 John Morgan, president of the Southern States Mission, arrived with seventy members of the Latter-day Saints Church in Pueblo, Colorado. His flock, most of whom were converts from the South, set up camp on an island in the Arkansas River, while church leaders from Utah sought suitable land in the San Luis Valley which

The focal point of social as well as religious life in several towns in Conejos County is the Church of Jesus Christ of Latter-day Saints, members of which settled here a century ago.

could be purchased for a colony. In May 1878 the group that had wintered at Pueblo moved to their new home, where missionaries from Utah helped in establishing the settlement. One of these, Lawrence M. Peterson, previously had lived at Los Cerritos and had evangelized among the Spanish-speaking people there.[10]

The site awaiting the emigrants consisted of two ranches purchased from Mexicans on the south side of the Conejos River across from Los Cerritos. Buildings, farming, and irrigation were begun at once, and meetings were held in a rented schoolhouse. The Mormons received a hospitable welcome from Lafayette Head and some of the prominent Mexicans.

By the next spring, 1879, the group had decided to lease state mineral lands about three miles northwest of Los Cerritos and to establish a town called Manassa, the name of a son of the Israelite Joseph.[11] In the selection of this land for a permanent colony, church leaders were assured that the railroad, which already had reached Alamosa, soon would provide rail transportation through the southwestern portion of the valley. This service, in fact, began a year later with tracks passing three miles west of Manassa.

Additions from Utah and Arizona arrived, and Mormon settlers soon numbered nearly four hundred. Despite the inexperience of the Southern members in farming irrigated land and despite the short growing season to which these farmers were unaccustomed, the project soon showed evidence of success—at least, enough to arouse the hostility of some non-Mormon neighbors and Colorado's Republican newspapers. First, Mexicans dammed the Conejos River to prevent the Mormons from withdrawing water for irrigation, but this interference stopped when the Mormons boldly knocked out the dams. Next, a committee of stockmen from the Strip paid a call to share their advice that the land being cultivated by the Mormons was better suited to raising cattle. The usual rumors were bandied about to the effect that the Mormons were polygamists, thieves, or worse, while Denver's newspapers campaigned against permitting the Mormons to settle in the state. It was even claimed that the Mormons intended to set up bases all the way across Colorado and to take over the state. Nevertheless, the law-abiding colony in the San Luis Valley persisted and eventually earned the respect of their neighbors.

In addition to field peas, oats, and alfalfa, the early Mormon settlers grew soft, spring Sonora wheat, a type that had been introduced by Spanish colonists and was favored by Mexicans in the valley. Later this variety was replaced by another soft wheat, Australian Club, which had larger heads and produced better flour. It was grown extensively throughout the valley for a few years.[12]

The first public buildings in Manassa were a school and a church, quickly followed by a co-operative store and a flour mill. This was the pattern of priorities in other Mormon towns as well. Manassa's post office opened in 1879.

As additional converts arrived from the Southeastern states, one of the groups from Virginia included the family of Hiram Dempsey. Of his eleven children, the ninth was William Harrison Dempsey, born in 1895 in Manassa. He was called "Harry" by his family, but he became known as Jack Dempsey or the "Manassa Mauler," world heavyweight boxing champion.

Hiram Dempsey had more of a roving spirit in him than did most of his neighbors, and, as Jack Dempsey recalled in his autobiography *Round by Round*, teachers from the church visited the Dempsey home regularly to exhort Hiram "to do right."

"Manassa was strong on religion," Jack Dempsey admitted, but it also was a typical pioneer town, "tough and ready for anything." As a schoolboy he had plenty of opportunities to learn firsthand how to fight on Manassa's wide, dusty streets.

In 1881 Mormon newcomers began another settlement four miles from Manassa. The new town was Ephraim, named for another of the Israelite Joseph's sons. Here canals brought water for agriculture, but the drainage was poor and the 150 residents of Ephraim moved from the waterlogged location between 1886 and 1888. Some of them went to nearby Richfield, which first was settled in 1882. Richfield's irrigation caused the water table to rise there, too, and the people moved from this site also.

The next move was to Morgan, about fifteen miles northwest of Manassa. Land for Morgan was acquired through homesteading. First located in 1886, the town grew with additional families arriving from Utah. A unique feature in this Mormon settlement were the artesian wells that were drilled to provide nearly every family with a domestic water supply. As in other towns, the Mormons lived within the community and farmed their individual fenced plots, each of which received water from the main ditch. Here the principal feeder was the Morgan Ditch. Other Mormon ditches were the Little Manassa,

Ephraim, Richfield, Sanford, and Miller. Also, the Mormons bought one-third of the rights to the water of the old Guadalupe Ditch.[13]

By 1888 Sanford, only a half mile from Ephraim, was becoming the most prosperous community in the area. The new town was surveyed in 1885, and the majority of people from both Ephraim and Richfield gradually moved here. Ephraim's post office, which had opened in 1881, moved to Sanford in 1888, following the migration of houses, barns, cooperative store, and school. The residents of Sanford may have been religious, but they also enjoyed their social life. The upper floor of the store was used for a dance hall. Another building served not only for church meetings but also for social gatherings, while the citizens painstakingly constructed a stone church, which finally was completed in 1907.[14] An academy also opened at about the same time.

Zebulon Pike would have had difficulty imagining that a religious colony and pioneer farms would be located a half-dozen miles west of his stockade only eighty years after his arrest there by Spanish dragoons. The site of the stockade, part of Governor Albert W. McIntire's property, was purchased in 1924 by the state, and in 1952 a log fort was completed there to commemorate the site.

During the growth of settlements around Manassa and La Jara, Mormons also continued to take up land around the Conejos River, until Los Cerritos warranted a post office by 1889. As irrigable land between the Conejos River and La Jara Creek became scarce, though, additional acreage was sought for Mormons who still were arriving in the valley. One of the last Mormon towns on the west side of the Rio Grande was Mountain View, where Romeo now is located.

In 1888 and 1889 the Uracca venture had been undertaken near Blanca Peak. In 1890 the church began a settlement called Eastdale on the Costilla drainage southwest of San Luis. Separated from their fellow churchmen by the Rio Grande, the people of Eastdale could reach Manassa and Sanford only by the inconvenient and unscheduled service of the ferry located east of Antonito. This crossing was called variously Myers' or Conlon's or Costilla Ferry. Eastdale also was separated from rail service except by the long road to Fort Garland.

The Eastdale colony built a canal and reservoir and raised wheat, and they purchased the St. Vrain and Easterday flour mill at San Luis to process it.[15] They fired bricks to build a church, and they had a school, a store, and a post office. Despite their enterprise, the Eastdale Mormons

could not meet their land payments, especially as a result of competition for sufficient irrigation water. As a result, the Eastdale settlement was abandoned in 1909, and the residents moved to the west side of the Rio Grande. After the failure of this colony and Uracca, the Latter-day Saints in the San Luis Valley confined their activities to the well-established area around Manassa, Sanford, and La Jara.

The new town of La Jara, settled in the late 1870s by non-Mormons, quickly became a marketing and supply center for the Strip and for the neighboring Mormon towns. A railroad station encouraged the town's growth. A Presbyterian church was organized as early as 1879, but some of the other accoutrements of a well-established community were slow in appearing. The town company's plat was not filed until 1887, and the first newspaper in the area, *La Jara Tribune*, appeared only in 1888. The town was not incorporated until 1895, the same year when one of its citizens became the governor of the state.

Albert W. McIntire came from Pittsburgh to Denver and finally to La Jara in 1880. Here he became one of the stockmen of the Strip, developing a herd of Black Angus cattle. He also served as county judge and district judge before he was elected governor on the Republican ticket.

Several other non-Mormons had large-scale ranches in the area by this time, although Mexicans still outnumbered the newcomers by a large majority. John Harvey of Leadville bred Percheron horses on 3,300 acres near La Jara. The horses were used for freighting ore, coal, hay, and grain.[16] As with the introduction of purebred cattle, these horses were a vast improvement over the livestock previously raised in the valley. Until then many horse herds consisted merely of range horses that were rounded up once a year, branded, and sold for two dollars a head. It was popularly believed that these wild horses derived from Spanish *caballos*.

A prominent cattleman from La Jara was William A. Braiden, a native of Ohio who arrived in Conejos County in 1887 trailing a small herd of Shorthorn cattle. After selling the herd, he went to work for various dairy farmers and ranchers until, having acquired his own small herd of horses, he opened the Pioneer Livery Barn in La Jara. He also became a dealer in livestock, owned a retail store, operated a stage line, and had enterprises in Creede, too. Eventually he became a major Hereford cattle raiser and landowner in Conejos County with a large ranch east of Antonito.[17] This property, called the T-Bone Ranch, was at the old town of Cenicero, which became

Manassa's museum is proud of the town's pioneers, especially of the boy who became known as the "Manassa Mauler."

known as Lobatos when the post office there adopted the name of a local family in 1902. In recent years the T-Bone Ranch has been owned by John Hamilton, a founder of the Continental Oil Company.

Billy Adams also raised cattle in the area of La Jara, and Dan Newcomb had one of the largest dairy farms in the state. When the post office closed at old La Jara in 1884, it was moved to the Newcomb farm for a couple of years and was given the name of Newcomb. On Gato Creek stock raisers were served by a post office called Vadner, which was the name of a ranch west of Bowen.

The area around Bowen was settled by Presbyterians, attracted by an Iowan, F. W. Williams, who advertised the land for sale to people of his own religious background. Williams also named the neighborhood for Thomas M. Bowen, another

stalwart Presbyterian. The church at Bowen served the religious and educational functions in that area for several years. Nearby Rock Creek ranchers also organized a Presbyterian church in 1881 to serve both their own neighborhood and Lariat on the railroad. This congregation soon became known as the Henry Presbyterian Church and then the Monte Vista church.

In communities such as Capulin and La Sauses there were Catholic churches attended by the predominantly Spanish-speaking residents. La Sauses remained active for several years while some wagon traffic from the Fort Garland area still used the ferry at Stewart's Crossing. The post office at the sloughs of the Rio Grande was called La Sauses.

In the late 1880s the Sunflower post office opened at what became Romeo at the turn of the century. Romeo was developed by a real estate

Middle Westerners who settled around Bowen built themselves a pretty church which would remind them of home.

promoter from Denver. With its railroad siding, grain elevator, and potato exchange, Romeo became a shipping center for the Manassa region. In fact, wherever a siding was located—Estrella, Henry, La Jara, Bountiful, or Romeo—local farmers and ranchers shipped cattle and crops from this productive part of the San Luis Valley.

On the Denver and Rio Grande's line west of Alamosa, Lariat Siding had started its life in 1881 as a small shipping point for cattle, as its name implies. When Theodore C. Henry platted the town of Henry at this location in 1884, a shift from ranching to farming took place.

Henry, originally from New York State, had met with success in real estate promotion and in wheat farming before he moved to Denver in the early 1880s. There he immediately entered Colorado politics and even was a candidate for governor. He bought the *Denver Tribune* and organized the Colorado Loan and Trust Company, through which he invested about two million dollars in land and irrigation projects, much of his capital being borrowed from the Travelers' Insurance Company. His undertakings extended all the way from the Platte and Arkansas rivers in eastern Colorado to the Uncompahgre country and the

Grand Valley, where he founded the town of Fruita.[18] In the San Luis Valley he developed irrigation and real estate around Monte Vista, or Henry as it was then called, and the Mosca area.

Shortly before the arrival of T. C. Henry's projects, two large irrigation canals had been built in the valley—the Rio Grande and Piedra Valley Ditch, which served ranches around Rock Creek, and the Excelsior Ditch, which served ranches northwest of Alamosa. In addition, there were many older and smaller ditches in the area, several of which dated back to colonization of the Conejos Grant. Another noteworthy ditch provided water for a German gristmill at Del Norte, while the Enterprise Ditch fed water into the La Garita area.

T. C. Henry's first move when he entered the San Luis Valley was to entice the insurance company to lend enough money to buy state land in the name of the Del Norte Land and Canal Company. Next he built four major canals that incorporated many old ditch systems. The new network included the Rio Grande Canal, the San Luis Valley Canal, Citizen's Ditch (later called Monte Vista Canal), and Empire Canal.[19] These four canals alone totaled about 140 miles in

length, and they supplied water to a complex of laterals which, it was claimed, would be able to irrigate about 500,000 acres.[20]

Henry's land acquisitions were equally enormous. They were divided into two principal farms, the North Farm consisting of about seven thousand acres north of Monte Vista and the South Farm consisting of about three thousand acres south of the Rio Grande. These were subdivided into fourteen smaller company farms where wheat and cattle were raised while the land was being sold off at three to five dollars per acre. The show piece of the operation was the 2,000-acre La Garita Farm, which had been purchased from the titled Englishmen who had been raising sheep there for the past decade.

Out of the entire project T. C. Henry soon controlled only the Empire Canal and the Alamosa, Empire, and Excelsior farms, these having been financed in part by businessmen from Alamosa. The rest of the property passed into the hands of the Travelers' Insurance Company when Henry was unable to repay his loan due in 1885. The town of Henry, faced with unpaid wages and bills, in disgust changed its name to Monte Vista in 1886.

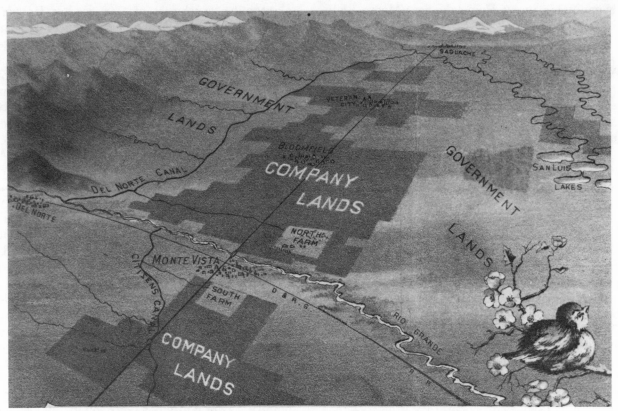

According to this map, T. C. Henry's agricultural projects would become the center of the universe, or of the San Luis Valley, at least.

Nevertheless, Monte Vista benefitted greatly by the undertakings of T. C. Henry, as it became headquarters for the larger part of the irrigated farmland in the region and became a prosperous agricultural center. During the first years of development a handful of small farm communities also appeared in the area. One of these was Parma, east of Monte Vista, with a post office in 1886, although its name changed to Liberty for one year in 1887. A short-lived colony called Rieckstadt was founded in 1885 by German Catholics about twenty miles northwest of Monte Vista.

As Monte Vista itself grew, the rather staid citizens rebuffed the sort of ruffians who set a lively pace in Del Norte and Alamosa during their early years. Monte Vista encouraged solid building—a three-story hotel, the Blanca, owned by the Hartford and Trust Company; a roller mill and an elevator; warehouses; a machine shop; creameries; banks; newspapers; a public library; six churches. The town also had electric lights and a Prohibition Club. A state experimental farm was located between Monte Vista and Del Norte in the early 1890s, and the State Soldiers' and Sailors' Home, now called the Colorado State Veterans' Center, was authorized in 1890 and began operation at Homelake near Monte Vista in 1893 or 1894.

Growth continued in the twentieth century. In 1915 a sugar beet factory was built in Monte Vista, and four years later the Sky-Hi Stampede presented its first rodeo, which became an annual event eagerly attended by the entire valley. But still, if anyone sold liquor anywhere in town, the deed to his property would be forfeited.

With the support of boosters and creditors in Alamosa, some of T. C. Henry's developments continued despite his setbacks elsewhere. Work in the Waverly district south of Alamosa proved unsuccessful, however, when irrigation caused seepage and alkaline residues. Thereafter the Henry operations concentrated on the Empire and Excelsior farms. Offices for their management were in Alamosa.

In response to promotions, settlers began to buy inexpensive land from the canal companies. Others took up government land through homesteading, pre-emption, or even by timber claims if the owner planted trees.

The first of the irrigation canals in this area was Henry's San Luis Valley Canal. Between 1886 and 1890 two cooperative projects—the Prairie Ditch and the Farmers' Union Canal—were constructed, bringing additional land under irrigation. In the meantime, many new arrivals struggled to start their farms without water.

McGinty, Streator, Goudy, and Coryell were the first communities north of Alamosa. Streator was assigned a post office in 1888, the name chosen by settlers who had come from Streator, Illinois. The designation changed to Mosca in 1890, when a vigorous campaign to develop the area began in the wake of the railroad extension from Villa Grove to Alamosa. The D&RG built a depot at Mosca, and large numbers of cattle and sheep from the area of Zapata and Medano were brought here to be shipped by freight.[21] It even was suggested that a railroad over Mosca Pass would transform Mosca into an important rail junction.

The Mosca Land and Farm Company boomed land sales and set up a tenant farm to attract labor with insufficient capital to buy their own land. By 1891 Mosca had the largest flour mill in the valley, two elevators, two lumberyards, two hotels, two blacksmiths, two barbers, two druggists, two churches, but only one saloon. The town's first newspaper, the *Herald*, was joined later by another, and both folded during the first decade of the 1900s.

Goudy was a nearby ranch community about eight miles southwest of Garrison, or Hooper. Goudy's name was changed to Garnett in 1888 when a post office opened. This postal service continued into the 1920s. At one time this hamlet boasted a school, the Hilltop, and a handful of crossroads businesses as well as a newspaper, the *Costilla News*, which was published at Garnett from 1888 until 1894 when it became Mosca's second journal.

Coryell was about five miles west of Mosca. A newspaper was published there for about a year. Apparently, an aspiring newspaperman with a case of lead type and a press existed for every new village with a promoter. And often the same man and press turned up in several different towns, in hopes that one of them would last. Coryell's name was changed to Stanley a few years later.

West of Coryell and Goudy was Lockett, while to the north of Hooper were La Garita station and Veteran. Veteran first had a post office in 1888. Several of the farmers around La Garita station and Veteran came from Michigan and Minnesota.

Of the numerous small towns in this vicinity Hooper proved to be most durable. This community was organized as Garrison in 1890, when Mosca also was being promoted. Besides Garrison and Howard's mercantile store, the town had

Although several other towns also had elevators and mills, Monte Vista became the agricultural center of the valley.

a branch of the Bank of Monte Vista, called the Bank of Garrison. The citizens supported a newspaper, a school, a Methodist church served by Mosca's preacher, but, like Monte Vista, no saloons were allowed. When the railroad built a siding, depot, and water tank fed by a large artesian well, the town's role as a shipping point for the surrounding agricultural area was assured.

The most productive acreage north of Alamosa at this time was in the region lying north and west of Garrison, the chief crop being wheat. In 1892 a flour mill was built, and a second joined it in a short time. Alamosa also milled flour from wheat grown around Garrison. Sun Light Flour was synonymous with Garrison.

This initial assurance of success was short-lived, for the financial panic of 1893 was disastrous not only to Colorado's mines but also to businesses indirectly dependent on them. Wheat prices dropped, and coincidentally a severe drought began. During this period of depression Garrison's bank failed, farmers gave up and left the area, and many of the small communities in the area disappeared.

However, encouraged by improved economic conditions and promises of advantageous rates from the railroad, the town of Garrison began a comeback in 1896. Signifying this fresh start, the town changed its name to Hooper. While its original newspaper remained and also began to serve the less fortunate town of Mosca, a second news sheet appeared in Hooper. Lodges were organized, and Hooper settled in for two more decades of prosperity before water again spelled its doom. Whereas the water problem in 1893 had been a shortage, now it was a surplus. The water table had been breaking through the valley floor in the Mosca-Hooper district for several years because of irrigation practices unsuited to land that had a high water table and no natural drainage. The procedure was to introduce enough irrigation water to raise the water table to a level where roots of crops could draw up water by capillary attraction. Although this method sounded good in theory, it also drew up salts that ruined the soil. By the middle of the second decade of the 1900s many acres had become either waterlogged or alkaline or both and had to be abandoned to

Hooper may not need Yellow Pages today, but it still has a town hall and a real park to serve its small population.

Above—In the 1890s Mosca had high hopes for the future, but drought and poor soil conditions caused the area's defeat as a farm center. *Denver Public Library, Western History Department photo.* Below—Hooper was a thriving business town as long as the railroad lasted, but removal of rail service on the Poncha Pass extension made milling and other farm-related enterprises unprofitable here.

greasewood and rabbitbrush. Many farmers had failed to survive the drought and low prices of the 1890s; now others departed and the few remaining communities in the area dwindled.

Between 1911 and 1921 several drainage systems were attempted, but these reclamation efforts resulted in damaged land elsewhere. In recent years a San Luis Closed Basin Water Project has been proposed to lower the water table in the area by pumping underground water into the Rio Grande. The goal of this controversial plan would be to restore the land in the sump to agricultural use while providing more water for irrigation downstream.

During the first few years after T. C. Henry entered the San Luis Valley, such problems were far from anyone's minds, and land under cultivation had doubled. Difficulties attending drought and seepage were already becoming apparent, however, when 350 Dutch immigrants, called the Holland American Land and Immigration Company, arrived to settle on land a few miles north of Alamosa in the winter of 1892-93. An agent had bought 15,000 acres from T. C. Henry, and two uncomfortable frame buildings had been built as temporary housing when the colonists arrived in Alamosa. Miserably cold and crowded, the immigrants came down with scarlet fever and diphtheria. Their plight captured the sympathy of Colorado's press, and the D&RG lent railroad cars for quarantine facilities during the emergency.

Even before this tragedy struck, the colony had felt that their new home was not going to be all that their agent had promised. The land company also was under public pressure to ensure the welfare of the group. As a result, land was offered on the South Platte River in northeastern Colorado, where many of the members of the colony settled, although a few remained in the valley, accepting other tracts of T. C. Henry's land in substitution for the original location.[22]

Farms in the Alamosa area were not alone in facing predicaments caused by water and difficult soil conditions during the 1890s. According to Colorado's system of prior appropriation, the valley's farms could use all the water they could get from canals tapping the Rio Grande. As cultivation in the valley increased, farmers in New Mexico, who also used water from the Rio Grande, were experiencing a shortage of water by 1890. When the drought of 1893 began, the riverbed at El Paso was dry, and the Juarez Valley suffered the loss of crops that usually were irrigated with Rio Grande water. Even farms in the San Luis Valley dried up as no water was available in any of the canals except the Rio Grande Canal, which took almost the entire flow.

Consequently, an International Boundary Commission met in 1896 to determine how in the future water could be distributed equitably to Colorado, New Mexico, Texas, and Mexico. Henceforth water of the Rio Grande was to be used in accord with controls agreed upon by this commission, and a series of dams were built in New Mexico by the United States for this allocation. Court battles continued for years afterward, and an embargo on building reservoirs and other diversion projects existed around the watershed of the Rio Grande until 1906.[23]

An alternative to diverting water through the canals was the drilling of artesian wells. The first of these in the San Luis Valley was at the Empire Farm in 1887, and within the next decade about three thousand were drilled. With the underflow at only one hundred to two hundred feet, such wells were inexpensive. Although some were used for irrigation, most provided domestic water supplies. Since 1950 a large number of wells have been drilled southwest of Alamosa, also. The San Luis Valley has capitalized on its being Colorado's major artesian basin.

Even in the case of artesian water, there can be too much of a good thing. When it was noticed that some of these wells gave off a gas, it was hoped that oil might be found beneath the valley floor, and an "oil well" was drilled near Hooper. All that came in was more water—in this instance, hot water. It eventually was used for a swimming pool.

Although the San Luis Valley has an annual precipitation of only eight to sixteen inches, an abundance of subsurface and spring water exists. Added to the thousands of artesian wells, several natural springs occur in the northern half of the valley where various cures once were promised to imbibers and bathers. Shaw's Magnetic Springs near Del Norte had marvelous qualities verified by a judge of the U.S. Circuit Court, a physician from New York, and Thomas M. Bowen himself. Numerous springs bubbled from volcanic formations around Saguache—Mishak Lakes, Russell Lakes, Hunt Springs, and O'Neil Hot Springs. Bathhouses were built for visitors at most of the hot springs. A resort called Chamberlin Springs became known later as either Valley View Hot Springs or Fairview Hot Springs, and what once was called San Luis Hot Springs may have become the latter-day Mineral Hot Springs.

With many streams flowing from the mountains that surround the north end of the valley, much of Saguache County employed irrigation

In the late 1800s and early 1900s thousands of wells were drilled in the San Luis Valley, Colorado's major artesian basin.

without using water from the Rio Grande, thereby avoiding some of the problems experienced elsewhere in the valley. Also, drainage was adequate. In this part of the valley Moffat was established during the boom that accompanied the extension of the D&RG. Its livelihood derived from shipping cattle and occasionally ore from the Crestone Estate, as the old Baca Grant was called now. Moffat also was a junction point for freight to the town of Saguache, which had been cut off from rail service. With a depot, three hotels, a large school, and a series of newspapers from 1891 until 1918, Moffat was a center for this area for several years. Its neighbors were Gibson, Dune, or La Garita to the south, Mirage to the north, and the mining camps around Crestone to the east.

In 1910 a short-lived land boom took place near La Garita station when the Oklahoma Land Company sponsored a promotion called the Oklahoma Lottery, foreshadowing other similar real estate ventures of recent years. Mineral Hot Springs also received attention from developers early in the twentieth century and attracted local postal service in 1911. This resort had a cottage camp and an enclosed pool. By 1948 activity had declined to a point that the post office was closed.

Saguache County enjoyed successful agriculture in the region of Saguache and Homan's Park despite the cooler climate experienced in this higher part of the valley. Because of its elevation the most successful products from this area were cattle, sheep, and hay. However, some vegetables were raised in the Kerber Creek area to sell in the mining camps around Bonanza during the boom years. As ranching became the dominant activity in northern Saguache County, most of the original homesteads were consolidated into large enough holdings to support grazing.

In the central part of the valley diversified farming was practiced after the devastating events of the 1890s. Large-scale cultivation of vegetables began in this area in the first decades of the twentieth century, and truck gardening developed around Center. Center, platted in 1898 as Center View, was organized by James L. Hurt, who had raised Percheron horses and Angus cattle in the region. A newspaper called the *Center Post* appeared, and the post office, previously called Centerview, changed its name to Center in 1899.

For the raising of vegetables a plentiful supply of labor was as vital as water. Around Center, Alamosa, Monte Vista, Del Norte, and Fort Garland farmers began to hire local Spanish-Americans and immigrants from Mexico for day laborers as the vegetable industry expanded. These workers built small adobe homes near the towns where they worked.[24]

Within a few years another group of "foreigners" arrived to farm in the southeastern part of the valley. In 1909 the Costilla Estate Development Company began to develop the high land around Culebra and Costilla creeks. Since this followed the moratorium of building water diversions, the company built Sanchez Reservoir and others to supplement Eastdale Reservoir and laid out the towns of San Acacio, Mesita, and Jarosa, using the names of earlier Mexican settlements.[25] Japanese farmers settled at San Acacio.

Before the Costilla Estate Development Company induced Japanese to farm in the area, the Seventh-Day Adventist Church was persuaded to establish a colony at Jarosa. They operated a cooperative farm and established in 1910 an academy specializing in agricultural training. A post office opened in 1911. Encouraged by the construction of the San Luis Valley Southern Railroad, business houses were erected in a solid, permanent fashion, but the town began to resemble a deserted village after the depression years of the 1930s.

Mesita, briefly called Hamburg by newcomers from a town of that name in Iowa, was north of Jarosa. It witnessed much activity on the part of the development company and had a depot for the railroad at one time, but today, as at Jarosa, most of its buildings, including its bank and school and stores, are empty.

Of these three towns San Acacio was the most promising. Here the Costilla Estate Development Company and the Sanchez Ditch and Reservoir Company located their offices, and a post office was established in 1909. In 1910 the San Luis Southern Railroad arrived, and a two-story depot and other facilities were constructed. To enable shipment of agricultural produce from San Acacio to Blanca and D&RG rails, a vegetable warehouse operated at San Acacio until about 1950. San Acacio also had a hotel (the Beaubien) and a bank.

Some residents in the region must have assumed that major amounts of cash passed through the bank, for it was robbed in 1922. The

Developers of the Costilla Estate could promise purchasers plenty of elbow room.

bandits, from Sunshine Valley in nearby northern New Mexico, carried off about $4,000, some of which they hid in an inner tube and the rest in a mitten. The sheriff of Costilla County, a well-known sheepshearer named J. C. Lobato, received a tip from a bootlegger about the whereabouts of the thieves and their loot. The money, minus only five dollars, which probably had been spent on bootlegged liquor, was restored to the bank.

During the 1920s the development company encouraged Japanese, who wished to emigrate from California because of adverse land laws there, to work the farms on the estate. Some came as tenant farmers, while others moved into a cooperative colony called Culebra Village. These Japanese perfected the practice of truck farming in the San Luis Valley. Among the vegetable crops cultivated was spinach, which proved so successful that the area became a major producer for the nation.

When World War II broke out and Japanese were forced to leave their homes on the West Coast, many settled in the San Luis Valley, where some had relatives in the neighborhood of San Acacio. Some of the newcomers occupied abandoned buildings at Eastdale and Waverly, but most settled around Blanca and Fort Garland.

Another relocation of farmers had occurred at Waverly in the late 1930s when the Farm Security Administration moved nearly one hundred families from eastern Colorado's dust bowl to Waverly southwest of Alamosa, where T. C. Henry's experiments had found the soil and drainage unsuitable for irrigated farming. The San Luis Valley Farmers' Project, as the federal program was called, provided farmers with eighty-acre tracts and small houses that could be leased with an option to buy. The plots quickly proved to be too small, and some were combined. When most of the farmers left, some of the buildings, including a community hall, were sold.

Blanca at the north end of the San Luis Southern Railroad got off to a spectacular start in 1908 as part of a land developer's scheme, drawing hundreds of people who camped out in the area to await a lottery. An earlier Blanca at the western foot of Blanca Peak had been the location of a post office in the 1890s, but that hamlet was long forgotten when the sweepstakes took place at new Blanca. Purchasers of five-acre tracts took a chance on winning larger pieces of land. Those who lost quickly learned that they could grow nothing on five acres, especially when water rights were unavailable. Nevertheless, the town itself took root, largely because of railroad facilities, including a shop. Blanca soon had a hotel,

newspaper, churches, and a school, although Blanca's school now is consolidated with Fort Garland's and the hotel and newspaper are defunct. Nevertheless, Blanca remains an important shipping point for vegetables which are grown in the vicinity and for volcanic scoria which is mined at Mesita.

During the 1920s the vegetable industry expanded from its original centers in Alamosa and Costilla counties to Rio Grande and Saguache counties. Lettuce, spinach, peas, and cauliflower were important vegetable crops being shipped from the valley, while barley, beans, oats, and hay also were produced extensively. In recent years Rio Grande County has grown more potatoes than any other county in Colorado, and Alamosa and Saguache counties are not far behind Rio Grande's output.

A few years after DeWitt C. Travis raised the first commercial crop of potatoes in the valley, other farmers in Saguache and Rio Grande counties began to produce them for resale in Leadville and in other mining centers. In 1886 a Del Norte farmer, Peter Barkley, planted a crop of Barkley's Prolifics, which he started from six tubers obtained in Canada. From this variety Brown Beauty potatoes were developed, and these became the type most commonly grown in the valley for several years. When the Travelers' Insurance Company farms seeded vast numbers of acres with Brown Beauties, their fame was assured, although they were not grown outside the San Luis Valley, strangely enough.[26] In 1925 a bumper crop yielded more than seven thousand carloads of potatoes.[27] By the 1930s Brown Beauties were being replaced by Red McClures as the principal variety.

Production and shipping were managed efficiently by the growers who organized into four local cooperative units with one selling agency, later called the Colorado Potato Growers' Exchange when it grew to include other agricultural areas of the state. This exchange also incorporated a warehousing cooperative for grading and packing. In the San Luis Valley early warehouses were located at Del Norte, Center, Monte Vista, Hooper, and La Jara. Recently Monte Vista has been chosen the location of a large processing plant for conversion to frozen food products.

During the early years of rural settlement in the San Luis Valley, schooling presented handicaps for children in small villages and on farms. One-room schoolhouses appeared on many ranches, where a teacher was hired by a group of neighbors to educate their offspring. Sometimes

When the valley produced a bumper crop of potatoes, bumper-to-bumper wagons created a traffic jam in Monte Vista, beside the L. L. Fassett store.

The schoolhouse at Estrella proudly wore a star, as well as the Stars and Stripes.

in small towns, as in Hooper for example, school met in an empty room in a business building. Teachers themselves often had little more than an eighth-grade education. In order to upgrade the quality of instruction, teachers' institutes were held in various towns such as Antonito and Monte Vista, and trainees had to pass a teachers' examination to become certified.

As rural schools struggled to provide opportunities comparable to those routinely offered in large school systems, the advantages of consolidation of schools became apparent. The advent of motor transportation made this transition practical. In 1914 the districts near La Jara consolidated, and others followed at Hooper, Center, Del Norte, and Monte Vista. More than four hundred inadequate school buildings were abandoned as pupils arrived at their new schools by free auto bus, although a few horse-drawn vehicles helped out for several years. For the first time many young people in these districts had the opportunity of four-year high school educations.

The most remarkable example of this new trend in public education occurred at Sargent in 1918. Between Center and Monte Vista, the Sargent Consolidated School was built where there had been only a one-room schoolhouse previously.[28] As part of this project homes for teachers and a community center were constructed. Even religious activities were integrated in the all-inclusive undertaking, which attracted the attention of educators not only in Colorado but elsewhere as a model for rural schools. As consolidation of schools has gone on, the location of the Sargent school in open country has been typical of recent districts, but the attempt to provide everything from homes to churches has been dropped. The Sargent district itself encountered some public disapproval of this omnifariousness.

A progressive outlook on education, exemplified by consolidation in the second decade of the 1900s, took on another dimension when the Adams State Normal School, now known as Adams State College, opened in Alamosa in 1921. Billy Adams, himself the product of an eighth-grade education, had introduced a bill in the state legislature as early as 1893 to have a teacher's training school located in the valley. For more than a half-century the college has provided an immeasurable service to the San Luis Valley.

Despite several ruinous setbacks agriculture became established as the principal industry of the San Luis Valley through the tenacity and courage of hundreds of rural settlers from all parts of the United States and from many foreign lands as well. Through their homes, towns, churches, and schools these newcomers transformed the face of the valley and many of the habits of the valley, and with these people the valley crossed the threshold from pioneer life to modern life. If the people of Manassa were "strong on religion," so too were they strong on education and other cultural values characteristic of agricultural communities at the turn of the century. And so too were their neighbors in scores of other towns of the San Luis Valley.

La Garita once was the headquarters for a large Catholic mission, and a convent was built of adobe brick near the church. This photograph shows the second church at the site, and this one is now deserted.

XVI

"They Do It In Good Faith"

It was only a short time that the Spanish-speaking people had lived in the valley before intermingling with the cultures of the newcomers took place. Perhaps that brevity is one reason why the resulting changes were so disastrous for the earlier colonizers—not because roots had sunk so deeply already but because they had such a tenuous hold.

When the Spanish-speaking settlers came from New Mexico, they gave the names of their old homes to the new land, and they lived in the traditional ways of their old homes. These links with the past were a necessary formula for life, and the formula was changed when cultures in the valley collided.

Most, though not all, of the Spanish-speaking people still were poor and functioned in habits which would keep them poor, especially in competition with more progressive agricultural and commercial techniques. For example, the Spanish-speaking farmers still tilled their small plots with oxen and sharpened sticks as plows, cut their crops by hand, and ground much of their grain with stone *manos* and *metates*. Although some early visitors to the settlements thought the peasants charmingly quaint and happy-go-lucky, their economic and cultural survival was doomed to a heartbreaking struggle.

Not only did the Mexican settlers differ from the newcomers in their agriculture, but they also had a different church, which divided the Protestant emigrants sharply against the old settlers. In the Conejos area the Catholic Church had become even more strongly entrenched when in 1871 the energetic, black-robed Jesuits assumed responsibilities previously carried out by brown-robed Franciscans.

Until then schools had been almost nonexistent among Spanish-speaking Catholics, for education was a luxury enjoyed by a privileged minority of well-to-do families who could afford to hire a teacher for their own children or for a small group of families. In 1875 Catholics around Conejos requested the Jesuits to provide a school. In response, the Sisters of Loretto arrived in 1877. Each *placita* participating in the system contributed to the cost of building an adobe convent and school at Conejos. Two separate programs were initiated, first one for girls followed by another for boys.[1]

These parochial schools were handicapped by the poverty of the people who supported them and by divisions within the church due to restrictions against Penitentes. In the 1930s economic conditions forced the closing of Antonito's schools, but in 1934 Benedictine sisters assumed teaching in Antonito, where they continued until the 1970s, when widely publicized complaints changed the school system's employment practices. Ironically in this age when women have rebelled against unfair unemployment practices, a male applicant at Antonito charged that the district discriminated against him on the basis of sex and religion.[2]

Until the turn of the century the Jesuits were confronted with the spiritual waywardness of the numerous Penitentes in the area. Father Salvatore Personé, one of the first Jesuit missionaries at Conejos, attempted to overcome the appeal of the Penitentes by providing more magnificent religious activities, but the Penitentes continued stubbornly in their habitual, rigorous customs. Of their extreme acts of penance Father Personé wrote: "Some of them count on buying heaven with such indiscretions, and maybe they do, because they do it in good faith. The chiefs do it for political reasons. They use these simple brethren for their votes in the elections."[3] The political power of the brotherhood was a reality, for two-thirds of the Spanish-speaking men in the valley were Penitentes at that time. Lafayette Head himself, "father" of Conejos and first lieutenant governor of the State of Colorado, was a member of the brotherhood.

The official position of the church regarding "these simple brethren" was more stern than Father Personé's words imply, and the sacraments and other benefits of the church were denied Penitentes. Such restrictions were slow to erode the strength of the brotherhood, however. As evidence of their lingering activity in the 1900s, craftsmen around Mogote and San Rafael, where Penitente activity was strong, continued to carve their religious sculptures, called *santos*, until recent years.

Protestants also were concerned about the salvation of Catholics in general and Penitentes in particular. In 1876 a Presbyterian church, which became the Antonito congregation, was organized. Later another Presbyterian church was built at Mogote. This church, which was served by a Spanish-speaking graduate of the seminary at Del Norte, became an influential Protestant center in this predominantly Catholic part of the valley. An important part of its program was a mission school where English was taught. Meanwhile, the Reverend Alexander Darley was conducting a relentless crusade against the Penitentes and wrote volatile tracts denouncing their excesses.[4]

In the long run, religious contests had less impact on the way of life than did the transfer of land into the hands of newcomers north and east of Conejos. A wholesale loss of real estate, with far-reaching implications for the county's treasury, occurred when Archuleta County was created in the 1880s, eliminating Conejos County's jurisdiction west of the Continental Divide. That the Conejos County courthouse was built as solidly as it was in 1893 was due to the arrival of the railroad and of Anglo-owned enterprises in the county.

The presence of the railroad encouraged not only the development of Anglo cattle ranches in the county but also the expansion of Mexican sheep raising. Sheep traditionally belonged to the Spanish-speaking population, and sheep outnumbered cattle in Conejos County for many years. Most farmers had small flocks that grazed around the plaza of Lado or San Rafael and other villages near Conejos. In the foothills to the west were found the large flocks, and Mogote and nearby Las Mesitas prided themselves as the homes of several respected *borregeros*, the sheepherders.

The valley southwest of Antonito also became a major sheep-raising area. In this pocket are the villages of San Antonio and Ortiz. Ortiz, one of the most prosperous Spanish-speaking communities, got its start when a veteran of the Civil War, José Maria Casias, took up a homestead there. In the early 1870s Nestor Ortiz joined him at this location, opened a store, and became a wool broker for his neighbors.[5] For an avocation he took up silversmithing. When a post office opened in 1885 in Ortiz's store, the name of the community was established officially. Both Baptist and Presbyterian mission schools functioned in Ortiz in the early 1900s but soon succumbed to financial problems that afflicted other schools in Ortiz.

The railroad facilitated shipment of wool and animals to market in Denver and, thus, encouraged the development of sheep production into a major industry. Osier, where the Cumbres Pass line had a station on Los Pinos Creek, became an important shipping point, but Antonito was the principal shipping center for the county.

Originally the sheep raised were a mixed breed called Navajos, with comparatively poor wool and meat. These sold for about a dollar a head. As Merino and Cotswold rams were introduced to improve the stock during the 1880s, the price per head doubled. These improved sheep produced wool that was shipped chiefly to mills on the East Coast.[6]

Although some of the biggest sheep growers were Spanish-speaking ranchers, many smaller owners lost their flocks when they accepted financial assistance they could not repay. Some of these unsuccessful people then worked as sheepherders for bigger operations. A system that encouraged the growth of the industry on the one hand but the economic failure of small operators on the other hand was the *partido* system, a method common in northern New Mexico and the San Luis Valley at that time.[7] A sheepherder could borrow ewes from a flock with no initial cost, but he was obligated to reimburse the owner with one-fourth of his spring lambs and one-fourth of the wool sheared. If the yield was poor, he could not survive financially. Then taxes or bank loans might become delinquent, too.

Two non-Spanish enterprises in Antonito—the Jordan Sheep Company and Warshauer-McClure—became the major dealers in wool and sheep in Conejos County. Fred Warshauer, who also was a banker, built a fortune with high interest rates at his bank and skillful use of the *partido* system.[8] A Polish immigrant who arrived in the valley in the 1880s, Warshauer was a wealthy man by the early 1900s. After his home burned in 1911, he built an elegant house with murals, fine woodwork, and expensive furniture. This showpiece of Antonito, which later became a restaurant, was scarcely finished when the price of sheep dropped, in 1913, and Warshauer committed suicide. The home was occupied by his family for several years and later belonged to a Catholic order.

Warshauer's family still has ties in Conejos County through his nieces, the Menke sisters. After a career as a traveling vaudeville team, the popular song-and-dance trio returned to Conejos County where they operated a mountain lodge and ran an abstract business.[9]

In the neighborhood of Capulin north of Antonito, sheep were introduced by the original Mexican settlers in the late 1860s. When Anglo ranchers entered the Strip in the next decade, cattle took over most of the land east of Capulin. Although Capulin survived and even had a post office beginning in 1881, many Spanish-speaking families between Capulin and Del Norte lost their land. They formed the nucleus of a group of settlers on Ramon Creek northwest of Del Norte. When some of these people failed to establish their own farms again, they took jobs on Anglo ranches.[10]

Despite the failure of some Spanish-speaking settlers, others amassed much land and great flocks of sheep and enjoyed the privileges of *ricos*. The Montoya family, for example, settled on Los Pinos Creek near the later site of Del Norte in the 1860s, bringing with them the usual flock of sheep. One member of this family, Luis Montoya, wandered around the West for several years, working as a buffalo hunter, interpreter, and freighter before he was persuaded to move to Los Pinos Creek to settle down. Only two miles east of his farm Del Norte was booming by then. Within a few years Luis Montoya built up his livestock interests to fifteen thousand head of sheep, and he was the leading sheepman in southern Colorado, although his own ranch consisted of only 360 acres.

In Saguache County, also, sheep were an important asset to Spanish-speaking ranchers. When Susano Trujillo and Domacio Espinoza settled on La Garita Creek in 1858, they had about three thousand sheep with them. Their flocks grazed in the nearby foothills, with the lower land reserved for farming and other livestock.[11]

When Mark Biedell took up land on the lower part of the creek, he too raised sheep, and it was one of his sheepherders who showed Biedell the unusual rocks north of La Garita that started the mining activity there. The sheepherder himself got a team and wagon and a little cash from his boss as a reward.

So many Catholics were in the area around La Garita and Carnero creeks by the 1870s that the Jesuits at Conejos decided to establish a separate parish with headquarters at La Garita, although the parish was called Carnero. Catholics already had been meeting in homes, and the Penitentes had an active morada in La Garita Canyon. In succession other moradas were built around La Garita, and the last one still is standing. In 1879 the Church of St. John the Baptist was built about a mile north of the old town of La Garita at the mouth of the canyon. Nuns lived in an adobe convent just east of the church and were responsible for religious instruction. This parish covered a wide area, north to Bonanza and Villa Grove, east to Cotton Creek, south to Monte Vista, and west to include the entire San Juan mining country. In 1889 the headquarters for this mission moved to Del Norte.[12]

The original church building burned and was replaced in the 1920s by another structure that served the area until the 1960s when pastoral duties were transferred to Center. The La Garita church property, now decaying, belongs to descendants of donors of the land where the church was built.[13] In the cemetery between the church and the present town of La Garita are the broken headstones and crucifixes where the pioneers of this district are buried. Today no records are kept, but the cemetery, overgrown with cacti and weeds, still is used. A bouquet of plastic roses or a religious picture framed in tin is the token left at a grave to signify that the past is honored, nonetheless.

Originally La Garita's school met at the Torrez Trading Post at the mouth of the canyon. Later schools were located in both La Garita and Carnero canyons. A grade school was built in the present town of La Garita nearby in 1932, but this district has been consolidated with Center.

In addition to farming and ranching, the people of this area supplemented their income with timber cutting. Over the years their wagon wheels wore deep ruts in the limestone of the hills west of town, as they hauled out firewood and railroad ties. A sawmill operated here for a while, also.

At both La Garita and Carnero post offices operated from the 1870s into the 1890s. Also, a

West of the Anglo ranches on the Strip, Spanish-speaking Capulin supports an active church and parochial schooling for local children. Capulin's handsome stone church was built in 1912.

A sweeping view of the San Luis Valley and the distant peaks of the Sangre de Cristo Mountains is enjoyed from the hills behind La Garita, where the Indians had a lookout.

post office served Los Mogotes on Carnero Creek in the 1880s. A town called Plaza appears on some maps of the old stage road between Saguache and Del Norte, and this designation may have referred to La Garita.

During these active decades in the district the interests of Trujillo and Espinoza were growing. Their bookkeeper, José Adolpho White, eventually became a full partner. In the 1890s he established ranches on La Garita Creek and in Carnero Canyon and built up his sheep to three thousand head. He was a stockholder in the Bank of Del Norte and was president of the La Garita school board.[14]

Building up a successful sheep operation was not without obstacles. As early as the 1880s range disputes were occurring in the San Luis Valley, and local enmity between sheep and cattle raisers was typical of other areas of the old West. In an attempt to compromise their differences, the ranchers on the west side of the valley agreed to partition the range for grazing. Sheep were allowed between Saguache and La Garita creeks with cattle south of this range to the Rio Grande. Between the Rio Grande and San Francisco Creek sheep were permitted, while cattlemen used the land between San Francisco and Rock creeks. In Del Norte during the fall shipping season, cowboys used one street while sheepherders used another to drive their livestock to the railroad yard.

At first sheep grazed in the high mountains without much competition, but by 1900 these ranges were becoming overgrazed. Also, as cattle were driven to summer pastures in the mountains by the turn of the century, conflicts between Anglo cattlemen and Mexican sheepmen became serious. From time to time there were beatings and murders or the scattering of livestock.

In order to protect timber and watersheds in the public domain and to control their use, Congress authorized the creation of timber reserves in the 1890s. One of these, established in

1905, was the Cochetopa Timber Reserve. In 1907 timber reserves became national forests when Congress changed the terminology of the program and its responsibilities. At this time Rio Grande, Cochetopa, and San Isabel National Forests were among the areas around the San Luis Valley so designated. Because of its extensive use for grazing, Rio Grande National Forest figured prominently in the establishment of practicable management of grazing rights.

When the new forest supervisor called the opposing ranchers together, the meeting nearly degenerated into a physical battle between the two factions. Eventually it was agreed that sheep would be confined to the high pastures in the forest while cattle would use lower ones.[15] Until the mid-thirties owners simply respected each other's areas without further regulation. Since then stricter management practices have been in effect. Great bands of stock used the driveways through the forest to specified areas, where owners leased permits for summer grazing. As herders passed a gate at the foot of a driveway, they paid five to six cents per head for sheep or thirty-five cents per head for cattle and were assigned an area for grazing. At one time 100,000 sheep used La Garita Driveway alone. This route gave access to La Garita Mountains around Wheeler Geologic Area. From there a continuation of the trail led to Creede, Lake City, and the Silverton region.[16] Offices for the supervision of Rio Grande National Forest are at Monte Vista, while ranger stations are located at Del Norte, Alamosa, La Jara, and Saguache.

In Costilla County, where the livestock industry was of less economic importance than in Conejos, Rio Grande, or Saguache counties, a few ranchers assembled large tracts of land and herds of livestock. Cristoval Lobato of San Pablo, became a wealthy sheepman with a large home that had a big *sala* for entertaining and carpets on the floors. When he died he was buried near the altar of his church, an honor accorded generous patrons of Catholic churches. Another of the valley's important sheepmen was from the Garcia family of Plaza de Los Manzanares. When the name of the plaza was changed to Garcia, the designation honored this prosperous rancher. Sheep belonging to him grazed as far away as Nevada.

J. C. Lobato, later the intrepid sheriff of Costilla County, was one of Garcia's sheepshearers in Nevada before he moved to the San Luis Valley, where he continued to shear. This skill required stamina and speed, and Lobato calculated that he usually sheared 115 to 120 sheep per day, or 139,708 in his 42 years as a shearer. His prowess with clippers, combined with his leadership with shearers, resulted in his becoming captain of a crew of shearers. As he commented, a lot of them were just "wool trompers." According to his analysis, wool trompers could "shear sheep because they have a grip, but they do not know how to fix the sheep shears."[17]

Although the old Plaza de Los Manzanares was closely linked with the town of Costilla, where a post office and a store and the Catholic Church were located, the smaller village had an independent character. They had their own flour mill, built by Pedro Manzanares, and the Penitentes maintained an active morada. In the 1880s the Methodist Church opened a mission, and the pastor, a converted Catholic priest, taught a night school for adults. A public school for the children of Plaza de Los Manzanares had met in the 1870s, too.[18] Encouraged by these signs of enlightenment, the Presbyterians opened a church, also. Nevertheless, to the outsider today the plaza known as Garcia seems as thoroughly Spanish-oriented as any land-grant plaza. The slight realignment of the state line in 1925 that placed Costilla in New Mexico but Garcia in Colorado seems inconsequential.

Retarding the changes that would have accompanied an acceleration of settlement on the old Sangre de Cristo Grant was the question of valid land titles. The machinations of William Gilpin and the United States Freehold Land and Emigration Company scarcely had altered the mode of day-to-day life in southern Costilla County. True, the shelves of the Salazar store were stocked with all sorts of things that Dario Gallegos only dreamed of—shoes for men, ladies, or children; shawls and corsets and bustles; kettles; saddles; gunpowder; Arbuckles coffee as well as green coffee; whiskey or wine; sheep shears or sheepskins. Salazar even dealt in sheep and steers and land. San Luis had matured a bit, but it had not changed.

An evidence of reluctance to alter the traditional ways was the absence of schools. Although the Church of Most Precious Blood, a stone structure now used for the Jaquez grocery store, was built in the 1860s, a parochial school did not open until 1909, in contrast to the earlier school at Conejos.[19] Instead, at San Luis education remained the privilege of a few well-to-do families. Exceptions were day schools organized in San Luis and San Pablo through Presbyterian missions in 1889.[20] Until 1955 the only high school in the area was Mercy Academy at San Luis. Since then Centennial Union High School has served the southern half of the county. A two-year college program and a four-year vocational school called the San Luis Institute of Arts and Crafts also operated in the 1930s and 1940s at San Luis.

Politics in Costilla County also reflected fixed traditions. While Anglo miners and farmers were settling elsewhere in the valley and voicing their political sentiments, Costilla County remained almost solidly Spanish-speaking Republican. A conspicuous exception was William Meyer of Zapata and Fort Garland who took over as head of the party in the county. When the small courthouse was built in 1883 in San Luis, it was considered adequate for the times. Later as the county's potential for growth dwindled and part of the county's jurisdiction was lost to Alamosa County, the same small courthouse continued to serve Costilla County's offices.

Toward the end of the nineteenth century a few newcomers settled but scarcely altered the character of the county. A Frenchman, Armand Choury, who had been working around Medano Creek moved to San Luis and became the postmaster, bookkeeper, surveyor, and, eventually, teacher and superintendent of schools. Two Anglo veterans of the Civil War set up a sawmill at El Puertecito between San Luis and Vallejos. Louis Cohn, a stalwart Democrat, had his store in San Luis. To the north were Fort Garland for a few declining years and the railroad, and to the southwest were the Mormons at Eastdale. These were a minority, however, and little intermingling of cultures occurred around San Luis.

Juniper smoke curling from the chimneys of Chama, Los Fuertos, San Pedro, San Pablo, or San Francisco, then as now, told the visitor that he was in Mexican country. La Valley and San Pablo may have had United States post offices by the turn of the century, but most of the letters posted there would have been written in Spanish, and a Catholic layman in any of the villages was as likely to meet at a morada as at a church. On an autumn day in Costilla County, with a trickle of water gurgling through an irrigation ditch and cottonwood leaves rattling overhead, it is easy to recall that less than a century and a half ago this area was settled as a Mexican land grant.

A small adobe building in San Luis, Chama, Costilla, or Capulin, or a white-washed structure in Antonito may catch the eye with its bold letters "S.P.M.D.T.U." These buildings belong to the *Sociedad Proteccion Muta de Trabajadores Unidas*, Society for the Mutual Protection of United Workers, organized in Antonito in 1900 and which came to include more than one thousand members, most of whom were from the southern part of the valley. Although this fraternal organization has benevolent and social functions, too, it provides direct benefits to its members through an insurance program. Yet, the primary motivation of this group when it first met was to develop a cohesive organization to voice resistance to discrimination that already was being experienced by Spanish-speaking workers in the valley.

At that time inequity in opportunities was becoming recognized. No public high schools existed yet for Spanish-speaking residents, and in some towns such as Del Norte segregation existed between English- and Spanish-speaking pupils. These conditions can be explained in part by the desire of many Catholic families to send their children to parochial school, and as late as 1949 the Benedictine Sisters opened a new school in Monte Vista. Health-care facilities for the Spanish-speaking people of the family also were scarce or nonexistent, although the United Presbyterian Church supports a health center at San Luis, the only clinic in the entire county.

One might argue that Costilla County needs few schools and doctors since its population has dropped to about three thousand, but the citizens who remain need more help, not less. More than four-fifths of the county's residents have poverty-level incomes, and seventy percent of the male population are unemployed. Similarly, in Conejos County ninety percent of the people receive welfare assistance.

In 1973 Costilla County expressed its wish, more or less facetiously, to secede from Colorado and to re-establish its ties with New Mexico. The legislature in Santa Fe, enjoying the compliment, said that both Costilla and Conejos counties would be welcome. The governor in Denver merely replied, "The best is yet to come."[21] Probably the people in the southern end of the valley agreed, for things could scarcely get worse.

In the central portion of the San Luis Valley a different set of circumstances has influenced the malcontent of the Spanish-speaking people. Here most came to the valley not as colonizers of land grants but as more recent migrants from Mexico, California, or Denver. These are the people who call themselves Chicanos. Many are products of mixed blood and impoverished backgrounds. As the number of Mexicans crossing the border increased in the early twentieth century, their arrival was greeted as a qualified blessing that offered cheap labor in the fields but, too often, hostility among local residents.

Around Monte Vista, Center, and Alamosa, many Chicanos found jobs where vegetables,

The tradition of manufacturing adobe bricks is encouraged at San Luis through a project sponsored by the Office of Economic Opportunity.

which require a large labor force, were being raised. Whereas many Japanese who took similar work in the valley became independent farmers, the Chicanos were less apt to break out of their role of farm laborers. This economically and socially oppressed group constitutes a somewhat homogeneous unit that has organized in the valley, the state, and the nation to voice its own needs, hopes, and protests. Instead of petitioning the legislature to secede from the state, these Spanish-speaking people of the valley carry placards and shout slogans. *"Viva La Huelda!"* "Long live the strike!"

It may seem a long time ago that the Chicanos' predecessors, the land-grant colonizers, came to the San Luis Valley. Yet, it was only yesterday compared to the times when Utes, Navajos, and their ancient precursors roamed the valley. Even allowed centuries, no person or group or nation can hope to win, finally and irrevocably, the endless cycle of struggle to dominate land and goods. Nor is there any consolation for those who lose what once was theirs. If there is hope, it lies in the quality of the people who find themselves, by choice or not, sharing a place for their brief moment in history.

As Thornton Wilder wrote in *The Bridge of San Luis Rey:* "We do what we can. It isn't for long, you know. Time keeps going by. You'll be surprised at the way time passes."

The six-armed cross of La Garita.

Epilogue

The Six-Armed Cross

On the deserted church at La Garita is a cross. This is not the usual religious emblem with arms pointing in only two directions from the central support. The cross at La Garita has two additional horizontal arms, set at right angles to the others, so that one sees a complete cross from any side of the structure.

One wooden arm extends toward the hazy hills and mountain passes beyond Saguache. Another points across the broken churchyard fence to the neglected cemetery and the Sangre de Cristos, shimmering far across the valley. Southward pastures and potato fields are sighing in the wind. Behind the church rise La Garita Mountains and the trails of ill-fated explorers and solitary sheepherders. Upward the main staff beckons toward the impalpable, blue, Colorado sky, and downward it clings to the crumbling belfry and the alluvium of eroded earth.

This six-armed cross seems symbolic of a concept of place which is not indicated by the traditional points of the compass but which is all-embracing. Like the Indian concept of space, which is unconfined and limitless, a place is neither two- nor three-dimensional but four.

At what particular moment and at what particular spot did this valley and its story begin? When and where will it cease? Perhaps there is no beginning and no ending but a continuum of time and place to which all life belongs. In this valley finite concepts of time and place seem inadequate. The most recent occupant is brother of the earliest, and unknown feet will walk within the changing valley tomorrow.

157

Endnotes

Chapter I

1. Zebulon Montgomery Pike, *The Southwestern Expedition of Zebulon M. Pike,* ed. Milo Milton Quaife (Chicago: Lakeside Press, 1925), pp. 109-12. These excerpts from the journal were written from January 27 through February 5, 1807.

2. Estimates of the valley's size vary because of physiographic irregularities. The smallest estimate is 90-by-65 miles; George P. Merk, "Great Sand Dunes of Colorado," in Robert J. Weimer and John D. Haun, eds., *Guide to the Geology of Colorado* (Denver: Rocky Mountain Association of Geologists, 1960), p. 127. An estimate of 150-by-50 miles is given by J. E. Upson, "Physiographic Subdivisions of the San Luis Valley, Southern Colorado," in H. L. James, ed., *Guidebook of the Rio Grande Basin, Colorado* (N.p.: New Mexico Geological Society, 1971), p. 113; first published in *Journal of Geology,* 47 (1939): 721-36. An estimate of 100-by-65 miles is given by David William Lantis, "The San Luis Valley, Colorado: Sequent Rural Occupance in an Intermontane Basin" (Ph.D. dissertation, Ohio State University, 1950), p. 4. The greatest difference is caused by Upson's inclusion of an area of northern New Mexico. Merk and Lantis include the extension along the Rio Grande west to South Fork.

3. The Cochetopa Hills have been called the Saguache Mountains and the Sierra Mimbres.

4. The Taos Plateau south of the Colorado state line is the fifth division of the San Luis Valley in Upson, "Physiographic Subdivisions."

5. An area comprising fifty-seven square miles was set aside by presidential proclamation on March 17, 1932, as Great Sand Dunes National Monument, administered by the National Park Service. The dunes are described as the "highest piled inland sand dunes in the United States."

6. Ross B. Johnson, "The Great Sand Dunes of Southern Colorado," in *Geological Survey Research, 1967,* U.S. Geological Survey Professional Paper 575-C (Washington, D.C.: Government Printing Office, 1967), pp. 177-78.

7. Further information is found in Upson, "Physiographic Subdivisions," and in Esper S. Larsen, Jr., and Whitman Cross, *Geology and Petrology of the San Juan Region, Southwestern Colorado,* U.S. Geological Survey Professional Paper 258 (Washington, D.C.: Government Printing Office, 1956), p. 88.

8. Upson, "Physiographic Subdivisions," and W. W. Atwood and K. F. Mather, *Physiography and Quaternary Geology of the San Juan Mountains, Colorado,* U.S. Geological Survey Professional Paper 166 (Washington, D.C.: Government Printing Office, 1932), pp. 23, 25, 99.

9. Thomas A. Steven, *Critical Review of the San Juan Peneplain, Southwestern Colorado,* U.S. Geological Survey Professional Paper 594-I (Washington, D.C.: Government Printing Office, 1968), p. 14.

10. The Rio Grande's original course was west of its present channel in the valley. The stream has moved in a southeasterly direction as it forced its way through the San Luis Hills. This cut through hard, volcanic material is said to have drained a saline lake from the center of the valley, a residuum of an ancient sea, but this theory is open to argument.

11. C. E. Siebenthal, *Geology and Water Resources of the San Luis Valley, Colorado,* U.S. Geological Survey Water-Supply Paper 240 (Washington, D.C.: Government Printing Office, 1910), pp. 54-55; William J. Powell, *Ground-Water Resources of the San Luis Valley, Colorado,* U.S. Geological Survey Water-Supply Paper 1379 (Washington, D.C.: Government Printing Office, 1958), pp. 1-27.

Chapter II

1. Ruth M. Underhill, *Red Man's Religion: Beliefs and Practices of the Indians North of Mexico* (Chicago: University of Chicago Press, 1965), pp. 30-39, 205.

2. Edgar L. Hewett and Bertha P. Dutton, *The Pueblo Indian World: Studies on the Natural History of the Rio Grande Valley in Relation to Pueblo Indian Culture* (Albuquerque: University of New Mexico and the School of American Research, 1945), pp. 23-24.

3. Ruth M. Underhill, *The Navajos* (Norman: University of Oklahoma Press, 1956), pp. 19-20.

4. C. T. Hurst, "A Folsom Location in the San Luis Valley, Colorado," *Southwestern Lore,* 7 (1941): 31-34; H. H. Wormington, *Ancient Man in North America* (4th ed.; Denver: Museum of Natural History, 1957), pp. 29-30; Frank H. H. Roberts, Jr., "Prehistoric Peoples of Colorado," *The Colorado Magazine,* 23 (1946): 145.

5. E. B. Renaud, "Prehistory of the San Luis Valley," *The Colorado Magazine,* 20 (1943): 51-52; Dorothy D. Wilson, "They Came to Hunt," *San Luis Valley Historian,* 3, no. 3 (1971): 12-13.

6. E. B. Renaud, "The Rio Grande Points," *Southwestern Lore,* 8 (1942): 33-36.

7. E. B. Renaud, *Archaeology of the Upper Rio Grande Basin in Southern Colorado and Northern New Mexico,* University of Denver Archaeological Series, Paper No. 6 (Denver: University of Denver, 1946), pp. 27-42.

8. Ibid., p. 43.

9. Wilson, "They Came to Hunt," p. 13.

10. Frank H. H. Roberts, Jr., "Prehistoric Peoples," in LeRoy R. Hafen, ed., *Colorado and Its People,* 4 vols. (New York: Lewis Publishing Co., Inc., 1948), 2:51.

11. Renaud, "Prehistory of the San Luis Valley," pp. 52-53. Mrs. F. W. Boyd of Saguache and Jack Nelson of Monte Vista are credited with finding most of these sites. On the authority of Henry P. Mera, Renaud stated in this article that pottery sherds recovered at these sites were of Pueblo origin. Earlier, however, Dr. Mera said that the pottery was not Pueblo but that it represented some other intrusion from the south, in E. B. Renaud, *Indian Stone Enclosures of Colorado and New Mexico,* University of Denver Archaeological Series, Paper No. 2 (Denver: University of Denver, 1942), p. 28. Renaud found this type of enclosure to be comparable with others discovered in the Arkansas River area of southeastern Colorado and Fountain Creek near Pueblo, Colorado.

12. Garrick Mallery, *Picture-Writing of the American Indians* (1893; New York: Dover Publications, Inc., 1972), 1:72, quoting E. L. Berthoud. *See also* Jean Allard Jeancon, "Pictographs of Colorado," *The Colorado Magazine,* 3 (1926):38-40.

13. Alfred J. Pearsall, "Evidence of Pueblo Culture in the San Luis Valley," *Southwestern Lore,* 5 (1939):7-9.

14. James Rose Harvey and Mrs. James Rose Harvey, "Turquoise among the Indians and a Colorado Turquoise Mine," *The Colorado Magazine,* 15 (1938):187, 188.

15. In 1936 W. L. King of Manassa donated relics to the State Historical Society of Colorado; *see* Acquisition No. 07388.17. Prehistoric tools were found in a trench 15 feet deep and 300 feet long.

16. Jean Allard Jeancon, *Archaeological Research in the Northeastern San Juan Basin of Colorado,* ed. Frank H. H. Roberts (Denver: State Historical and Natural History Society of Colorado and the University of Denver, 1922), p. 30.

17. Sydney H. Ball, *Mining of Gems and Ornamental Stones by American Indians,* Bureau of American Ethnology, Anthropological Paper No. 128 (Washington, D.C.: Government Printing Office, 1941), p. 24.

18. A necklace in the possession of the owner of the mine is considered to contain some of the highest quality stone, this coming from 130 feet down.

19. Edna Mae Bennett, *Turquoise and the Indian* (Denver: Sage Books, 1966), pp. 37, 56.

20. Marvin K. Opler, "The Southern Utes of Colorado," in Ralph Linton, ed., *Acculturation in Seven American Indian Tribes* (New York: D. Appleton-Century Co., 1940), p. 122.

21. Lantis, "The San Luis Valley," p. 104.

22. With the expansion of agriculture and urbanization which occurred in the twentieth century, waterfowl traveling this Central Flyway were threatened with the loss of their nesting grounds. In 1952 and 1962, as a result, two wildlife refuges were established to ensure suitable nesting habitats for them. Monte Vista National Wildlife

Refuge is south of Monte Vista, and Alamosa National Wildlife Refuge is south of Alamosa.

23. Frank C. Spencer, *The Story of the San Luis Valley* (1925; Alamosa: San Luis Valley Historical Society, 1975), p. 51.

24. Hazel Bean Petty, "The History of Costilla County as Revealed by its Cemeteries" (M.A. thesis, Adams State College, 1971), p. 57.

Chapter III

1. George P. Hammond and Agapito Rey, *Don Juan de Onate, Colonizer of New Mexico, 1595-1628* (Albuquerque: University of New Mexico, 1953), 2:335, quoting the "Act of Taking Possession of New Mexico."

2. Rex W. Strickland, "Moscoso's Journey through Texas," *Southwestern Historical Quarterly*, 46 (1942):109-37; J. W. Williams, "Moscoso's Trail in Texas," ibid., pp. 138-57.

3. Florence Hawley Ellis, "San Gabriel del Yungue, Window on the Pre-Spanish World," paper read before the Eleventh Annual Western History Association Conference, Santa Fe, New Mexico, October 14, 1971.

4. W. Storrs Lee, ed., *Colorado: A Literary Chronicle* (New York: Funk and Wagnalls, 1970), pp. 17-21.

5. John Francis Bannon, *The Spanish Borderlands Frontier, 1513-1821* (New York: Holt, Rinehart and Winston, 1970), p. 6.

6. Oakah L. Jones, Jr., *Pueblo Warriors and Spanish Conquest* (Norman: University of Oklahoma Press, 1966), p. 68.

7. J. Manuel Espinosa, ed., "Journal of the Vargas Expedition into Colorado, 1694," *The Colorado Magazine*, 16 (1939):84; Espinosa, "Governor Vargas in Colorado," *New Mexico Historical Review*, 11 (1936):179-87.

8. Report of Don Antonio Valverde de Cossio, June 4, 1720, in "References in Spanish Archives to Expeditions in the 18th and 19th Centuries to the Territory Now Included in the State of Colorado, Secured by Irving Howbert in the Library of Congress" (typescript, Tutt Library, Colorado College), no pagination. The Jicarilla Apaches occupied an area across the mountains directly east of Taos. *See* Jack D. Forbes, *Apache, Navajo and Spaniard* (Norman: University of Oklahoma Press, 1960), p. 77.

9. Letter of Juan Domingo de Bustamente, 1724, in "References in Spanish Archives."

10. Report of Don Antonio Valverde de Cossio.

11. Spencer, *Story of the San Luis Valley*, p. 20.

12. For some of these treasure tales see "Mystery Caves in Colorado," *Rocky Mountain News*, September 21, 1921, p. 6; Allan Haarr, "Marble Mountain Caves (Custer County, Colorado)," *Speleo Digest, 1959* (Pittsburgh: Pittsburgh Grotto, National Speleological Society, 1961), pp. 270-71; William R. Halliday, *Adventure Is Underground: The Story of the Great Caves of the West and the Men Who Explore Them* (New York: Harper and Brothers, 1959), pp. 98-111.

13. Jones, *Pueblo Warriors and Spanish Conquest*, p. 140.

14. Ibid.

15. Alfred Barnaby Thomas, trans. and ed., *Forgotten Frontiers: A Study of the Spanish Indian Policy of Don Juan Bautista de Anza, Governor of New Mexico, 1777-1787* (Norman: University of Oklahoma Press, 1932), pp. 373-74.

16. Thomas, in *Forgotten Frontiers*, placed this crossing near Alamosa rather than Del Norte.

17. This account, taken from Anza's journal of the campaign, is found in Thomas, *Forgotten Frontiers*, pp. 123-39.

18. Report of Provisional Governor Manrique, March 21, 1810, in "References in Spanish Archives."

19. Petty, "History of Costilla County," p. 37.

Chapter IV

1. Eleanor L. Richie, "The Disputed International Boundary in Colorado, 1803-1819," *The Colorado Magazine*, 13 (1936):171.

2. Report of Governor Real Alencaster, November 20, 1805, in "References in Spanish Archives."

3. Ibid.

4. Report of Joaquin Real Alencaster, January 4, 1806, ibid. Since Pike saw no fort or settlement there in 1806, it can be assumed that Alencaster's request was not filled.

5. W. Eugene Hollon, *The Lost Pathfinder: Zebulon Montgomery Pike* (Norman: University of Oklahoma Press, 1949), p. 135.

6. Zebulon Montgomery Pike, *The Journals of Zebulon Montgomery Pike,* ed. Donald Jackson (Norman: University of Oklahoma Press, 1966), p. 375n.

7. Hollon, *The Lost Pathfinder,* pp. 101-02.

8. Ibid., pp. 112-14.

9. These springs issued from the foot of a hill east of the present town of Sanford. Later the site was part of a ranch belonging to A. W. McIntire, a governor of Colorado in the 1890s.

10. Pike, *The Southwestern Expedition,* p. 111.

11. Carrol Joe Carter, *Pike in Colorado* (Fort Collins, Colorado: The Old Army Press, 1978), pp. 39-43; "The Pike Stockade Site and its Purchase by the State of Colorado," *The Colorado Magazine,* 4 (1927):28-32.

12. Ibid. Purchased in 1925, this site is maintained by the state and may be visited by the public.

13. A detailed discussion of this controversy is found in Hollon, *The Lost Pathfinder,* pp. 41-53, 90-100.

14. Pike, *The Southwestern Expedition,* p. 122.

15. Report of Orders of Real Alencaster, April 1807, in "References in Spanish Archives." The identity of Almagre Creek is uncertain, but it may have been Fountain Creek.

16. *Lt. Zebulon Pike's Notebook of Maps, Traverse Tables, and Meteorological Observations, 1805-07,* Microfilm Publication T-36, Federal Archives and Records Center, Denver.

17. Frank Hall, *History of the State of Colorado,* 4 vols. (Chicago: Blakely Printing Co., 1889-95), 4:94.

18. Exceptions to this agreement gave three areas west of the Continental Divide to the United States. These were Middle Park, the valley of the Blue River, and a small area west of Hoosier Pass, none of which affected the development of the San Luis Valley.

Chapter V

1. Janet Lecompte, "Jules De Mun," in LeRoy R. Hafen, ed., *The Mountain Men and the Fur Trade in the Far West,* 10 vols. (Glendale, California: Arthur H. Clark Co., 1965-72), 8:97. The original source was the *Missouri Gazette,* July 29, 1815, from Dale L. Morgan, "The Mormons and the West" (transcripts in Beinecke Library, Yale University, New Haven, Connecticut). De Mun had gone to Santa Fe to obtain permission to trap east of the mountains.

2. Letter from De Mun to William Clark, cited in Alfred C. Thomas, "An Anonymous Description of New Mexico, 1818," *Southwestern Historical Journal,* 33 (1929):51.

3. Richie, "The Disputed International Boundary," p. 176.

4. Thomas, "An Anonymous Description," pp. 62-63.

5. Chauncey Thomas, "The Spanish Fort in Colorado, 1819," *The Colorado Magazine,* 14 (1937):82.

6. Ibid., pp. 83-85. These Indians are thought to have been Pawnees.

7. Jacob Fowler, *The Journal of Jacob Fowler,* ed. Elliott Coues with preface and additional notes by Raymond W. and Mary Lund Settle and Harry R. Stevens (Lincoln: University of Nebraska Press, 1970). In note 12 for Fowler's account there appear the names of these trappers, all but one of whom were in the San Luis Valley in 1822: Robert Fowler, Jacob's brother; Baptiste Roy, the party's interpreter; Baptiste Peno; George Douglas; Nathaniel Pryor, who had traveled with Lewis and Clark; Richard Walters; Eli Ward; Jesse van Biber (van Bibber); Dudley Maxwell; Baptiste Moran; Slover (Isaac Slover); five men whose first names are not given—Beno, Barbo, Taylor, Simpson, and Findley; Jacob Fowler's negro, Paul; and Lewis Dawson, who was killed by a bear before the expedition entered the San Luis Valley.

8. Harry R. Stevens, "Hugh Glenn," in Hafen, ed., *The Mountain Men and the Fur Trade*, 2:173.

9. David J. Weber, *The Taos Trappers: The Fur Trade in the Far Southwest* (Norman: University of Oklahoma Press, 1968), p. 57.

10. Harvey L. Carter, "The Mountain Men," *San Luis Valley Historian*, 3, no. 1 (1971):20.

11. Ibid., p. 22.

12. Forbes Parkhill, "Antoine Leroux," in Hafen, ed., *The Mountain Men and the Fur Trade*, 4:174; *see also* Parkhill, *The Blazed Trail of Antoine Leroux* (Los Angeles: Westernlore Press, 1965).

13. Blanche C. Grant, ed., *Kit Carson's own Story of his Life as Dictated to Col. and Mrs. D. C. Peters about 1856-57* (Santa Fe: Santa Fe New Mexican Publishing Corp., 1926), p. 10.

14. Ibid., p. 11.

15. Harvey L. Carter, "Ewing Young," in Hafen, ed., *The Mountain Men and the Fur Trade*, 2:385-86.

16. Luther E. Bean, *Land of the Blue Sky People* (Monte Vista, Colorado: *Monte Vista Journal*, 1962), p. 34.

17. Harvey L. Carter, "Tom Tobin," in Hafen, ed., *The Mountain Men and the Fur Trade*, 4:360.

18. Harvey L. Carter, "Aaron B. Lewis," ibid., 5:175.

19. Weber, *The Taos Trappers*, pp. 160-61.

20. A military expedition that went north to the San Luis Valley in 1829 to deal with hostile Indians is referred to by Donaciano Vigil in "Surveyor-General Records," Case No. 93, New Mexico State Records Center and Archives.

21. Janet Lecompte, "John Hawkins," in Hafen, ed., *The Mountain Men and the Fur Trade*, 4:142.

22. "Alexander Barclay Papers" (typescript from microfilm, in State Historical Society of Colorado Library), p. 35.

23. Janet Lecompte, "Charles Town," in Hafen, ed., *The Mountain Men and the Fur Trade*, 1:393.

24. Hall, *History of the State of Colordo*, 4:304.

25. "Alexander Barclay Papers," p. 51.

26. Map (1839) by David H. Burr, geographer to the U.S. House of Representatives, which appears in Maurice S. Sullivan, *The Travels of Jedediah Smith* (Santa Ana, California: Fine Arts Press, 1934).

27. Daniel Tyler, *A Concise History of the Mormon Battalion in the Mexican War* (Washington, D.C.: n.p., 1891), pp. 113, 169-94.

28. Carter, "Tom Tobin," pp. 360-61.

29. LeRoy R. Hafen, "Mountain Men—John D. Albert," *The Colorado Magazine*, 10 (1933):56-62.

30. George F. Ruxton, *Adventures in Mexico and the Rocky Mountains* (New York: Harper and Brothers, Publishers, 1848), pp. 206-07. The publication of Ruxton's book provided more information about this area than had been available concerning the population and its way of life.

31. Ibid., pp. 208-17.

Chapter VI

1. Frederic E. Voelker, "William Sherley (Old Bill) Williams," in Hafen, ed., *The Mountain Men and the Fur Trade*, 8:365, 386-87.

2. Charles Preuss, *Exploring with Frémont: The Private Diary of Charles Preuss, Cartographer for John C. Frémont on the First, Second, and Fourth Expeditions to the Far West* (Norman: University of Oklahoma Press, 1958), p. 143. If Williams ever had been in the San Luis Valley, no evidence has come to light; *see* Voelker, "William Sherley (Old Bill) Williams," pp. 386-87.

3. Frank C. Spencer, "The Scene of Frémont's Disaster in the San Juan Mountains, 1848," *The Colorado Magazine*, 6 (1929):141.

4. LeRoy R. Hafen and Ann W. Hafen, *Frémont's Fourth Expedition: A Documentary Account of the Disaster of 1848-49*, vol. 11, *The Far West and the Rockies*

Historical Series, 1820-1875 (Glendale, California: Arthur W. Clark Co., 1960), pp. 20-21.

5. "Statements on Responsibility for the Disaster," ibid., p. 242.

6. Ibid., pp. 22-25. In addition to the Hafen edition covering the fourth expedition, see William E. Brandon, *The Men and the Mountain: Frémont's Fourth Expedition* (New York: William Morrow and Co., 1955).

7. Preuss, *Exploring with Frémont*, p. 144.

8. Ibid.

9. Neither pass would appear to recommend itself for a railroad.

10. Ibid.

11. Ibid., p. 145.

12. Thomas E. Breckenridge, "The Story of a Famous Expedition," as told to J. W. Freeman and Charles W. Watson, *The Cosmopolitan*, 21 (1896):400-08, and reprinted in Hafen and Hafen, *Frémont's Fourth Expedition*, p. 184.

13. Preuss, *Exploring with Frémont*, p. 147.

14. "Diary of Benjamin Kern" in Hafen and Hafen, *Frémont's Fourth Expedition*, p. 106.

15. Preuss, *Exploring with Frémont*, p. 149.

16. Ibid., pp. 149-50.

17. Letter, LeRoy R. Hafen to A. F. Hoffman, supervisor, Rio Grande National Forest, September 3, 1935, in Workbook, Rio Grande National Forest Headquarters, Monte Vista, Colorado.

18. Spencer, in "The Scene of Frémont's Disaster," discusses the location of a camp at the head of Wannamaker Creek, where he found a soldier's belt buckle, a mule's foot shod with an ox shoe, and mule bones. When this site was visited by Ranger E. S. Erickson, Albert Pfeiffer, and Frank Spencer in 1928, they found no equipment. The other site containing the sleds was not located on this occasion. Memo, E. S. Erickson to Forest Supervisor, March 30, 1932, Workbook, Rio Grande National Forest Headquarters. Directions for reaching this site were given in a memo from Ranger William F. Cummings, May 2, 1937, ibid.: "On the divide between Bellows Creek and Embargo Creek where the Bellows and Embargo and Sky City trails join—go north about one mile then northeasterly to the divide between the first and second creeks. Follow south down the east side of the ridge along the edge of the timber."

19. Letter, William E. Brandon to Ambrose Burkhart, August 12, 1951, Workbook, ibid. Photographs made by Ambrose Burkhart on September 8, 1950, at Embargo Creek, show the sleds and the stumps with axe marks six feet above the ground.

20. Memo, Mark R. Ratliff to Ambrose Burkhart, September 12, 1950, ibid. The sleds with these characteristics were identified in 1950 from photographs made in 1931 by E. S. Erickson. These sleds have been in the collections of the Rio Grande County Museum since 1953.

Chapter VII

1. L. R. Hafen, "Status of the San Luis Valley," *The Colorado Magazine*, 3 (1926):46-49.

2. Morris F. Taylor, "Fort Massachusetts," *The Colorado Magazine*, 45 (1968):120-21.

3. Grant Foreman, "Antoine Leroux, New Mexico Guide," *New Mexico Historical Review*, 16 (1941):370-74.

4. *See* Gwinn Harris Heap, *Central Route to the Pacific, from the Valley of the Mississippi to California: Journal of the Expedition* (Philadelphia: Lippincott, Grambo, and Co., 1854).

5. Ibid., pp. 30-32.

6. Ibid., pp. 34-37.

7. Ibid., p. 37.

8. Ibid., p. 54.

9. Ibid., p. 57.

10. Ibid., p. 58.

11. William H. Goetzmann, *Army Exploration in the American West* (New Haven: Yale University Press, 1959), p. 283.

12. U. S. Congress, Senate, *Reports of Explorations and Surveys to Ascertain the Most Practicable and Economical Route for a Railroad from the Mississippi River to the Pacific Ocean, 1853-4*, 33rd Cong., 2d sess., 1:17.

13. Nolie Mumey, "John Williams Gunnison: Centenary of his Survey and Tragic Death," *The Colorado Magazine*, 31 (1954):27.

14. Senate, *Reports of Explorations and Surveys*, 1:17.

15. Mumey, "John Williams Gunnison," pp. 30-31.

16. Hall, *History of the State of Colorado*, 1:140.

17. For the account of this expedition *see* S. N. Carvalho, *Incidents of Travel and Adventure in the Far West with Colonel Frémont's Last Expedition* (New York: Derby and Jackson, 1857).

18. Hall, *History of the State of Colorado*, 1:141-42.

19. Marcy's account of this portion of the expedition appears in Lee, *Colorado*, pp. 141-48.

20. Hall, *History of the State of Colorado*, 1:143-44.

21. William L. Wessels, *Born To Be a Soldier: The Military Career of William Wing Loring of St. Augustine, Florida* (Fort Worth: Texas Christian University Press, 1971), pp. 46-48.

22. Ibid., p. 48.

23. Loring's journal appears in "Colonel Loring's Expedition across Colorado in 1858," *The Colorado Magazine*, 23 (1946):49-76. Loring served with the Confederate forces during the Civil War, as did Johnston.

Chapter VIII

1. "Petition for Confirmation by Cresencio Valdes," Papers Relating to New Mexico Land Grants, Claims Adjudicated by the U.S. Surveyor General and by the U.S. Court of Private Land Claims, *Los Conejos*, Case 109, File 112, microfilm reel 45, New Mexico State Records Center and Archives.

2. "Request for Renewal of Los Conejos Grant," translation no. 0021, Blackmore Papers, Los Conejos Grant, New Mexico State Records Center and Archives.

3. Ibid.

4. "Act of Governor Charles Bent," November 3, 1846, Papers Relating to New Mexico Land Grants, Claims Adjudicated by the U.S. Surveyor General and the U.S. Court of Private Land Claims, *Los Conejos*, File 80, microfilm reel 31, New Mexico State Records Center and Archives. A nucleus of settlement at Rincones, undertaken in the spring of 1849, is described in "Recollections of Tata Atanasio Trujillo," *The San Luis Valley Historian*, 8, no. 4 (1976):19.

5. Harold H. Dunham, "New Mexico Land Grants with Special Reference to the Title Papers of the Maxwell Grant," *New Mexico Historical Review*, 30 (1955):4.

6. A survey of this grant determined the size to be 998,780.46 acres, according to *Abstracts of Title to Trinchera Ranch Lands, Certified March 1st, 1917* (San Luis: Costilla County Abstract Co., n.d.), p. 3.

7. Beaubien's daughter Luz married Lucien Maxwell, who later owned the Beaubien-Miranda Grant, or the Maxwell Grant as it was then called.

8. Francis T. Cheetham, "The Early Settlements of Southern Colorado," *The Colorado Magazine*, 5 (1928):5.

9. Olibama Lopez Tushar, *People of the Valley: A History of the Spanish Colonials of the San Luis Valley* (Denver: Privately printed, 1975), p. 47. Based on the same author's previous work, Olibama Lopez, "The Spanish Heritage in the San Luis Valley" (M.A. thesis, University of Denver, 1942), this publication is a valuable source on the Spanish colonials.

10. Parkhill, "Antoine Leroux," in Hafen, ed., *The Mountain Men and the Fur Trade*, 4:178; James Warren Covington, "Relations between the Ute Indians and the United States Government, 1848-1900" (Ph.D. dissertation, University of Oklahoma, 1949), pp. 32-33.

11. Cheetham, "The Early Settlements," p. 5. This store belonged to Moritz, Bielschoski, and Koenig, who later were joined by Charles Deus, a German veteran of the Mexican War and an Indian fighter in the campaign of 1854. Having worked as a brewer in Santa Fe, Deus managed a distillery in Costilla for the store owners.

12. Hall, *History of the State of Colorado*, 3:329.

13. Tushar, *People of the Valley*, p. 49.

14. Hall, *History of the State of Colorado*, 3:329.

15. Beryl McAdow, *Land of Adoption* (Boulder, Colorado: Johnson Publishing Co., 1970), p. 71.

16. Emilia Gallegos Smith, "Reminiscences of Early San Luis," *The Colorado Magazine*, 24 (1947):25.

17. Colorado, Costilla County, Public Records, Book I, p. 256.

18. State Historical Society of Colorado, MSS XV-9b and Pamphlet 349, no. 18. The original San Acacio was east of the present town of the same name.

19. Alvin T. Steinel, *History of Agriculture in Colorado* (Fort Collins, Colorado: State Agricultural College, 1926), pp. 177-78.

20. Charlie A. Vigil, "History and Folklore of San Pedro and San Pablo, Colorado" (M.A. thesis, Adams State College, 1956), pp. 12-13.

21. Hall, *History of the State of Colorado*, 3:329.

22. Meliton Velasquez, "Guadalupe Colony Was Founded 1854," *The Colorado Magazine*, 34 (1957):264-65.

23. State Historical Society of Colorado, Pamphlet 349, no. 18.

24. Aurelio M. Espinosa, *The Spanish Language in New Mexico and Southern Colorado*, Historical Society of New Mexico, Publication 16 (Santa Fe: New Mexico Printing Company, 1911), pp. 6-8.

25. Morris F. Taylor, "Fort Massachusetts," *The Colorado Magazine*, 45 (1968):120-22.

26. M. L. Cummins, "Fort Massachusetts, First United States Military Post in Colorado," *The Colorado Magazine*, 14 (1937):130. An archaeological examination of the site was conducted in the 1960s by the State Historical Society of Colorado in cooperation with Trinidad State Junior College.

27. Heap, *Central Route to the Pacific*, pp. 32-33.

28. Harvey Lewis Carter, *'Dear Old Kit': The Historical Christopher Carson* (Norman: University of Oklahoma Press, 1968), pp. 139-42.

29. Accounts of these events are found in ibid., pp. 143-46; Rafael Chacon, "Campaign against Utes and Apaches in Southern Colorado, 1855, from the Memoirs of Major Rafael Chacon," *The Colorado Magazine*, 11 (1934):108-12; and Dewitt C. Peters, *The Life and Adventures of Kit Carson, The Nestor of the Rocky Mountains, from Facts Narrated by Himself* (New York: W. B. C. Clark & Co., 1858), pp. 466-507. Articles about the campaign also are found in LeRoy R. Hafen, "The Fort Pueblo Massacre and the Punitive Expedition against the Utes," *The Colorado Magazine*, 4 (1927):49-58; and Morris F. Taylor, "Action at Fort Massachusetts: The Indian Campaign of 1855," *The Colorado Magazine*, 42 (1965):292-310.

30. Velasquez, "Guadalupe Colony," p. 265.

31. Smith, "Reminiscences of Early San Luis," pp. 24-25.

32. Olibama Lopez, "Pioneer Life in the San Luis Valley," *The Colorado Magazine*, 19 (1942):161-67.

33. Steinel, *History of Agriculture*, p. 31.

34. Claire McMenamy, "Our Lady of Guadalupe at Conejos, Colorado," *The Colorado Magazine*, 17 (1940):180-81; Martin F. Hasting, "Parochial Beginnings in Colorado to 1889" (M.A. thesis, St. Louis University, St. Louis, Missouri, 1941), pp. 143-44.

35. In addition to Guadalupe these included Guadalupita, Mesitas, Canon, San Rafael, Cido, San Antonio, Piños, Puraria, Limpia, Isla, Cenicero, Rincones, Sauces, Cerritos, Fuerticitos, Brazo, Servilleta, Jara, Alamosa, Casillas, Loma, Garita, Carnero, San Luis, and Saguatche.

36. Lorayne Ann Horka-Follick, *Los Hermanos Penitentes* (Los Angeles: Westernlore Press, 1969), pp. 3-11, 110.

37. Bill Tate, *The Penitentes of the Sangre de Cristos: An American Tragedy* (Truchas, New Mexico: Tate Gallery, 1968), pp. 14-15; Marta Weigle, *The Penitentes of the Southwest* (Santa Fe: Ancient City Press, 1970), pp. 14-15.

38. Frances J. Gomez, "Medical Folklore of the Spanish-Speaking People of the San Luis Valley" (M.A. thesis, Adams State College, 1970), p. 9.

39. "San Luis Store Celebrates Centennial," *The Colorado Magazine*, 34 (1957):256, 258.

40. H. E. Easterday to Ceran St. Vrain, April, 1860, in Francisco Collection, La Veta, Colorado, and printed in Steinel, *History of Agriculture*, pp. 37-38.

41. Lynn Robison Bailey, *Indian Slave Trade in the Southwest: A Study of Slave-taking and Traffic of Indian Captives* (Los Angeles: Westernlore Press, 1966), p. 19.

42. D. Gene Combs, "Enslavement of Indians in the San Luis Valley of Colorado" (M.A. thesis, Adams State College, 1970), pp. 16, 19.

43. Bailey, *Indian Slave Trade*, pp. 106-07.

44. For the complete list *see The San Luis Valley Historian*, 5, no. 1 (1973):22-29.

45. Combs, "Enslavement of Indians," p. 22.

46. Frank A. White, *La Garita* (La Jara, Colorado: Cooper Printing Co., 1971), pp. 21-23.

47. Patricia Joy Richmond, "La Loma de San Jose," *The San Luis Valley Historian*, 5, no. 2-4 (1973):1-63; 6, no. 1-2 (1974):66-118. This material first was written as an M.A. thesis at Adams State College, 1969. The site of La Loma de San Jose on the Jim Paulsen ranch, three miles east of Del Norte, has been the subject of an archaeological investigation conducted by Herbert W. Dick.

48. Spencer, *Story of the San Luis Valley*, p. 60. Tax records of the 1870s provide the names of other settlements nearby—Plaza de Abaja, Plaza de Arriba, Plaza de Don Hilario Abaja, Plaza de San Francisco, Los Pinos de La Loma, Plaza del Alto, and Plaza del Norte. Besides the Silvas and the Luceros, well-known families in this area included such names as Valdez, Chavez, Sanchez, Martinez, Vigil, Espinosa, Torres, Atencio, and Ortega. Lafayette Head's report of 1865 verifies place names for several other contemporary plazas south of here. These were Guadalupe, San Jose (near San Antonio Mountain), Servietta, Brazo, Seritas (Cerritos), Senisero (Cenicero, later called Lobatos), Santa Cruz, San Antonio, Los Pinos (near the present New Mexico state line), Guadalupita, Pinos, Mesitas, Canon, San Rafael (originally called Paisaje in 1857), and Pura y Limpia, meaning "clean and neat." In addition to Head's census, *see* Colton's Map (1865?). Many of the old plazas, such as La Placita de Las Meas, once on the south side of the Conejos River near its canyon mouth, are impossible to date or even to locate conclusively.

Chapter IX

1. U.S., Bureau of Indian Affairs, Letters Received 1824-80, Colorado Superintendency 1861-8, Microcopy 234, Roll 197 (1861-4), Federal Archives and Records Center, Denver.

2. "Colonel Loring's Expedition," p. 73.

3. John H. Nankivell, "Fort Garland, Colorado," *The Colorado Magazine*, 6 (1939):13-27; Duane Vandenbusche, "Life at a Frontier Post: Fort Garland," ibid., 43 (1966):132-48.

4. U.S., Bureau of Indian Affairs, Letters Received 1824-80, New Mexico Superintendency 1849-80, Microcopy 234, Roll 550 (1860-1), Federal Archives and Records Center, Denver.

5. Ibid., Colorado Superintendency 1861-8, Roll 197 (1861-4).

6. Covington, "Relations between the Ute Indians and the United States Government," p. 86.

7. *Rocky Mountain News*, February 24, 1861, p. 2.

8. James Rose Harvey, "El Cerrito de Los Kiowas," *The Colorado Magazine*, 19 (1942):213-15.

9. Harry E. Kelsey, Jr., *Frontier Capitalist: The Life of John Evans* (Denver and Boulder: Colorado State Historical Society and Pruett Publishing Co., 1969), p. 132.

10. Additional biographical information is found in Carter, *'Dear Old Kit'*, passim; Pauline S. Sharp, "Kit Carson at Fort Garland, C.T.," *The San Luis Valley Historian*, 2, no. 2 (1970):12-20.

11. Christopher Carson, "Report on Fort Garland Made by Christopher (Kit) Carson to Major Roger James, June 10, 1866," ed. Gene M. Gressley, *The Colorado Magazine*, 32 (1955):216.

12. Ibid., pp. 222-23.

13. U.S., Bureau of Indian Affairs, Letters Received 1824-80, Colorado Superintendency 1861-8, Microcopy 234, Roll 199.

14. A. C. Hunt, Report of 1868, in *Annual Report of the Commissioner of Indian Affairs for 1868* (Washington, D.C.: 1868), pp. 642-43.

15. Covington, "Relations between the Ute Indians and the United States Government," p. 112; Edward E. Hill, *Historical Sketches for Jurisdictional and Subject Headings Used for the Letters Rec'd. by the Office of Indian Affairs, 1824-80* (Washington, D.C.: National Archives and Records Service, 1967), p. 2.

16. Edward M. McCook, *Report of 1870*, in *Annual Report of the Commissioner of Indian Affairs for 1871* (Washington, D.C.: 1871), pp. 627-28.

17. Erl H. Ellis, *International Boundary Lines across Colorado and Wyoming* (Boulder, Colorado: Johnson Publishing Co., 1966), p. 9.

18. White, *La Garita*, p. 22.

19. Gerald C. Smith, "Colonel Albert H. Pfeiffer," *The San Luis Valley Historian*, 2, no. 2 (1970):7-11.

Chapter X

1. Thomas L. Karnes, *William Gilpin, Western Nationalist* (Austin and London: University of Texas Press, 1970), pp. 118-20.

2. Hubert Howe Bancroft, *History of Arizona and New Mexico, 1530-1888* (1889; Albuquerque, New Mexico: Horn & Wallace, Publishers, 1962), pp. 419-23.

3. William Gilpin, "Pike's Peak and the Sierra San Juan," in *Guide to the Kansas Gold Mines at Pike's Peak, from Notes of Capt. J. W. Gunnison . . .* (1859; Denver: Nolie Mumey, 1952), p. 34. The word *bayou* is a Creole corruption of the Spanish word *valle*, meaning "valley."

4. Karnes, *William Gilpin*, p. 243n.

5. *Rocky Mountain News*, August 27, 1860, p. 2.

6. Ibid.

7. Ibid., June 25, 1861, p. 2.

8. Another account of this expedition is found in Virginia McConnell, "Captain Baker and the San Juan Humbug," *The Colorado Magazine*, 48 (1971):59-75.

9. Hall, *History of Colorado*, 3:329.

10. Ibid., 4:94.

11. William H. Bauer, James L. Ozment, and John H. Willard, *Colorado Postal History: The Post Offices* (Crete, Nebraska: J-B Publishing Co., 1971), pp. 39, 55, 116: Hall, *History of Colorado*, 4:93-94.

12. Ralph C. Taylor, *Colorado South of the Border* (Denver: Sage Books, 1963), pp. 166-70.

13. *Rocky Mountain News*, October 12, 1860, p. 2.

14. Richmond, "La Loma de San Jose," p. 68.

15. Lantis, "San Luis Valley," pp. 176, 196, quoting William Stewart, Jr. *La Sauses*, the name of the older town settled by New Mexicans, means "the willows."

16. *Rocky Mountain News*, February 6, 1861, and *Canon City Times*, May 4, 1861, in the State Historical Society of Colorado clippings file.

17. Arthur Ridgway, "The Mission of Colorado Toll Roads," *The Colorado Magazine*, 9 (1932):167.

18. Frank C. Spencer, *The Story of the San Luis Valley*, p. 61.

19. Hall, *History of Colorado*, 4:304.

20. Ibid., 4:304-05.

21. *Rocky Mountain News*, October 12, 1860, p. 2.

22. Sidney Jocknick, *Early Days on the Western Slope of Colorado and Campfire Chats with Otto Mears the Pathfinder from 1870 to 1883, Inclusive* (1913; Glorieta, New Mexico: Rio Grande Press, Inc., 1968), pp. 236-37. For other biographical material on Mears, *see* Helen M. Searcy, "Otto Mears" in *Pioneers of the San Juan Country* (Durango: Outwest Printing and Stationery Co., 1942), 1:15-47; Allen duPont Breck, *The Centennial History of the Jews of Colorado, 1859-1959* (Denver: Hirschfeld Press, 1960), pp. 40-42; and Mears Papers, State Historical Society of Colorado Library.

23. Michael Kaplan, "Otto Mears and the Silverton Northern Railroad," *The Colorado Magazine*, 48 (1971):236.

24. Ridgway, "Mission of Colorado Toll Roads," pp. 168-69.

25. Beryl McAdow, *Land of Adoption*, pp. 9-10.

26. This diary is in the State Historical Society of Colorado Library. Part of it was published in *The Colorado Magazine* in the January, April, and July issues in 1961 and in the January issue in 1962.

27. Mrs. Eugene Williams, manuscript, Boyd Papers, envelope 6, Adams State College Library.

28. John L. Dyer, *The Snow-Shoe Itinerant* (Cincinnati: Cranston & Stowe, 1890), pp. 205-06.

29. Lantis, "San Luis Valley," pp. 102, 183.

30. William Hansen, as told to Velma West Sykes, "Pioneer Life in the San Luis Valley," *The Colorado Magazine,* 17 (1940):146-55.

31. *See* White, *La Garita,* passim, for an objective, firsthand view of these problems.

Chapter XI

1. Thomas T. Tobin, "The Capture of the Espinosas," dictated 1895, *The Colorado Magazine,* 9 (1932):59-62.

2. Ibid., pp. 62-65.

3. A reward of $2,500 was offered by Governor Evans, but of this only a total of $1,500 was paid and that by later administrations.

4. Petty, "The History of Costilla County," p. 40.

5. Conejos Tract, case no. 109, p. 160, reel no. 45, *Records of Private Land Claims Adjudicated by the Court of Private Land Claims, New Mexico Land Grant Microfilm Collection* (Albuquerque: University of New Mexico); *Surveyor General of Colorado, 1861-1925, Copies of Miscellaneous Letters Sent, 1861-73,* Federal Archives and Records Center, Denver; ibid., *Copies of Letters Sent to the Commissioner, 1861-68.* Hall, *History of Colorado,* 4:91, confirms that the documents were placed in the files of the Surveyor General of Colorado in Denver.

6. W. H. Lessig to Joseph S. Wilson, August 10, 1868, *Surveyor General of Colorado, Letters Sent to the Commissioner.*

7. Valdez et al. v. United States, *Records of Private Land Claims Adjudicated by the Court of Private Land Claims,* case 109, p. 127.

8. Karnes, *William Gilpin,* p. 302.

9. Gilpin is quoted as expressing this reason to Francis M. Case in Case, Surveyor General of Colorado, to J. M. Edmunds, Commissioner, General Land Office, February 24, 1863, in *Surveyor General of Colorado, Copies of Letters Sent to the Commissioner, 1861-1925.*

10. Ibid.

11. Karnes, *William Gilpin,* p. 302.

12. Herbert O. Brayer, *William Blackmore: The Spanish-Mexican Land Grants of New Mexico and Colorado, 1863-1878,* vol. 1 of *A Case Study in the Economic Development of the West* (Denver: Bradford-Robinson, 1949), p. 65.

13. San Acacio Abstract and Investment Company, *Abstract of Title, no. 1436,* as cited in Lantis, "The San Luis Valley," p. 163.

14. Karnes, *William Gilpin,* p. 320.

15. William Blackmore, *Colorado: Its Resources, Parks and Prospects as a New Field for Emigration* (London: Sampson, Low, Son, and Marston, 1869).

16. Brayer, *William Blackmore,* 1:91-93.

17. Ibid., p. 99. The association between Blackmore and Hayden continued with Blackmore donating funds and accompanying the geologist to Yellowstone the following year.

18. Ibid., p. 109.

19. Vigil, "History and Folklore of San Pedro and San Pablo," p. 47.

20. William Hubert Jones, *The History of Catholic Education in the State of Colorado* (Washington, D.C.: Catholic University of America Press, 1955), pp. 84-85.

21. Brayer, *William Blackmore,* 1:210.

Chapter XII

1. D. H. Cummins, "Toll Roads in Southwestern Colorado," *The Colorado Magazine,* 29 (1952):99-102; Arthur Ridgway, "The Mission of Colorado Toll Roads," *The Colorado Magazine,* 9 (1932):164, 167.

2. Morris F. Taylor, *First Mail West: Stagecoach Lines on the Santa Fe Trail* (Albuquerque: University of New Mexico Press, 1971), passim.

3. For the background of these intricacies see Herbert O. Brayer, *William Blackmore:*

The Spanish-Mexican Land Grants of New Mexico and Colorado, 1863-1878 and William Blackmore: Early Financing of the Denver and Rio Grande Railway and Ancillary Land Companies, vols. 1 and 2, A Case Study in the Economic Development of the West (Denver: Bradford-Robinson, 1949); Karnes, William Gilpin; and Robert G. Athearn, Rebel of the Rockies: A History of the Denver and Rio Grande Western Railroad (New Haven: Yale University Press, 1962).

4. Brayer, William Blackmore, 2:197.

5. "Place Names in Colorado," The Colorado Magazine, 18 (1941):61. Helen Hunt Jackson described this scene in Bits of Travel at Home (Boston: Little, Brown & Co., 1878), under the pen name "H. H."

6. "Agreement, Morton Fisher, etc.," December 22, 1876, Abstracts of Title, Sangre de Cristo Grant, p. 11.

7. Hall, History of Colorado, 4:99-100.

8. Spencer, Story of the San Luis Valley, p. 56.

9. Riverside Station was east of Wayside, which had a post office in 1875.

10. Ellen F. Walrath, "Stagecoach Holdups in the San Luis Valley," The Colorado Magazine, 14 (1937):30-31.

11. For detailed coverage of this extension, see Haldon W. Lindfelt, "The Chili Line: The Santa Fe Branch of the Denver and Rio Grande Western" (M.A. thesis, Adams State College, 1966); and John A. Gjeore, Chili Line: The Narrow Rail Trail to Santa Fe (Espanola, New Mexico: Rio Grande Sun Press, 1969).

12. Spencer, Story of the San Luis Valley, p. 63.

Chapter XIII

1. C. G. Gunther, "The Gold Deposits of Plomo, San Luis Park, Colo.," Economic Geology, 1 (1906):143, 152-53.

2. H. B. Patton, Charles E. Smith, G. Montague Butler, and Arthur J. Hoskin, "Geology of the Grayback Mining District, Costilla County, Colorado," Colorado Geological Survey Bulletin, 2 (1910):83.

3. Cram's Map of 1891.

4. Patton et al., "Geology of the Grayback Mining District," passim.

5. Hall, History of Colorado, 4:291.

6. Manuscript, Del Norte file, Adams State College Library.

7. H. B. Patton, "Geology and Ore Deposits of the Platoro-Summitville Mining District, Colo.," Colorado Geological Survey Bulletin, 13 (1917):105.

8. Bill Fassett, "The Fassett Store in Jasper," The San Luis Valley Historian, 7, no. 2 (1975):16-17.

9. Cockrell in Conejos County was a post office from 1879 to 1892. Cram's Map of 1891 shows it about half way between the railroad and Stunner.

10. "Place Names in Colorado," The Colorado Magazine, 19 (1942):149.

11. Patton et al., "Geology and Ore Deposits of the Platoro-Summitville Mining District," p. 89.

12. Sedgwick's post office moved three miles to Parkville in 1885, but service continued only until 1886. The post office at Bonanza operated with only two brief interruptions until 1938. Another camp in this area was Claytonia, which appeared on Thayer's Map of Colorado in 1882. This town was between Villa Grove and Bonanza.

13. Anne Ellis, The Life of an Ordinary Woman (Boston and New York: Houghton Mifflin Company, 1929), p. 24.

14. Anne Ellis, "My First Bath Tub," Los Angeles Times Sunday Magazine, December 20, 1931, pp. 5, 16.

15. S. E. Kortright, "Historical Sketch of the Bonanza Mining District," The Colorado Magazine, 22 (1945):75; see also, Helen A. Kempner, "Bonanza and the Kerber Creek District," The San Luis Valley Historian, 3, no. 2 (1971):1-46.

16. W. S. Burbank and Charles W. Henderson, Geology and Ore Deposits of the Bonanza Mining District, Colorado, U.S. Geological Survey Professional Paper 169 (Washington, D.C.: Government Printing Office, 1932), p. 1.

17. Ellis, The Life of an Ordinary Woman, p. 23.

18. Robert Born, interview, in Place Names file, La Garita, State Historical Society of Colorado Library. Green probably was named for rancher Russell Green.

19. Thomas A. Steven and C. L. Bieniewski, *Mineral Resources of the La Garita Wilderness, San Juan Mountains, Southwestern Colorado,* Geological Survey Bulletin 1420 (Washington, D.C.: Government Printing Office, 1977), pp. 60-61.

20. Irene Flom Cox, "Development of Baca Grant Number Four" (M.A. thesis, Adams State College, 1948), pp. 75-76.

21. Mrs. A. H. Major, "Pioneer Days in Crestone and Creede," *The Colorado Magazine,* 21 (1944):214-15.

22. Rand, McNally and Company, Map of 1882; Denver and Rio Grande Railway, undated map (1883-86?).

23. Herbert H. Oba, "Source Material for Teaching History of the East-Central Section of the San Luis Valley" (M.A. thesis, Adams State College, 1961), pp. 28-31.

24. Robert B. Fisher, "An Historical Study of the Orient Mine and its Impact on the San Luis Valley" (M.A. thesis, Adams State College, 1969), pp. 11-13, with special reference to John B. Stone, "Limonite Deposits at the Orient Mine," *Economic Geology,* 29 (1934).

25. A. R. Pelton, *The San Luis Valley, with Illustrations of its Public Buildings . . .* (Salida, Colorado: Carson, Hurst, and Harper, 1891), p. 23.

26. Steven and Bieniewski, *Mineral Resources of the La Garita Wilderness,* pp. 40-41.

27. A post office called Hirst served the camp at the Commodore. Orean was at or very near the same location as Montville, which succeeded the mining camp. At the foot of Mosca Pass, Montville was a post office until 1898.

28. Colorado, Mineral Resources Board, *Mineral Resources of Colorado* (Denver: Colorado Mining Association, 1947), pp. 183-96; ibid. (Denver: Publishers Press, 1960), pp. 62-63, 102-04, 259-61, 266-71.

Chapter XIV

1. J. Cary French, "Diary, 1871," *The San Luis Valley Historian,* 8, no. 1 (1976):3-13; Arthur French, letter to Salome French Wilson, ibid., pp. 16-17.

2. Hall, *History of Colorado,* 4:291-92.

3. These springs were taken up in 1872 by Henry Henson and others; ibid., 4:294-95. Hot water from the springs recently has been piped into a swimming pool at a dude ranch operated by the Allan Phipps family of Denver.

4. Douglas C. McMurtrie and Albert H. Allen, *Early Printing in Colorado, 1859-1876* (Denver: A. B. Hirschfeld Press, 1935), p. 127; Donald E. Oehlerts, *Guide to Colorado Newspapers, 1859-1963* (Denver: Bibliographical Center for Research, 1964), pp. 126-27.

5. Hall, *History of Colorado,* 4:298.

6. William B. Faherty, "Regional Minorities and the Woman Suffrage Struggle," *The Colorado Magazine,* 33 (1956):212-17.

7. Mary Louise Coolbroth, "Early Church Buildings of the San Luis Valley," *The San Luis Valley Historian,* 7, no. 3 (1975):13-18.

8. Norman J. Bender, "A College Where One Ought to Be," *The Colorado Magazine,* 49 (1972):196-218.

9. Ellis, *Life of an Ordinary Woman,* pp. 25-26.

10. William H. Rideing, *A-Saddle in the Wild West* (London: J. C. Nimmo and Bain, 1879), pp. 28-34.

11. Ibid., p. 32.

12. H. H., *Bits of Travel at Home* (Boston: Little, Brown & Co., 1878), p. 389.

Chapter XV

1. Mrs. Eugene Williams, manuscript, Boyd Papers, envelope 6, Adams State College Library.

2. Steinel, *History of Agriculture in Colorado,* pp. 86-87.

3. Lantis, "The San Luis Valley," p. 191.

4. Forbes Parkhill, "Colorado's Earliest Settlements," *The Colorado Magazine,* 34 (1957):243-53.

5. Lantis, "The San Luis Valley," p. 191.

6. Oba, "Source Material for Teaching History," p. 34.

7. Cox, "Development of Baca Grant Number Four," pp. 72-84.

8. Oba, "Source Material for Teaching History," pp. 6-8.

9. Ibid., p. 20.

10. Nicholas G. Morgan, "Mormon Colonization in the San Luis Valley," *The Colorado Magazine,* 27 (1950):278.

11. Andrew Jenson, "The Founding of Mormon Settlements in the San Luis Valley, Colorado," *The Colorado Magazine,* 17 (1940):176-77.

12. Steinel, *History of Agriculture in Colorado,* p. 446; Lantis, "The San Luis Valley," p. 213.

13. Lantis, "The San Luis Valley," p. 204.

14. Fred T. Christensen, "Early History of Sanford, Colorado," *The Colorado Magazine,* 36 (1959):221.

15. Hall, *History of Colorado,* 3:330.

16. Ibid., 4:101, 468.

17. William A. Braiden, as told to Irma S. Harvey, "Early Days in the San Luis Valley," *The Colorado Magazine,* 21 (1944):41-51. *See also* Gladys Shawcroft, "A Brief History of the Alamosa River and La Jara River Valley," *The San Luis Valley Historian,* 2, no. 1 (1970):4-12.

18. Hall, *History of Colorado,* 4:464-65.

19. Lantis, "The San Luis Valley," pp. 239-44.

20. George A. Crofutt, *Crofutt's Grip-Sack Guide of Colorado* (1885; Denver: Cubar, 1966), 2:29.

21. Pelton, *The San Luis Valley,* pp. 79-81. Both Pelton, *The San Luis Valley,* and Crofutt, *Crofutt's Grip-Sack Guide of Colorado,* vol. 2, are useful sources of information on towns of the 1880-90 period.

22. Dorothy Roberts, "A Dutch Colony in Colorado," *The Colorado Magazine,* 17 (1940):229-36.

23. Norris Hundley, Jr., *Dividing the Waters: A Century of Controversy between the United States and Mexico* (Berkeley and Los Angeles: University of California Press, 1966), passim.

24. Lantis, "The San Luis Valley," p. 484.

25. Petty, "The History of Costilla County," p. 21.

26. Ernie Phillips, Farmers' Home Administration, Denver, personal communication, September 21, 1972.

27. Steinel, *History of Agriculture in Colorado,* pp. 431-33. *See also* Irwin Thomle, "Rise of the Vegetable Industry in the San Luis Valley," *The Colorado Magazine,* 26 (1949):112-35.

28. C. G. Sargent, *Consolidated Schools of the Mountains, Valleys and Plains of Colorado,* Colorado Agricultural College Bulletin, series 21, number 5 (June 1921), pp. 26-57.

Chapter XVI

1. Jones, *History of Catholic Education in the State of Colorado,* pp. 85-86.

2. *Rocky Mountain News,* August 4, 1971, p. 8.

3. E. R. Vollmar, S. J., "Religious Processions and Penitente Activities at Conejos, 1874," *The Colorado Magazine,* 31 (1954):172-79.

4. *See,* for example, Alex. M. Darley, *The Passionists of the Southwest, or the Holy Brotherhood* (Pueblo, Colorado: Privately printed, 1893).

5. Monica Romero, "Ortiz," in *Memories of South Conejos,* a compilation of essays written by students in the Gifted and Talented Program of School District South Conejos RE-10 (1976?). The booklet contains several informative contributions on regional history.

6. Ernest Ingersoll, *The Crest of the Continent* (Chicago: R. R. Donnelley and Sons, Publishers, 1885), p. 79.

7. Spencer, *Story of the San Luis Valley,* p. 68.

8. Lantis, "The San Luis Valley," pp. 434-35.

9. Roland Robins, Antonito, personal communication, August 27, 1972.

10. Lantis, "The San Luis Valley," p. 388.

11. White, *La Garita*, pp. 21, 34.

12. Hasting, "Parochial Beginnings in Colorado," pp. 153-54.

13. Charles Atencio, La Garita, personal communication, July 23, 1972.

14. White, *La Garita*, p. 26.

15. Spencer, *Story of the San Luis Valley*, p. 69.

16. White, *La Garita*, p. 28.

17. J. C. Lobato, "My Forty-Two Years as a Sheep Shearer," *The Colorado Magazine*, 28 (1951):215-18.

18. Lopez, "The Spanish Heritage in the San Luis Valley," p. 18.

19. Jones, *History of Catholic Education in the State of Colorado*, pp. xiv-xxviii.

20. Petty, "History of Costilla County," p. 5.

21. *Denver Post*, March 8, 1973, p. 51.

Bibliography

Government Publications and Public Records

Atwood, W. W., and Mather, K. F. *Physiography and Quaternary Geology of the San Juan Mountains, Colorado.* U.S. Geological Survey Professional Paper 166. Washington, D.C.: Government Printing Office, 1932.

Ball, Sydney H. *Mining of Gems and Ornamental Stones by American Indians.* Bureau of American Ethnology Anthropological Paper 128. Washington, D.C.: Government Printing Office, 1941.

Burbank, W. S. "The Bonanza (Kerber Creek) Mining District, Saguache County." In Colorado, Mineral Resources Board, *Mineral Resources of Colorado.* Denver: Colorado Mining Association, 1947.

Burbank, W. S., and Henderson, Charles W. *Geology and Ore Deposits of the Bonanza Mining District, Colorado.* U.S. Geological Survey Professional Paper 169. Washington, D.C.: Government Printing Office, 1932.

Colorado, General Assembly, Legislative Council. *The Status of Spanish-Surnamed Citizens in Colorado.* 1967.

Colorado. *General Laws, Joint Resolutions, Memorials, and Private Acts of the Legislative Assembly of the Territory of Colorado, 1861-76.*

Colorado, Mineral Resources Board. *Mineral Resources of Colorado,* 1947 ed. Denver: Colorado Mining Association, 1947.

————. *Mineral Resources of Colorado.* 1960 ed. Denver: Publishers Press, 1960.

Gilpin, William. "Report of 1861." In U.S., Bureau of Indian Affairs, *Annual Report of the Commissioner of Indian Affairs for 1861,* pp. 99-100. Washington, D.C.: N.p., 1862.

Hayden, F. V. *Geological and Geographical Atlas of Colorado.* (Dept. of Interior) N.p.: Julius Bien, 1881.

Hill, Edward E. *Historical Sketches for Jurisdictional and Subject Headings Used for the Letters Rec'd. by the Office of Indian Affairs, 1824-80.* Washington, D.C.: National Archives and Records Service, 1967.

Johnson, Ross B. "The Great Sand Dunes of Southern Colorado." In *Geological Survey Research, 1967.* U.S. Geological Survey Professional Paper 575-C, pp. 177-83. Washington, D.C.: Government Printing Office, 1967.

Kappler, Charles J., ed. *Indian Affairs, Laws, and Treaties.* Vol. II. Washington, D.C.: Government Printing Office, 1904.

Larsen, Esper S., Jr., and Cross, Whitman. *Geology and Petrology of the San Juan Region, Southwestern Colorado.* U.S. Geological Survey Professional Paper 258. Washington, D.C.: Government Printing Office, 1956.

Lt. Zebulon Pike's Notebook of Maps, Traverse Tables, and Meteorological Observations, 1805-07. Microfilm Publication T-36. Federal Archives and Records Center, Denver Federal Center.

McCook, Edward M. "Report of 1870." In U.S., Bureau of Indian Affairs, *Annual Report of the Commissioner of Indian Affairs for 1870,* pp. 627-28. Washington, D.C.: N.p., 1871.

Papers Relating to New Mexico Land Grants, Claims Adjudicated by the U.S. Surveyor General and by the U.S. Court of Private Land Claims, "Los Conejos," File 80, Microfilm Reel 31; and Case 109, File 112, Microfilm Reel 45. New Mexico State Records and Archives Center.

Patton, H. B. *Geology and Ore Deposits of the Bonanza District, Saguache County, Colo.* Colorado Geological Survey Bulletin 9. 1916.

————. *Geology and Ore Deposits of the Platoro-Summitville Mining District, Colo.* Colorado Geological Survey Bulletin 13. 1917.

Patton, H. B.; Smith, Charles E.; Butler, G. Montague; and Hoskin, Arthur J. *Geology of the Grayback Mining District, Costilla County, Colorado.* Colorado Geological Survey Bulletin 2. 1910.

Powell, William J. *Ground-Water Resources of the San Luis Valley, Colorado.* U.S. Geological Survey Water-Supply Paper 1379. Washington, D.C.: Government Printing Office, 1958.

Request for Renewal of Los Conejos Grant. Translation 0021. Blackmore Papers, Los Conejos Grant. New Mexico State Records Center and Archives.

Siebenthal, C. E. *Geology and Water Resources of the San Luis Valley, Colorado.* U.S. Geological Survey Water-Supply Paper 240. Washington, D.C.: Government Printing Office, 1910.

Steven, Thomas A. *Critical Review of the San Juan Peneplain, Southwestern Colorado.* U.S. Geological Survey Professional Paper 594-I. Washington, D.C.: Government Printing Office, 1968.

Steven, Thomas A., and Bieniewski, C. L. *Mineral Resources of the La Garita Wilderness, San Juan Mountains, Southwestern Colorado.* U.S. Geological Survey Bulletin 1420. Washington, D.C.: Government Printing Office, 1977.

Surveyor General of Colorado, 1861-1925. Copies of Miscellaneous Letters Sent, 1861-73. Copies of Letters Sent to the Commissioner, 1861-68. Federal Archives and Records Center, Denver Federal Center.

U.S., Bureau of Indian Affairs. *Letters Received, 1824-80. New Mexico Superintendency, 1849-80. Colorado Superintendency, 1861-8.* Microcopy 234. Federal Archives and Records Center, Denver Federal Center.

U.S., Forest Service, Rio Grande National Forest. *Workbook Containing Files Pertaining to Fremont's Fourth Expedition.* Rio Grande National Forest Headquarters, Monte Vista, Colorado.

U.S., General Land Office. *Del Norte Land Office, 1875-1925.* Tract Books. Vols. I-XV. Federal Archives and Records Center, Denver Federal Center.

―――. *Descriptive Notes of the Sangre de Cristo Grant, 1860.* Costilla County, Colorado, Courthouse.

―――. *Pueblo Land Office, 1871-1949.* Vol. XXXVIII: *Abstract of Pre-Emption Declaratory Statements.* Federal Archives and Records Center, Denver Federal Center.

U.S., General Records of the United States Government. *Ratified Indian Treaties, 1722-1869.* M-668, Roll 16. Federal Archives and Records Center, Denver Federal Center.

U.S., House. *Letter from the Secretary of the Interior in Relation to an Agreement Concluded with the Ute Indians in Colorado, September 13, 1873.* 43d Cong., 1st sess., 1874.

U.S., Post Office Department. *Records of Appointments of Postmasters, Colorado, 1860-1929.*

―――. *Official Postal Guide.*

―――. *Post Office Directory.*

U.S., Senate. *Reports of Explorations and Surveys to Ascertain the Most Practicable Route for a Railroad from the Mississippi River to the Pacific Ocean, 1853-4.* 33d Cong., 2d sess., 1854.

U.S. *Statutes at Large.* Vol. X. Boston: Little, Brown and Company, 1855.

―――. *Statutes at Large. Treaties and Proclamations of America from December 5, 1859, to March 3, 1863.* Vol. XII.

U.S., War Department, Department of the Missouri. *Atlas of Detailed Sheets of the Reconnaissance in the Ute Country.* Washington, D.C., 1873.

Books

Abstract of Title, "Costilla Estate," Sangre de Cristo Grant. N.p.: Costilla Estates Development Company, n.d.

Abstract of Title, Jaroso Garden Tracts, "Costilla Estate," Sangre de Cristo Grant. N.p.: Costilla Estates Development Company, n.d.

Abstract of Title, "The Trinchera Estate," The Sangre de Cristo Grant. San Luis, Colorado: Costilla County Abstract Company, n.d.

Athearn, Robert G. *Rebel of the Rockies: A History of the Denver and Rio Grande Western Railroad.* New Haven: Yale University Press, 1962.

Bailey, Lynn Robison. *Indian Slave Trade in the Southwest: A Study of Slave-taking and Traffic of Indian Captives.* Los Angeles: Western Lore Press, 1966.

Bancroft, Hubert Howe. *History of Arizona and New Mexico, 1530-1888.* 1889; Albuquerque, New Mexico: Horn and Wallace Publishers, 1962.

Bannon, John Francis. *The Spanish Borderlands Frontier, 1513-1821.* New York: Holt, Rinehart and Winston, 1970.

Bauer, William H.; Ozment, James L.; and Willard, John H. *Colorado Postal History: The Post Offices.* Crete, Nebraska: J-B Publishing Company, 1971.

Bean, Luther E. *Land of the Blue Sky People.* Monte Vista, Colorado: Monte Vista Journal, 1962.

Bennett, Edna Mae. *Turquoise and the Indian.* Denver: Sage Books, 1966.

Blackmore, William. *Colorado: Its Resources, Parks and Prospects as a New Field for Emigration.* London: Sampson, Low, Son, and Marston, 1869.

————. *Investments in Land in Colorado and New Mexico.* London: Witherby and Company, 1955.

Brayer, Herbert O. *A Case Study in the Economic Development of the West.* Vol. I: *William Blackmore: The Spanish-Mexican Land Grants of New Mexico and Colorado, 1863-1878.* Vol. II: *William Blackmore: Early Financing of the Denver and Rio Grande Railway and Ancillary Land Companies.* Denver: Bradford-Robinson, 1949.

Breck, Allen duPont. *The Centennial History of the Jews in Colorado, 1859-1959.* Denver: Hirschfeld Press, 1960.

Campa, Arthur L. *Treasure of the Sangre de Cristos: Tales and Traditions of the Spanish Southwest.* Norman: University of Oklahoma Press, 1963.

Carter, Carrol Joe. *Pike in Colorado.* Fort Collins, Colorado: The Old Army Press, 1978.

Carter, Harvey Lewis. *'Dear Old Kit': The Historical Christopher Carson.* Norman: University of Oklahoma Press, 1968.

Carvalho, S. N. *Incidents of Travel and Adventure in the Far West with Fremont's Last Expedition.* New York: Derby and Jackson, 1857.

Crofutt, George A. *Crofutt's Grip-Sack Guide of Colorado.* Vol. II. 1895; Denver: Cubar, 1966.

Darley, Alex. M. *The Passionists of the Southwest, or the Holy Brotherhood.* Pueblo, Colorado: Privately printed, 1893.

Denver and Rio Grande Railroad. *Slopes of the Sangre de Cristo; A Book of the Resources and Industries of Colorado.* Denver: Carson-Harper, 1896.

Description of the Parks of Colorado and the Estate of the Colorado Freehold Land Association Limited. London: F. Straher, 1868.

Dyer, John L. *The Snow-Shoe Itinerant.* Cincinnati: Cranston and Stowe, 1890.

Ellis, Anne. *The Life of an Ordinary Woman.* Boston and New York: Houghton Mifflin Company, 1929.

Ellis, Erl H. *International Boundary Lines across Colorado and Wyoming.* Boulder, Colorado: Johnson Publishing Company, 1966.

Espinosa, Aurelio M. *The Spanish Language in New Mexico and Southern Colorado.* Historical Society of New Mexico Publication 16. Santa Fe: New Mexican Printing Company, 1911.

Feitz, Leland. *Alamosa: The San Luis Valley's Big City.* Colorado Springs, Colorado: Little London Press, 1976.

Forbes, Jack D. *Apache, Navajo and Spaniard.* Norman: University of Oklahoma Press, 1960.

Fowler, Jacob. *The Journal of Jacob Fowler.* Ed. by Elliott Coues with preface and additional notes by Raymond W. and Mary Lund Settle and Harry R. Stevens. Lincoln: University of Nebraska Press, 1970.

Gilpin, William. "Pike's Peak and the Sierra San Juan." In *Guide to the Kansas Gold Mines at Pike's Peak, from Notes of Capt. J. W. Gunnison...* 1859; Denver: Nolie Mumey, 1952.

Gjeore, John A. *Chili Line: The Narrow Rail Trail to Santa Fe.* Espanola, New Mexico: Rio Grande Sun Press, 1969.

Goetzmann, William H. *Army Exploration in the American West.* New Haven: Yale University Press, 1959.

Grant, Blanche C., ed. *Kit Carson's Own Story of His Life as Dictated to Col. and Mrs. D. C. Peters about 1856-57.* Santa Fe: Santa Fe New Mexican Publishing Corporation, 1926.

H. H. [Helen Marie Hunt Jackson]. *Bits of Travel at Home.* Boston: Little, Brown and Company, 1878.

Haarr, Allan. "Marble Mountain Caves (Custer County, Colorado)." In *Speleo Digest, 1959,* pp. 270-71. Pittsburgh, Pennsylvania: Pittsburgh Grotto, National Speleological Society, 1961.

Hafen, LeRoy R., ed. *Colorado and Its People: A Narrative and Topical History of the Centennial State.* 2 vols. New York: Lewis Historical Publishing Company, Inc., 1948.

————. *The Mountain Men and the Fur Trade of the Far West.* 10 vols. Glendale, California: Arthur H. Clark Company, 1965-72.

Hafen, LeRoy R., and Hafen, Ann W., eds. *The Far West and the Rockies Historical Series, 1820-1875.* Vol. XI: *Fremont's Fourth Expedition: A Documentary Account of the Disaster of 1848-49.* Glendale, California: Arthur H. Clark Company, 1960.

Hall, Frank. *History of the State of Colorado.* 4 vols. Chicago: Blakely Printing Company, 1889-95.

Halliday, William R. *Adventure Is Underground: The Story of the Great Caves of the West and the Men Who Explore Them.* New York: Harper and Brothers, Publishers, 1959.

Hammond, George P., and Rey, Agapito, eds. *Coronado Cuarto Centennial Publications, 1540-1940.* Vols. V and VI: *Oñate, Colonizer of New Mexico, 1595-1628.* Albuquerque: University of New Mexico Press, 1953.

Heap, Gwinn Harris. *Central Route to the Pacific, from the Valley of the Mississippi to California: Journal of the Expedition.* Philadelphia: Lippincott, Grambo, and Company, 1854.

Herstrom, Guy M. "Sangre de Cristo Grant, 1843-1880." In *The 1960 Brand Book,* pp. 73-102. Denver: Denver Posse of the Westerners, 1961.

Hewett, Edgar L., and Dutton, Bertha P. *The Pueblo Indian World: Studies on the Natural History of the Rio Grande Valley in Relation to Pueblo Indian Culture.* Handbooks of Archaeological History Series. Albuquerque: University of New Mexico and the School of American Research, 1945.

Hollon, W. Eugene. *The Lost Pathfinder: Zebulon Montgomery Pike.* Norman: University of Oklahoma Press, 1949.

Horka-Follick, Lorayne Ann. *Los Hermanos Penitentes.* Los Angeles: Western Lore Press, 1969.

Hundley, Norris, Jr. *Dividing the Waters: A Century of Controversy between the United States and Mexico.* Berkeley and Los Angeles: University of California Press, 1966.

Ingersoll, Ernest. *The Crest of the Continent.* Chicago: R. R. Donnelley and Sons, Publishers, 1885.

Jackson, Donald, ed. *The Journals of Zebulon Montgomery Pike.* Norman: University of Oklahoma Press, 1966.

James, H. L., ed. *Guidebook of the San Luis Basin, Colorado.* N.p.: New Mexico Geological Society, 1971.

Jeancon, Jean Allard. *Archaeological Research in the Northeastern San Juan Basin of Colorado.* Ed. by Frank H. H. Roberts. Denver: State Historical and Natural History Society of Colorado and the University of Denver, 1922.

Jocknick, Sidney. *Early Days on the Western Slope of Colorado and Campfire Chats with Otto Mears the Pathfinder from 1870 to 1883, Inclusive.* 1913; Glorieta, New Mexico: Rio Grande Press, Inc., 1968.

Jones, Oakah L., Jr. *Pueblo Warriors and Spanish Conquest.* Norman: University of Oklahoma Press, 1966.

Jones, William Hubert. *The History of Catholic Education in the State of Colorado.* Washington, D.C.: Catholic University of America Press, 1955.

Karnes, Thomas L. *William Gilpin, Western Nationalist.* Austin and London: University of Texas Press, 1970.

Kelsey, Harry E., Jr. *Frontier Capitalist: The Life of John Evans.* Denver and Boulder: State Historical Society of Colorado and Pruett Publishing Company, 1969.

Lee, W. Storrs, ed. *Colorado: A Literary Chronicle.* New York: Funk and Wagnalls, 1970.

Mallery, Garrick. *Picture-Writing of the American Indians.* Vol. I. 1893; New York: Dover Publications, Inc., 1972.

McAdow, Beryl. *From Crested Peaks: The Story of Adams State College of Colorado.* Denver: Big Mountain Press, 1961.

————. *Land of Adoption.* Boulder, Colorado: Johnson Publishing Company, 1970.

McMurtrie, Douglas C., and Allen, Albert H. *Early Printing in Colorado.* Denver: A. B. Hirschfeld Press, 1935.

Memories of South Conejos. Antonito, Colorado: School District South Conejos RE-10, 1977.

Merk, George P. "Great Sand Dunes of Colorado." In Weimer, Robert J., and Haun, John D., eds., *Guide to the Geology of Colorado.* Denver: Rocky Mountain Association of Geologists, 1960.

Oehlerts, Donald E. *Guide to Colorado Newspapers, 1859-1963.* Denver: Biblio-graphical Center for Research, 1964.

Opler, Marvin K. "The Southern Utes of Colorado." In Linton, Ralph, ed., *Acculturation in Seven American Indian Tribes.* New York: D. Appleton-Century Company, 1940.

O'Ryan, William, and Malone, Thomas H. *History of the Catholic Church in Colorado.* Denver: C. J. Kelly, 1889.

Parkhill, Forbes. *The Blazed Trail of Antoine Leroux.* Los Angeles: Western Lore Press, 1965.

Pelton, A. R. *The San Luis Valley with Illustrations of Its Public Buildings, Summer Resorts, and Some of Its Residences, Business Blocks, Manufactories, and Citizens.* Salida, Colorado: Carson, Hurst and Harper, 1891.

Peters, Dewitt C. *The Life and Adventures of Kit Carson, the Nestor of the Rocky Mountains, from Facts Narrated by Himself.* New York: W. B. C. Clark and Company, 1858.

Pike, Zebulon M. *The Southwestern Expedition of Zebulon M. Pike.* Ed. by Milo Milton Quaife. Chicago: Lakeside Press, 1925.

Porter, Clyde and Mae Reed, comps. *Ruxton of the Rockies.* Ed. by LeRoy R. Hafen. Norman: University of Oklahoma Press, 1950.

Preuss, Charles. *Exploring with Frémont: The Private Diaries of Charles Preuss, Cartographer for John C. Frémont on his First, Second, and Fourth Expeditions to the Far West.* Trans. and ed. by Erwin G. and Elizabeth K. Gudde. Norman: University of Oklahoma Press, 1958.

Renaud, E. B. *Archaeology of the Upper Rio Grande Basin in Southern Colorado and Northern New Mexico.* University of Denver Archaeological Series, Paper 6. Denver: University of Denver, 1946.

Reynolds, Matthew G. *Spanish and Mexican Land Laws: New Spain and Mexico.* St. Louis: Buxton and Skinner Stationery Company, 1895.

Rideing, William H. *A-Saddle in the Wild West.* London: J. C. Nimmo and Bain, 1879.

Rockwell, Wilson. *The Utes, A Forgotten People.* Denver: Sage Books, 1956.

Ruxton, George F. *Adventures in Mexico and the Rocky Mountains.* New York: Harper and Brothers, Publishers, 1848.

Salpointe, J. B. *Soldiers of the Cross: Notes on the Ecclesiastical History of New Mexico, Arizona, and Colorado.* 1898; Albuquerque: Calvin Horn, Publisher, Inc., 1967.

Sanchez, George I. *Forgotten People: A Study of New Mexicans.* Albuquerque: University of New Mexico Press, 1940.

Sargent, C. G. *Consolidated Schools of the Mountains, Valleys and Plains of Colorado.* Colorado Agricultural College Bulletin. Fort Collins: Colorado Agricultural College, 1921.

Searcy, Helen M. "Otto Mears." In *Pioneers of the San Juan Country.* Vol. I, pp. 15-47. Durango, Colorado: Out West Printing and Stationery Company, 1942.

Spencer, Frank C. *The Story of the San Luis Valley.* 1925; Alamosa, Colorado: San Luis Valley Historical Society, 1975.

Steinel, Alvin T. *History of Agriculture in Colorado.* Fort Collins: State Agricultural College, 1926.

Tate, Bill. *The Penitentes of the Sangre de Cristos: An American Tragedy.* Truchas, New Mexico: Tate Gallery, 1968.

Taylor, Morris F. *First Mail West: Stagecoach Lines on the Santa Fe Trail.* Albuquerque: University of New Mexico Press, 1971.

Taylor, Ralph C. *Colorado South of the Border.* Denver: Sage Books, 1963.

Thomas, Alfred Barnaby, trans. and ed. *Forgotten Frontiers: A Study of the Spanish Indian Policy of Don Juan Bautista de Anza, Governor of New Mexico, 1777-1787.* Norman: University of Oklahoma Press, 1932.

Tushar, Olibama Lopez. *People of the Valley: A History of the Spanish Colonials of the San Luis Valley.* Intro. by Daniel T. Valdes. Denver: Privately printed, 1975.

Tyler, Daniel. *A Concise History of the Mormon Battalion in the Mexican War.* Washington, D.C.: N.p., 1891.

Underhill, Ruth M. *The Navajos.* Norman: University of Oklahoma Press, 1956.

———. *Red Man's Religion: Beliefs and Practices of the Indians North of Mexico.* Chicago: University of Chicago Press, 1965.

Weber, David J. *The Taos Trappers: The Fur Trade in the Far Southwest.* Norman: University of Oklahoma Press, 1968.

Weigle, Marta. *The Penitentes of the Southwest.* Santa Fe, New Mexico: Ancient City Press, 1970.

White, Frank A. *La Garita.* La Jara, Colorado: Cooper Printing Company, 1971.

Wessels, William L. *Born To Be a Soldier: The Military Career of William Wing Loring of St. Augustine, Florida.* Fort Worth: Texas Christian University, 1971.

Wormington, H. M. *Ancient Man in North America.* 4th ed. Denver: Denver Museum of Natural History, 1957.

Periodicals

Bender, Norman J. "A College Where One Ought to Be," *The Colorado Magazine*, 49 (1972):196-218.

Braiden, William A. "Early Days in the San Luis Valley," as told to Irma S. Harvey, *The Colorado Magazine*, 21 (1944):41-51.

Breckenridge, Thomas E. "The Story of a Famous Expedition," as told to J. W. Freeman and Charles W. Watson, *The Cosmopolitan*, 21 (1896):400-08.

Carson, Christopher. "Report on Fort Garland Made by Christopher (Kit) Carson to Major Roger James, June 10, 1866," ed. by Gene M. Gressley, *The Colorado Magazine*, 32 (1955):215-45.

Carter, Harvey L. "The Mountain Men," *The San Luis Valley Historian*, 3, no. 1 (1971):2-26.

Chacon, Rafael. "Campaign against Utes and Apaches in Southern Colorado, 1855, from the Memoirs of Major Rafael Chacon," *The Colorado Magazine*, 11 (1934):108-12.

Cheetham, Francis T. "The Early Settlements of Southern Colorado," *The Colorado Magazine*, 5 (1928):1-8.

Christensen, Fred T. "Early History of Sanford, Colorado," *The Colorado Magazine*, 36 (1959):214-22.

"Colonel Loring's Expedition across Colorado in 1858," *The Colorado Magazine*, 23 (1946):49-75.

Coolbroth, Mary Louise. "Early Church Buildings of the San Luis Valley," *The San Luis Valley Historian*, 7, no. 3 (1975):13-18.

Cummins, D. H. "Toll Roads in Southwestern Colorado," *The Colorado Magazine*, 29 (1952):98-104.

Cummins, M. L. "Fort Massachusetts, First United States Military Post in Colorado," *The Colorado Magazine*, 14 (1937):128-35.

Davis, Donald G. "Important New Finds on Marble Mountain, Colo.," *National Speleological Society News*, 18 (1960):133-34.

———. "More about Colorado's Marble Mountain Caves," *National Speleological Society News*, 19 (1961):45-47.

Dunham, Harold H. "New Mexican Land Grants with Special Reference to the Title Papers of the Maxwell Grant," *New Mexico Historical Review*, 30 (1955):1-22.

Ellis, Anne. "My First Bath Tub," *Los Angeles Times Sunday Magazine*, December 20, 1931, pp. 5, 16.

Espinosa, J. Manuel. "Governor Vargas in Colorado," *New Mexico Historical Review*, 11 (1936):179-87.

———, ed. "Journal of the Vargas Expedition into Colorado, 1694," *The Colorado Magazine*, 16 (1939):81-90.

Faherty, William B. "Regional Minorities and the Woman Suffrage Struggle," *The Colorado Magazine*, 33 (1956):212-17.

Fassett, Bill. "The Fassett Store in Jasper," *The San Luis Valley Historian*, 7, no. 2 (1975):16-17.

Foreman, Grant. "Antoine Leroux, New Mexico Guide," *New Mexico Historical Review*, 16 (1941):370-74.

French, J. Cary. "Diary, 1871," *The San Luis Valley Historian*, 8, no. 1 (1976):3-13.

Gunther, C. G. "The Gold Deposits of Plomo, San Luis Park, Colo.," *Economic Geology*, 1 (1906):143-54.

Hafen, LeRoy R. "The Fort Pueblo Massacre and the Punitive Expedition against the Utes," *The Colorado Magazine*, 4 (1927):49-58.

———. "Mountain Men—John D. Albert," *The Colorado Magazine*, 10 (1933):56-62.

——— "Status of the San Luis Valley, 1850-1861," *The Colorado Magazine*, 3 (1926):46-49.

Hansen, William. "Pioneer Life in the San Luis Valley," as told to Velma West Sykes, *The Colorado Magazine*, 17 (1940):146-55.

Harvey, James Rose. "El Cerrito de Los Kiowas," *The Colorado Magazine*, 19 (1942):213-15.

Harvey, James Rose, and Harvey, Mrs. James Rose. "Turquoise among the Indians and a Colorado Turquoise Mine," *The Colorado Magazine*, 15 (1938):186-92.

Hill, Joseph J. "Antoine Robidoux, Kingpin in the Colorado River Fur Trade, 1824-1844," *The Colorado Magazine,* 7 (1930):125-32.

Hurst, C. T. "A Folsom Location in the San Luis Valley, Colorado," *Southwestern Lore,* 7 (1941):31-34.

Jeancon, Jean Allard. "Pictographs of Colorado," *The Colorado Magazine,* 3 (1926):33-45.

Jenson, Andrew. "The Founding of Mormon Settlements in the San Luis Valley, Colorado," *The Colorado Magazine,* 17 (1940):174-80.

Kaplan, Michael. "Otto Mears and the Silverton Northern Railroad," *The Colorado Magazine,* 48 (1971):235-54.

Kempner, Helen A. "Bonanza and the Kerber Creek District," *The San Luis Valley Historian,* 3, no. 2 (1971):1-46.

Kortright, S. E. "Historical Sketch of the Bonanza Mining District," *The Colorado Magazine,* 22 (1945):68-76.

Lobato, J. C. "My Forty-Two Years as a Sheep Shearer," *The Colorado Magazine,* 28 (1951):215-18.

Lopez, Olibama. "Pioneer Life in the San Luis Valley," *The Colorado Magazine,* 19 (1942):161-67.

Major, Mrs. A. H. "Pioneer Days in Crestone and Creede," *The Colorado Magazine,* 21 (1944):212-17.

McConnell, Virginia. "Captain Baker and the San Juan Humbug," *The Colorado Magazine,* 48 (1971):59-75.

McMenamy, Claire. "Our Lady of Guadalupe at Conejos, Colorado," *The Colorado Magazine,* 17 (1940):180-83.

Morgan, Nicholas G. "Mormon Colonization in the San Luis Valley," *The Colorado Magazine,* 27 (1950):269-93.

Mumey, Nolie. "John Williams Gunnison: Centenary of His Survey and Tragic Death," *The Colorado Magazine,* 31 (1954):19-32.

Nankivell, John H. "Fort Garland, Colorado," *The Colorado Magazine,* 16 (1939):13-27.

Parkhill, Forbes. "Colorado's Earliest Settlements," *The Colorado Magazine,* 34 (1957):241-53.

Pearsall, Alfred J. "Evidence of Pueblo Culture in the San Luis Valley," *Southwestern Lore,* 5 (1939):7-9.

"Recollections of Tata Atanasio Trujillo," *The San Luis Valley Historian,* 8, no. 4 (1976):11-19.

Renaud, E. B. "Prehistory of the San Luis Valley," *The Colorado Magazine,* 20 (1943):51-55.

————. "The Rio Grande Points," *Southwestern Lore,* 8 (1942):33-36.

Richie, Eleanor L. "The Disputed International Boundary in Colorado, 1803-1819," *The Colorado Magazine,* 13 (1936):171-78.

Richmond, Patricia Joy. "La Loma de San Jose," *The San Luis Valley Historian,* 5, no. 2-4 (1973):1-63; 6, no. 1-2 (1974):64-118.

Ridgway, Arthur. "The Mission of Colorado Toll Roads," *The Colorado Magazine,* 9 (1932):163-69.

Roberts, Dorothy. "A Dutch Colony in Colorado," *The Colorado Magazine,* 17 (1940):229-36.

Roberts, Frank H. H., Jr. "Prehistoric Peoples of Colorado," *The Colorado Magazine,* 23 (1946):145-56, 215-29.

"San Luis Store Celebrates Centennial," *The Colorado Magazine,* 34 (1957):256-62.

The San Luis Valley Historian. Vols. I-X, 1969-78.

Sharp, Pauline S. "Kit Carson at Fort Garland, C.T.," *The San Luis Valley Historian,* 2, no. 2 (1970):12-20.

Shawcroft, Gladys. "A Brief History of the Alamosa River and La Jara River Valley," *The San Luis Valley Historian,* 2, no. 1 (1970):4-12.

Smith, Emilia Gallegos. "Reminiscences of Early San Luis," *The Colorado Magazine,* 24 (1947):24-25.

Smith, Gerald C. "Colonel Albert H. Pfeiffer," *The San Luis Valley Historian,* 2, no. 2 (1970):7-11.

Smith, Victoria. "The Shangri La of the Rockies," *Denver Westerners Roundup,* 26 (November-December 1970):3-17.

Spencer, Frank C. "The Scene of Fremont's Disaster in the San Juan Mountains, 1848," *The Colorado Magazine,* 6 (1929):141-46.

————. "The Wheeler National Monument," *The Colorado Magazine,* 1 (1924):97-103.

Strickland, Rex W. "Moscoso's Journey through Texas," *Southwestern Historical Quarterly,* 46 (1942):109-37.

Taylor, Morris F. "Action at Fort Massachusetts: The Indian Campaign of 1855," *The Colorado Magazine*, 42 (1965):292-310.

———. "Fort Massachusetts," *The Colorado Magazine*, 45 (1968):120-42.

Thomas, Alfred B. "An Anonymous Description of New Mexico, 1818," *Southwestern Historical Quarterly*, 33 (1929):51.

———. "Documents Bearing upon the Northern Frontier of New Mexico, 1818-1819," *New Mexico Historical Review*, 4 (1929):146-63.

Thomas, Chauncy. "The Spanish Fort in Colorado, 1819," *The Colorado Magazine*, 14 (1937):81-85.

Tobin, Thomas T. "The Capture of the Espinosas," dictated 1895, *The Colorado Magazine*, 9 (1932):59-66.

Upson, J. E. "Physiographic Subdivisions of the San Luis Valley, Southern Colorado," *Journal of Geology*, 47 (1939):721-36.

Vandenbusche, Duane. "Life at a Frontier Post: Fort Garland," *The Colorado Magazine*, 43 (1966):132-48.

Velasquez, Meliton. "Guadalupe Colony Was Founded 1854," *The Colorado Magazine*, 34 (1957):264-67.

Vollmar, E. R., S.J. "Religious Processions and Penitente Activities at Conejos, 1874," *The Colorado Magazine*, 31 (1954):172-79.

Wallrath, Ellen F. "Stagecoach Holdups in the San Luis Valley," *The Colorado Magazine*, 14 (1937):27-31.

"The Wheeler Expedition in Southern Colorado," *Harper's New Monthly Magazine*, 52 (1876):798-807.

Williams, J. W. "Moscoso's Trail in Texas," *Southwestern Historical Quarterly*, 46 (1942):138-57.

Wilson, Dorothy. "They Came to Hunt," *The San Luis Valley Historian*, 3, no. 3 (1971):12-18.

Unpublished Material

Barclay, Alexander. Papers. (Typescript from microfilm copies.) State Historical Society of Colorado Library.

Boyd, Mrs. W. F. Papers. Adams State College Library.

Burford, Arthur Edgar. "Geology of the Medano Peak Area, Sangre de Cristo Mountains, Colorado." Ph.D. dissertation, University of Michigan, 1960.

Christensen, Fred. Taped interview by Mrs. Hugh Kingery. 1962. State Historical Society of Colorado Library.

Combs, D. Gene. "Enslavement of Indians in the San Luis Valley." M.A. thesis, Adams State College, 1970.

Covington, James Warren. "Relations between the Ute Indians and the United States Government, 1848-1900." Ph.D. dissertation, University of Oklahoma, 1949.

Cox, Irene Flom. "Development of Baca Grant Number Four." M.A. thesis, Adams State College, 1948.

Ellis, Florence Hawley. "San Gabriel del Yungue, Window on the Pre-Spanish World." Paper read before the Eleventh Annual Western History Association Conference, Santa Fe, New Mexico, October 14, 1971.

Fisher, Robert B. "An Historical Study of the Orient Mine and Its Impact on the San Luis Valley." M.A. thesis, Adams State College, 1969.

Flower, Judson Harold, Jr. "Mormon Colonization of the San Luis Valley, Colorado, 1878-1900." M.A. thesis, Brigham Young University, 1966.

Gibson, Charles E., Jr. "Alamosa, Conejos, and Costilla Counties: Interviews Collected during 1933-1934 for the State Historical Society of Colorado by Civil Works Administration Workers." State Historical Society Library.

Gomez, Francis J. "Medical Folklore of the Spanish-Speaking People of the San Luis Valley." M.A. thesis, Adams State College, 1970.

Hasting, Martin F. "Parochial Beginnings in Colorado to 1889." M.A. thesis, St. Louis University, 1941.

Inouye, Ronald K. "Alamosa, Colorado: Some Highlights on Its Early History." M.A. thesis, Adams State College, 1968.

Lantis, David William. "The San Luis Valley, Colorado: Sequent Rural Occupance in an Intermontane Basin." Ph.D. dissertation, Ohio State University, 1950.

Lawrence, John. "Diary, 1867-1907." State Historical Society of Colorado Library.

Lindfelt, Haldon W. "The Chili Line: The Santa Fe Branch of the Denver and Rio Grande Western." M.A. thesis, Adams State College, 1966.

Oba, Herbert H. "Source Material for Teaching History of the East-Central Section of the San Luis Valley." M.A. thesis, Adams State College, 1961.

Petty, Hazel Bean. "The History of Costilla County as Revealed by Its Cemeteries." M.A. thesis, Adams State College, 1971.

"References in Spanish Archives to Expeditions by Spaniards in the 18th and 19th Centuries to the Territory Now Included in the State of Colorado, Secured by Irving Howbert in the Library of Congress." (Typescript.) Colorado College, Tutt Library.

Schwarzbeck, Dorothy. "The History of Monte Vista." (Typescript.) Adams State College Library.

Thomle, Irwin. "The Developmental Period in San Luis Agriculture, 1898-1930." Ph.D. dissertation, Northwestern University, 1948.

Trujillo, Luis M. *"Diccionario del Espanol del Valle de San Luis de Colorado y Del Norte de Nuevo Mexico."* M.A. thesis, Adams State College, 1961.

Vigil, Charlie A. "History and Folklore of San Pedro and San Pablo, Colorado." M.A. thesis, Adams State College, 1956.

Maps

Burr, David H. Map, 1839. In Sullivan, Maurice S., *The Travels of Jedediah Smith.* Santa Ana: Fine Arts Press, 1934.

Colton, J. H. Map of Colorado and New Mexico [1865?].

Cram. Map of Colorado, 1891.

Denver and Rio Grande Railroad. Map of Colorado [1883-86?].

Hayden, F. V. *Geological and Geographical Atlas of Colorado,* 1881.

Misc. maps in State Historical Society of Colorado Library, including *Map of the Trenchara and Costilla Estates Forming the Sangre de Christo Grant.*

Mitchell, S. Augustus, Jr. Map of Kansas, Nebraska, and Colorado, 1861.

Thayer. Map of Colorado, 1882.

U.S., Forest Service. Map of Rio Grande National Forest. GPO 834-921.

U.S. Geographical Survey West of the 100th Meridian. Topographical Atlas Sheets, 1877 ed. and 1878 ed.

U.S. Geological Survey. Topographic Maps of Colorado. Quadrangle Maps in 1:250,000 Series, 15-Minute Series, and 7.5-Minute Series.

Index

Brooks, Horace, Lt. Col. 52
Brown Beauty Potatoes 143
Brown's Hole 40
Bruce, William, Judge 79
Buena Vista 21
Buffalo Pass 41. *See also* Coche-topa Pass
Burnt Creek 105
Burr, Aaron 22
Byers, William N. 71

Caliente *see* Ojo Caliente, N.M.
Camels 9
Canby, E.R.S., Maj. 64
Canon 166, 167
Canon City 21, 63, 72, 73, 79, 85
Canon City, Grand River and San Juan Road Company 85
Canyon de Chelly, Ariz. 10, 66
Capote Ute Indians 66
Captain Jack 67
Capulin 74, 128, 133, 149, 150, 153
Carat, Simon 27
Carnero 105, 149, 166
Carnero Canyon 11, 151
Carnero Creek 10, 11, 39, 41, 61, 75, 105, 149, 151
Carnero Pass 39, 52
Carson, Christopher (Kit), Gen. 27, 31, 32, 34, 35, 46, 49, 52, 60, 64, 66, 69, 74, 80, 129
Carson, Josefa 60, 66
Carson, Juan 60
Carson, William 80, 129
Casias, Jose Maria 148
Casillas 166
Cathcart, Andrew, Capt. 34
Cenisero 132-33, 166, 167
Center 96, 141-42, 143, 145, 149, 153
Center Post 142
Center View 141. *See also* Center-view
Centerview 142. *See also* Center View
Cerritos *see* Los Cerritos
Chaco Canyon, N.M. 10
Chama, Colo. 48, 54, 83, 153
Chama, N.M. 91, 92
Chama River (Colo.) 4
Chama River (N.M.) 72
Chamberlin Springs 140
Chamito, N.M. 91
Chaves, Jose Andres 75
Cheyenne Indians 11
Chicanos 153, 155
Chili Line 91. *See also* Denver and Rio Grande Railway
Choury, Armand 153
Churches
  Baptist 119, 148
  Catholic 53, 58, 60, 76, 83, 91, 114, 119, 133, 136, 146, 147-48, 149, 152

Church of Jesus Christ of Latter-day Saints *see* Mormons
Church of Most Precious Blood 152
Church of St. John the Baptist 149
Congregational 109
Dunkard 128
Episcopal 114
Methodist 76, 91, 114, 119, 136, 137, 152
Our Lady of Guadalupe 54
Presbyterian 88, 91, 115, 119, 124, 132, 133, 148, 152
Seventh-Day Adventist 142
Unitarian 119
United Presbyterian 153
Centennial Union High School 152
Cibola, Seven Cities of 13, 101
Cido 166
Citizen's Ditch *see* Monte Vista Canal
Civil War 60, 63, 64, 66, 68, 69, 71, 72, 74, 76, 81, 85, 124, 127, 153, 165
Claytonia 170
Cochetopa Hills 4, 103, 159
Cochetopa National Forest 152
Cochetopa Pass 4, 11, 15, 27, 38, 39, 40-41, 52, 53, 67, 74, 85, 99, 105, 111, 113, 118, 119
Cochetopa Timber Reserve 151-52
Cohn, Louis 46-47, 153
Colorado, State 72, 92
Colorado, Territory 63, 64, 65, 67, 72, 74, 82-83, 85
Colorado Coal and Iron Company 101, 106, 108. *See also* Colorado Fuel and Iron Company
Colorado Fuel and Iron Company 107, 108. *See also* Colorado Coal and Iron Company
Colorado Independent 88
Colorado Loan and Trust Company 134
Colorado Potato Growers' Exchange 143
Colorado River 27
Colorado Springs 86, 111
Colorado State Veterans' Center *see* State Soldiers' and Sailors' Home
Colorado Volunteers 64, 74
Comanche Indians 11, 14, 15, 16, 20
Conejos 46-51, 54, 61, 72, 73, 74, 75, 76, 83, 88, 91, 124, 125, 128, 147, 148
Conejos County 56, 60, 73, 78, 79, 91, 113, 124, 130, 132, 148-49, 152, 153. *See also* Guadalupe County

Conejos Grant 43-44, 48-51, 53, 54, 60-61, 73, 76, 80, 83, 128-29, 135
Conejos Indian Agency 64, 66, 67, 73, 79
Conejos River 6, 7, 16, 21, 26, 34, 43, 44, 48, 53, 72, 102, 131, 132
Conejos Road 73
Conlon's Ferry *see* Myers' Ferry
Copper Creek 103
Cornwall 102, 112
Cornwall, John 102
Cornwall Mountain 102
Coronado, Francisco 13
Cortez, Hernando 13
Coryell 136. *See also* Stanley
Costilla, N.M. 46, 47, 52, 58, 59, 73, 74, 79, 80, 82, 88, 124, 152, 153, 165
Costilla County 56, 60, 61, 72, 73, 75, 129, 143, 152-53
Costilla Creek 6, 29, 46, 47, 48, 51, 86, 132, 142
Costilla Estate 82-83, 86, 96, 129, 142-43
Costilla Estate, Map of ix
Costilla Estate Development Company 142
Costilla Ferry *see* Myers' Ferry
Costilla News 136
Costilla Plains 4, 6
Cotswold sheep 148
Cotton Creek 88, 105, 149
Cotton Creek (town) 127
Cottonwood 95, 105, 106
Creede 72, 94, 108-09, 111, 115, 128, 132, 152
Creede, Nicholas 108
Creede Mining District 108-09
Crestone 31, 81, 95, 96, 105, 106, 141. *See also* Cristonie
Crestone Estate 94, 96, 141
Crestone Needle 105
Crestone Peak 105
Creutzfeldt, Frederick 33, 34, 40
Cristonie 105. *See also* Crestone
Crystal Hill Pilot 105
Cucharas Junction 86
Cuerno Verde, Chief 16
Culebra 59, 122. *See also* San Luis
Culebra Creek 6, 14, 16, 22, 23, 25, 26, 28, 29, 47, 48, 51, 73, 101, 142
Culebra Mountain Range 4, 42, 46, 81, 86, 101, 110
Culebra Re-entrant 4, 6
Culebra Village 143
Cumbres and Toltec Scenic Railroad 92, 93
Cumbres Pass 4, 11, 92, 93, 99, 122, 148
Cummings, Alexander, Gov. 66-67

189

Villa Grove 7, 11, 88, 95, 102, 106, 107, 110, 127, 136, 149. *See also* Garibaldi

Villa Grove Headlight 106

Vincenthaler, Lorenzo 34

Vulcano, N.M. 91

Wagon Wheel Gap 26, 72, 94, 108, 111, 113, 115, 125, 128

Walsen, Fred 74, 75

Walsenburg 74

Walters, Lieutenant 74

Walters, Richard 162

Wannamaker Creek 34, 35, 105, 164

Ward, Eli 162

Warman, Cy 109

Warshauer, Fred 148-49

Warshauer-McClure Commission House 148

Washington Springs 88, 95

Wason, Martin Van Buren 111, 128

Water, irrigation canals and ditches 48, 49, 61, 76, 94, 105, 129, 131, 132, 135, 136, 140, 142

Water resources 6-7, 137, 140-41

Watts, John S. 86

Waverly 136, 143

Wayside (station) 170

Weminuche Ute Indians 66

Wet Mountain Valley 4, 15, 21, 33, 40, 52

Wet Mountains 33

Wetmore 79

Wetmore, T.C. 63

Wheeler, George M., Lt. 111

Wheeler Geologic Area 125, 152. *See also* Wheeler National Monument

Wheeler National Monument 125. *See also* Wheeler Geologic Area

Wheeler Survey *see* United States Geographical Surveys West of the Hundredth Meridian

Whiplash Curve 92

White, José Adolpho 151

White Mountains 3. *See also* Sangre de Cristo Mountain Range

White River 67, 68

Whitsitt Hotel 113

Whittlesey, J.H., Lt. 46

Wightman, James 101

Wightman, William 101

Wilcox 106

Wildlife 2, 9, 11, 14, 18, 26, 160-61

Wilkinson, James, Gen. 20, 21, 22

Williams, F.W. 133

Williams, John 129

Williams, William Sherley (Parson Bill) 31, 33, 34, 35, 46, 163

Williams Pass (San Juan Mountains) 35. *See also* Leroux Pass, Summer Pass

Williams Pass (Sangre de Cristo Mountains) 33. *See also* Medano Pass

Willow Creek 108, 128

Windy Bill 105

Wolf Creek 11, 111

Woodson, Andres 75

Woodson, Gabriel 75

Woodson, James B. 75

Wootton, Dick 27-28

Xicarilla 15. *See also* Jicarilla Apache Indians

Young, Ewing 27

Yuma Culture 10

Zapata 61, 83, 88, 109, 129, 153

Zapata Creek 129, 130

Zapata Ranch 129, 136

Zapata Site 10

Zuni Indians 11. *See also* Pueblo Indians